HOW TO T
ABOUT TH
CLIMATE (

HOW TO THINK ABOUT THE CLIMATE CRISIS

A philosophical guide to saner ways of living

Graham Parkes

BLOOMSBURY ACADEMIC
LONDON • NEW YORK • OXFORD • NEW DELHI • SYDNEY

BLOOMSBURY ACADEMIC
Bloomsbury Publishing Plc
50 Bedford Square, London, WC1B 3DP, UK
1385 Broadway, New York, NY 10018, USA
29 Earlsfort Terrace, Dublin 2, Ireland

BLOOMSBURY, BLOOMSBURY ACADEMIC and the Diana logo are
trademarks of Bloomsbury Publishing Plc

First published in Great Britain 2021
Reprinted 2021 (twice)

Cover design by Louise Dugdale
Cover image: *Gaia Rising over Punished Prometheus* by Setsuko Aihara

A catalogue record for this book is available from the British Library.

Library of Congress Cataloging-in-Publication Data
Names: Parkes, Graham, 1949– author.
Title: How to think about the climate crisis : a philosophical guide to saner ways
of living / Graham Parkes. Description: London ; New York : Bloomsbury
Academic, 2021. | Includes bibliographical references and index.
Identifiers: LCCN 2020033556 (print) | LCCN 2020033557 (ebook) |
ISBN 9781350158863 (hardback) | ISBN 9781350158870 (paperback) |
ISBN 9781350158887 (ebook) | ISBN 9781350158894 (epub)
Subjects: LCSH: Climatic changes–Philosophy. | Philosophy, Comparative.
Classification: LCC QC903 .P375 2021 (print) | LCC QC903 (ebook) |
DDC 363.738/74—dc23
LC record available at https://lccn.loc.gov/2020033556
LC ebook record available at https://lccn.loc.gov/2020033557

ISBN: HB: 978-1-3501-5886-3
       PB: 978-1-3501-5887-0
       ePDF: 978-1-3501-5888-7
       eBook: 978-1-3501-5889-4

Typeset by RefineCatch Ltd, Bungay, Suffolk
Printed and bound in Great Britain

To find out more about our authors and books, visit www.bloomsbury.com
and sign up for our newsletters.

To the students I've taught – from whom I've learned. For the students I won't have the opportunity to teach, in the hope that they'll learn some things that will help.

And in memory of Martin Schönfeld (1963–2020), a dear friend and treasured colleague, whose tragic death has deprived us of someone who knew well how to think about the climate crisis.

Contents

CONTENTS

Preface

Because of the radical transformation of the world that began shortly after I finished writing this book, it needs a new preface. On completing the manuscript at the end of 2019, part of a project I'd been working on for a decade, I realized to my dismay that an unusual conjuncture of circumstances had rendered it redundant. Let me recount the relevant events.

Having followed developments in the environmental sciences for over forty years, it became all too clear to me that reports of ecosystem destruction, biodiversity loss and species extinction were becoming steadily more dire. The evidence was overwhelming: by persisting in consuming the natural world to death, we are eliminating the 'natural resource base' on which our lives depend.[1] The enterprise was breathtaking in its irrationality – almost impossible to imagine such collective stupidity – but we were actually doing it.

I had also been following the climate sciences, and the message from that quarter, too, had changed radically in import and urgency. Some of the top experts in Earth System Science had identified several 'planetary boundaries' in the system, and 'tipping points' in the spheres of earth, oceans and air, beyond which cascades of effects would push the climate irrevocably into a very different condition. Everything we know about the interactions among these various systems suggests that we *don't* know whether we might not have pushed too far already.[2] And when positive feedbacks kick in, this increases the chances of tripping over other tipping points. Then you get 'runaway' global heating, which makes the Earth steadily less habitable – and quicker than you'd care to imagine.

Being aware of this dual threat, the best-informed commentators on climate change were becoming more pessimistic – *Requiem for a Species*, *Why the Struggle against Climate Change Failed*, *Learning to Die in the Anthropocene*, *Out of the Wreckage*, *On Fire*, *Falter*, and so forth – and barely able to conceal their despair at the desperate nature of the situation. The discrepancies between stated goals for reducing greenhouse gas emissions (after the Paris Agreement of 2016) and what's actually needed if we're to avoid climate catastrophe were huge.[3] As this grim reality came into focus, it was hard to see how the developed countries could possibly achieve the required reductions in time – even if they tried. A feeling of dread was obtruding.

In the course of a career spent teaching philosophy, I had naturally experienced existential *Angst* in the face of death. (That was some *serious* philosophy.) But this was different: worse, because it wasn't so much *my* death as the demise – suicide, really – of the human species. Reason rightly resists the realization that humanity is on track to self-destruct by breaking the climate and destroying the natural world on which it depends for its survival, but it doesn't change the facts of the matter. Now we were actually managing it. Take those two undertakings together – wrecking the climate and destroying the biosphere – and the chances that many human beings will survive the resulting catastrophe look pretty slim. Believe me (after reading the first two chapters): I've been on this case for a long time, and I'm as far as you can get from being an alarmist.

But wait! Perhaps there was hope after all – generated by the younger generation. One of the few encouraging events in 2019 was the beginning of the 'school strikes for the climate', inspired by the formidable Greta Thunberg. In the autumn of that year, the Global Climate Strike brought several million young people onto the streets of almost twenty countries. For someone who had been teaching university courses on global warming for many years, and finding the students mostly (and understandably) more concerned with other things, it was wonderful to see such enthusiasm finally. When I looked at the websites of the various organizations and movements, and read about their aims and objectives, I was encouraged – in part because I thought the ideas and information in this book could help further their worthy cause. The outrage on the part of young people whose lives were going to be ravaged by the effects of global heating was totally justifiable – but would the world's leaders listen, and take appropriate action?

Every year for the past two decades I read about the results of the annual United Nations Climate Change Conference and am consistently depressed by the continued fruitlessness of those gatherings. But this time – the *twenty-fifth* conference, to be held in Madrid at the end of 2019 – it would surely be different. The year had been the second hottest since 1850, and filled with extreme weather events, including wildfires in the Amazon and Australia. The scientific evidence was more incontrovertible than ever that we're destroying the natural basis of our very survival as a species, and are on the point of tipping the climate system into irreversible collapse. On top of that, leaders of developing countries were protesting more forcefully than ever the gross injustice of the situation, now with vocal support from schoolchildren and students all over the world.

And what did that year's conference achieve? *Less than nothing*, because major players – Australia, Brazil, China, India, Russia, Saudi Arabia and the United States – continued to drag their feet and obstruct meaningful progress on tackling the climate crisis. An utter disgrace, to have such losers for 'leaders'.

A couple of weeks later, I had to send off the manuscript – but in the face of catastrophe, what was the point? I was on the point of burning the damned thing and deleting every last kilobyte of the electronic files. Yet, even if it were too late to help avert climate catastrophe, could the book perhaps contribute to minimizing the misery? It was the end of the decade, and to hit 'send' would afford some kind of closure to what had seemed an interminable project. I did hit 'send', oblivious to something else that happened that day, something momentous that would make the book relevant again.

On 31 December 2019, a 'pneumonia of unknown cause detected in Wuhan' was reported to the World Health Organization's office in China. The cause would turn out to be a new coronavirus.

For decades we have chosen to ignore clear signals from the geosphere, natural reactions to our overheating of the planet, signifying that we're overdoing it as a species. In addition, scientists have been warning for years that human activities – deforestation and habitat destruction, wildlife trade and animal markets – are increasing the incidence of infectious diseases such as Covid-19 crossing from animals to humans.[4] And global heating is making the situation worse. The message is simple: there are natural limits in the Earth's various systems, and we humans have been pushing them too hard for too long. We have encroached upon the natural realm so obtrusively as to provoke a devastating pushback. We need to restrain ourselves, regulate our extreme rates of 'resource extraction', if we're to get back to a world of fewer pandemics – or to anything like a normal climate.

In the case of climate change, the mainstream view has been that it's *impossible* for the developed world to renounce its late capitalist and high-consumerist lifestyle, and make the required changes in land use and cuts in greenhouse gas (GHG) emissions. But then a natural reaction in the form of the Covid-19 outbreak brought about in a matter of weeks something they assured us could never happen: large parts of the globalized economy were shut down almost overnight. Bruno Latour expressed it nicely: 'All along, within the world economic system, hidden from us all, there was a bright red alarm signal with a nice big stainless-steel lever that the heads of state could pull, one after the other, to instantly stop the "train of progress" with a loud screeching of brakes.'[5] Who would have guessed? But it actually happened!

It's a tragedy that it had to happen this way: so many people sick, thrown out of work by shutdowns, ruined by failed businesses and by failing governments, victims of all ages dead. People want to work again – but they need to be given new and better positions in a different kind of economy that's the basis for a Green New Deal.

It was libertarian individualists and free market fundamentalists that got us into the climate crisis, and now a global public health crisis has exposed their impotence and the baseness of their ideas. Just as they ignored the warnings of the climate scientists, they now endanger their fellow citizens by refusing to listen to the experts in epidemiology.

Libertarian and faux populist leaders are aiming for a replay of the fiasco that followed the last big global upheaval, the financial crisis of 2008: bail out the big industries, and let ordinary taxpayers and ill-paid 'necessary workers' foot the bill. The richest 1 per cent are already profiting from the pandemic, and they desperately want to get the train of progress going again so that they can profit even more.[6] Lockdowns preclude people from taking to the streets to protest such colossal injustice – but what if enough of us decline to reboard the train?

It's time to *resist 'return to normal'*, for the simple reason that our former 'normal' was on course to heat up the planet so much as to render it uninhabitable – or to make it so difficult to inhabit that only a fraction of the current world population would survive.[7] The old normal was becoming lethal to the species, but the next normal needn't be. The International Energy Agency has estimated that all the government restrictions in response to the pandemic could result in an 8 per cent drop in carbon emissions for 2020 – remarkably just what the United Nations Environment Programme says will be necessary every year for the next decade if we're to prevent a temperature rise of over $1.5°C$.[8] That's what we need, and we could manage it if we tried.

This virus-enforced lull amidst the onrush of progress gives us an unprecedented opportunity to maintain the momentum toward a low- and eventually zero-carbon economy. If oil prices sink so low as to shut down a good chunk of the fossil fuel industry, just let it go; and if the airline industry has shrunk to a fraction of its previous size, let it be. Sensible governments will finance transitions to new employment for displaced workers. And the same with over-tourism, cruise ships, cities congested with cars, and other 'non-essentials': let them shrink to a size compatible with a planet that's inhabitable.

I honestly believed we were doomed, but then the pandemic suddenly opened a window of opportunity to forestall climate catastrophe. Now, however, powerful interests are doing their best to slam it shut. If they succeed, the resumption of normal will lead to species suicide. We must resist letting them seduce us down that fatal path. There are other, saner ways of living: let's try them out!

Vienna, May 2020

Acknowledgements

I have learned from conversations with many people over the years about the topics in this book, including: Setsuko Aihara (thanks to Romanization, my wife's name comes first), Dimitra Amarantidou, Ahinora Antova, Josef Aregger, Bai Tongdong, Jim Behunaik, Daniel A. Bell, Morris Berman, Baird Callicott, Lisa Carden, Ed Casey, El Casey, David Cooper, Danny Coyle, Paul D'Ambrosio, Deguchi Yasuo, Ľubomír Dunaj, Rolf Elberfeld, Rolf Elberfeld, Tim Engström, Hans Feger, Sarah Flavel, Joergen Fog, Tim Freeman, Jean-Claude Gens, John Grim, Helmut Heit, Fabian Heubel, Atsuko Ichijo, Simon James, Julia Jansen, David Jones, François Jullien, Leah Kalmanson, Tom Kasulis, Kobayashi Yasuo, David Krell, Hayo Krombach, Laurence Lampert, Titus Leber, Ronan Lebras, Eckardt Lindner, Sophie Loidolt, Jean-Michel Lou, Adam Loughnare, Lu Feng, Grazia Marchianò, James McRae, Suzanne Murphy, Nakajima Takahiro, Don Nilson, Ouyang Xiao, Brad Park, Helen Parkes, Margot Parkes, Randy Peerenboom, Franklin Perkins, Michael Puett, Matthew Ratcliffe, Rein Raud, Georg Schneider, Brian Schroeder, James Sellman, Geir Sigurðsson, Hans Sluga, Kenn Steffensen, Takada Yasunari, Mary Evelyn Tucker, Mostafa Vaziri, Andrew Whitehead, David Williams, Jason Wirth, Yu Lan, Zhu Hongzhao, Brook Ziporyn and Bernhard Zorzi. Thanks also to the students in my seminars at the University of Hawaii, University College Cork, East China Normal University in Shanghai, Tokyo University and the University of Vienna.

And with special gratitude to: Roger Ames, Caroline Davidson, James Heisig, Peter Hershock, Hunter McEwan, Hans-Georg Moeller, Martin Schönfeld †, Lee Siegel, Xenia Vargova, Anthony Wrixon – and to my editor at Bloomsbury, Colleen Coalter, for not losing faith in this protean project.

I am grateful to the Department of Philosophy at the University of Vienna for my affiliation as a Professorial Research Fellow, as well as to the University Botanical Garden and the City of Vienna Parks and Gardens Department (MA 42) for providing pleasant places in which to think and write.

And for the music – it influences the writing – thanks to (among many others): Laurie Anderson, Alfred Brendel, David Byrne, George Clinton,

Teodor Currentzis, Brian Eno, Mitsuko Uchida – and of course Rage against the Machine!

Unless otherwise noted, translations of quotations from texts in foreign languages are my own. I have occasionally modified extant translations where appropriate and, in the case of ancient Greek and Chinese texts, drawn from several versions in the light of the original. For the Romanization of Chinese terms I use the Pinyin system rather than the older (and more confusing) Wade-Giles system – for example, *Daodejing* rather than *Tao Te Ching*.

The text that follows is an excerpt from a decade-long project that addresses environmental problems from the standpoint of East Asian as well as Western philosophies. As the effects of global heating became more severe, I decided to make the first instalment a book that would be helpful for students, and others who are concerned about the situation. But so many interrelated topics required attention that the manuscript grew too long, and I was obliged to make extensive cuts. I have put relevant sections of the original manuscript on a webpage for the benefit of readers who are interested in seeing the evidence – facts, figures and sources – and more detailed discussions (http://www.bloomsbury.com/how-to-think-about-the-climate-crisis). The existence of an appendix is marked in the body of the text like this [1.2], referring to the second one for Chapter 1.

A brief remark concerning terminology. It used to be that people talked about 'global warming'. Then it became clear that one of the effects of steady warming was occasional extremes of *colder* weather in winter, so some began to talk of 'climate change' instead. Political considerations also came into play. Nevertheless it's the relentless warming that's pushing us toward some perilous 'tipping points'. In 2019, the worsening situation prompted the British newspaper *The Guardian* to modify its style guide to reflect more clearly the results of the science: now the favoured terms are 'climate emergency, crisis or breakdown' and 'global heating'.[1] As the book's title indicates, I'm going with 'crisis' – and on darker days, 'catastrophe'.

Introductions (Background and Book)

A man walks into a bar. He's hungry as well as thirsty, and so he orders a hamburger, which he eats with relish. The beef in the burger arrived in the kitchen via JBS S.A., the world's largest meat-processing company, with headquarters in Brazil. The slaughterhouses owned by JBS are operated by the Brazilian farming concern AgroSB, which owns huge cattle farms in the Amazon state of Pará. The owners of AgroSB have been involved in numerous corruption scandals, and the company and JBS have been paying millions of dollars in fines for illegal deforestation and buying cattle raised on farms in prohibited areas. Thousands of hectares of the Amazon rainforest are cleared every year for the purpose of producing beef and planting soybeans for animal feed. This fuels an increase in forest fires, threatening to turn the Amazon from 'the lungs of the earth', in which capacity it absorbs carbon dioxide and slows down global heating, to a source emitting *more* CO_2 – which will make the climate crisis even worse.[1]

Without intending to, the man in the bar is contributing to a system that's increasing global heating and also, due to the cutthroat capitalist policies of Brazil's President Bolsonaro, depriving the indigenous inhabitants of the Amazon of their land and livelihoods. This is just one of many instances where, thanks to globalization, the absurdly long supply lines of the global food system are associated with damage to the climate and harm to nature and the poor. Nor is it just the supply lines: now that the food system is largely industrialized, the whole thing relies heavily on fossil fuels – for petrochemical fertilisers, transport and so forth – and is a major contributor to global heating.[2]

This is no joke – but the example is *not* intended as a moral judgment on eating meat (though some ethical qualms about supporting an industrial agricultural system that inflicts pollution on neighbours of its factories, and gratuitous suffering on animals, are quite in order). The point is rather to highlight consequences of our actions that we might not be comfortable with. Just as buying a pair of running shoes may support businesses in South Asia that use child labour, so turning on the heating in your home usually contributes to carbon emissions. This latter isn't a matter of personal guilt, since those of us living in the developed countries are caught up in an energy system over which we have little control, and finding a way to live 'off the grid' isn't a viable option for most people.

But the main problem here, which is not so difficult to address, is our lack of awareness concerning the central insight of ancient philosophies and the modern science of ecology alike: it's *all interconnecting*. This idea is also germane to how to think about the climate crisis. It's not that interconnection is good and lack of connection is bad: the current globalized economy is a paradigm of interconnectedness, but one that delivers many ills along with the goods. It's rather that many interactions that we do well to understand are not immediately apparent. As finite beings, we can't possibly become aware of the consequences of every action we perform, but we can surely expand our awareness of interactivity to some extent. Let's consider some examples of interconnectedness in the context of weather and climate, by way of three stories from three months at the end of 2018.

'We live on the coast. It's cyclical,' said a North Carolina resident after Hurricane Florence blasted through the state in September of that year, leaving over fifty people dead and an estimated $15 billion in damage. The man denied that human-caused global warming could have fed the hurricane's unusual power. Instead, he said, 'There's a group of people that want to control things, and they're using climate change to control things, and they want to put a tax on things.'[3] Yes, some do think that we need to regulate GHG emissions, and environmental economists recommend a tax on carbon as one way of doing this. And the things they want to control are harmful: disruption of the climate and destruction of the natural environment on which human beings depend. The suspicion of *malicious* control, widespread in the United States, exemplifies the power of conspiracy theories to shape people's thinking.

A month after the blow from Florence, Hurricane Michael caused almost sixty deaths and some $25 billion of damage in Florida and neighbouring states. But when a reporter asked a 'programs specialist' at the Georgia Farm Bureau if he thought the force of the hurricane might be associated with global warming, the curt reply was, 'That's politics, and I don't want to get into it!' No, it's a matter for the climate sciences. In any case a pity, because this is really a *300 billion* dollar question – the record annual cost of extreme weather events to the US the previous year. Between 1980 and 2018, the country experienced 240 such events costing over $1 billion each, for a cumulative total of $1.6 *trillion*.[4] (Extreme weather has caused greater losses to life and property in Africa and Asia, but I'm focusing on the US because it has the greatest capability to improve the situation – for citizens of other countries as well as for its own.)

The key field of research here is 'attribution science', which examines the extent to which unusual weather can be attributed to climate change. As the new science gets more sophisticated, it becomes more evident that global heating *is* making extreme weather events more likely.[5] Nonetheless farmers in the US, whose livelihoods depend on their not being subject to destructive weather conditions, are *less* likely than most people to think that extreme weather events are connected with human-caused global heating – even after their crops have been destroyed by hurricanes, flooding or drought.[6] I suppose some of them *have* to think that way in order to keep going.

The month after Hurricane Michael, the US Global Change Research Program published the Fourth National Climate Assessment: *Impacts, Risks, and Adaptation in the United States*.[7] Four years in the making, the report is the work of over 300 scientists and experts from all relevant branches of the government and related institutions. It warns of disastrous social consequences if we continue to burn fossil fuels, and rising costs to the US economy that surpass the $300 billion of 2017. This would be a matter of great concern for a government that cared about the welfare of its people, but the response of the Trump administration was simply to ignore it. Trump himself claimed to have 'read some of it' (it's over 1,500 pages long), and on that basis he said simply, 'I don't believe it'. Since Trump thinks that climate change is 'a hoax', we're presumably supposed to believe that the Assessment is the product of some kind of conspiracy by government experts.[8]

These are three examples of how *not* to think about climate change: namely, by not thinking about it at all, pretending it doesn't exist, or imagining that climate scientists are conspiring to destroy our way of life. Insofar as conspiracy theories exemplify the power of preconceived *ideas*, a philosophical approach – which takes ideas seriously – is called for. But since the argument of the first half of this book might itself smack of conspiracy theory, let me recount my first encounter with the phenomenon fifty years ago, and with a number of themes in this book – as a prelude to showing that I've been thinking about these issues for a while.

First, some background

In 1970 I left the the United Kingdom for the University of California, to study for a Ph.D. in philosophy. On the evening after installing myself in a one-room apartment in a shingle-style house north of the university campus, there came a tentative knock on the door. I opened it to find a tall figure looking very much like Jesus, but rail thin and dressed in faded denim shirt and jeans. 'Hey man, welcome to Berkeley!' he said with a broad smile and extended hand. 'I'm Luke, your neighbour 'cross the hall. I heard you're from the UK: that's really cool, man.' I was thinking it was pretty cool to have a name like Luke.

I invited my new neighbour to come in, noticing that he was holding something behind his back. When he held it out to me, I saw it was a record by David Bowie with the unfamiliar title *Man of Words / Man of Music*. 'You know this album?' Luke asked. Taking it and turning it over to look at the list of songs on the back cover, I replied, 'Yes, I do. But where I come from it's called *Space Oddity*.' 'That's just it!' he said. 'And you know why they changed the title for US consumption *and* left out a 40-second track called "Don't Sit Down"?' When I admitted I didn't know, and asked if he'd like to sit down, he dropped casually to a cross-legged position on the carpet while motioning to me to do the same. 'Lemme tell you the story behind it, man.'

The story was long, and wove enigmatic connections among the missing forty-second track, the nonsense phrases at the end of Side 2 of the Beatles' *Sgt. Pepper's Lonely Hearts Club Band*, scenes from Stanley Kubrick's film *2001: A Space Odyssey,* themes from Erich von Däniken's *Chariots of the Gods?* and some other arcane things I can no longer recall.[9] Being unfamiliar with the von Däniken book, I had to confess at the end of the story that I didn't quite get the point. 'But don't you see, man?' said Luke, 'Bowie's an *alien*, from outer space – but they don't want us to know that.' I nodded sympathetically, wondering silently who 'they' might be. Six years later, Nicolas Roeg's film *The Man Who Fell to Earth* came out, starring David Bowie in a remarkable performance as a space alien. This prompted some pondering of the story according to Luke.

Much of Luke's mental life, it turned out, revolved around conspiracy theories, and in this respect he was not untypical of residents of the San Francisco Bay Area at the time. Most of them, though, were harmless enough: contact with UFOs and aliens from outer space didn't appear to endanger the health of believers or drive them to violence. Fifty years later, what used to be very much an American phenomenon has spread worldwide, infecting millions, and sometimes reaching the highest levels of government.[10] Conspiracy theories are now far darker, and (thanks to the Internet) more widespread, often with harmful effects on non-believers. If you dismiss the climate crisis as a fabrication, for example, and slow down progress on dealing with it, you thereby put other people's health, livelihoods, and even lives at risk.

At one level, conspiracy theorists exhibit in extreme form a tendency we all share as human beings: our worldviews point up certain things and screen out others, so that new events may be exaggerated or missed completely according to how they fit, or fail to fit, with our basic understanding of the world. The philosopher and statesman Francis Bacon stated it elegantly:

Once a man's understanding has settled on something (either because it is an accepted belief or because it pleases him), it draws everything else also to support and agree with it. And if it encounters a larger number of more powerful countervailing examples, it either fails to notice them, or disregards them, or makes fine distinctions to dismiss and reject them, and all this with much dangerous prejudice, to preserve the authority of its first conceptions.[11]

That was 500 years ago: the authority of first conceptions is far more powerful now that people enjoy the filtering functions of the Internet, which provide the comfort of customised 'information cocoons' or 'filter bubbles' that are penetrated only by voices that echo and reinforce what we already believe.[12]

I have always dismissed conspiracy theorists as sadly deluded – but then I came to realize that there actually *is* a conspiracy unfolding behind the scenes (in the sense of a secret plot to seize power), which is preventing us from tackling the climate crisis.[13] But how can I expect the reader, in a world where so many people's heads are buzzing with the looniest conspiracy theories, to believe *my* account of a real, billionaire-backed conspiracy going on behind the scenes? In a 'post-truth' age awash with fake news and alternative facts, how does an author convince the reader that he's writing in good faith, as a reliable guide to what's really going on?

It will help, I hope, if I give a sense of where I'm coming from (man), so the reader can judge the extent of any personal stake in the matter and my qualifications for treating it. And since I've just recounted a personal anecdote, there's an opportunity here for some disclosure of my interests.

It would perhaps be good if I could assure you that I'm not a 'nature person', because you could then rest assured that I would never respect nature more highly than the human, or God, society, the free market, or whatever. But I can't: I have to confess that for me – never having been introduced to organized religion – the natural world is a source of meaning in life, a phenomenon of profound beauty. From the time I went to university in the (then) idyllic town of Oxford, there's been a feeling of *belonging* among grasses and trees, rocks and hills and streams, grey clouds tinged orange by the sinking sun. Of course, such feelings are partial: the natural world is also, depending on your perspective and position, a dangerous and inhospitable place.[14]

Wondering about the meaning of these 'natural mystic' experiences, I began to study philosophies of nature, not only in Western traditions but also in Buddhism, Sufism and Daoism. The culture shock for a clueless young fellow from the UK landing in Berkeley in the early seventies was considerable – but also a great learning experience. Not only could you study with first-rate scholars at the university in areas from Greek and Roman classics to Buddhism and East Asian Studies, but you could also practise disciplines from Ayurveda to Zen with masters from India, China, Tibet and Japan.

People often dismiss the American counterculture movement of the sixties and seventies as hopelessly idealistic and narcissistic, and to some extent it was. (I confess to some navel-gazing and spiritual seeking myself, when young.) But the hedonistic triad of sex, drugs and rock 'n' roll was balanced by a concern with physical health (yoga, taiji, diet), mental well-being (meditation practices) and a flourishing artistic culture. There was also a healthy awareness of civic responsibility on the part of many activists at that time. The Berkeley City Council was an enlightened group of people who engaged in conscientious discussion of important social issues. In 1971 the city initiated (without meaning to) the 'sanctuary movement', by passing laws making local churches safe havens for sailors resisting the Vietnam War. There were neighbourhood recycling programmes, and broader initiatives for conservation of natural ecosystems around the city. Environmental issues were frequently discussed and debated, in the University as well as around it by concerned citizens.

This counter-cultural pushback against the American Dream took place within a larger scene of opposing tendencies. On the one hand there was growing awareness of the harm that human activities were inflicting on the natural world: increasing pollution, worldwide, of the air, water and soil; species extinction (a natural phenomenon, but we were clearly speeding it up); deforestation and desertification as a result of agricultural practices and pressures; and general over-exploitation of the planet's resources. (The list sounds sadly familiar.) On the other hand the government enacted some enlightened legislation, notably a series of Acts of Congress that furthered the spirit of the Clean Air Act from 1963: the Clean Water, Endangered Species, and Toxic Substances Control Acts (1972 to 1976).

In spite of these progressive pieces of legislation, the problems I just mentioned have become far more serious, in large part because the world's population has almost doubled since 1974 when it was 4 billion. The spirit of the laws and government back then, based on reliable science, was the antithesis of what now holds sway: a libertarian dismantling of all environmental regulations that might reduce industries' profits. Certain parties profit handsomely by exploiting the natural world, without caring that it's usually the poor who suffer the worst effects of this exploitation. This unfortunate characteristic of capitalism – some people getting rich at the expense of others and the environment – is more prevalent now than ever before.

Then good ideas

Some of the ideas that were earnestly discussed in those days have retained their relevance. In 1968 a professor of biology at the University of California by the name of Garrett Hardin had published an influential article in the journal *Science* titled 'The Tragedy of the Commons'.[15] His main concern was with 'the population problem', but his ideas have had most impact on discussions of environmental issues more broadly. Going against the popular economic endorsement of the 'free market' as advocated by figures like Milton Friedman, Hardin questions Adam

Smith's idea of the 'invisible hand' that seems to direct things so efficiently. (The idea that even though each individual may not intend to 'promote the publick interest', his commercial activity in a functioning economy, in which he 'intends only his own gain', ends up promoting precisely that.[16]) Hardin argues that the common assumption that reasonable 'decisions reached individually will, in fact, be the best decisions for an entire society' is very often false. Here's how it doesn't work.

Imagine the commons as a pasture on which residents of a village can graze their animals. It's in my self-interest to add another animal to my herd, since that gives me the benefit of an extra animal without having to bear much in the way of costs, which would be shared equally by all residents. This works just fine – except that when everyone makes similar decisions, the pasture will eventually become barren from over-grazing, and then everyone's herds go hungry. Hardin points out that the tragedy of the commons also applies to the oceans, where at that time the old idea of their 'inexhaustible resources' still held sway. The total collapse of the cod fisheries in the northwest Atlantic during the 1990s showed that the ocean's resources were by no means inexhaustible.

Hardin goes on to show that the tragedy of the commons also happens in the case of something like pollution, where it's 'not a question of taking something out of the commons, but of putting something in'. As many industrialists have realized, 'the rational man finds that his share of the costs of the wastes he discharges into the commons is less than the costs of purifying his wastes before releasing them'. But when too many rational men do this for too long, the system collapses. This is what's happening now on a global scale with the atmosphere: the industrial nations persist in emitting carbon dioxide even though economists keep saying that it will cost less to mitigate the problem now than to pay the costs of a catastrophe later. Since there's no higher power than the sovereign nation, they feel free to persist; but, as Hardin warned: 'Freedom in a commons brings ruin to all.'[17]

Hardin's pessimism concerning successful management of the commons had the unfortunate effect of bolstering the long-standing practice of *enclosure*, whereby private interests (or the state) appropriate common land for their own use and profit. But this doesn't legitimate such takeovers, because it *is* possible, as Elinor Ostrom has shown in her book *Governing the Commons*, to find ways to manage the commons fairly without resorting to top–down regulation. The problem is that this appears to work only on a small scale and on the basis of a grass-roots movement. On a scale as large as the oceans and the atmosphere, it's every businessman (and nation-state) for himself.[18]

The year before Hardin's article appeared, another University of California professor had published a landmark essay in the journal *Science*, Lynn White, Jr. His 'The Historical Roots of Our Ecologic Crisis' explored connections between understandings of the humans-nature relationship and treatment of the environment. An eminent historian of technology, White was prescient in warning of the effects of burning fossil fuels: 'it threatens to change the chemistry of the globe's atmosphere as a whole, with consequences which we are only beginning to guess'. His thinking – wishful, as it turned out – was that we'd be better equipped to handle the coming change of climate if we understood its historical roots.

White was one of the first to remark on 'the greatest event in human history since the invention of agriculture, and perhaps in nonhuman terrestrial history as well' – namely, 'the marriage between science and technology, a union of the theoretical and the empirical approaches to our natural environment'.[19] The roots of this synthesis lay in Francis Bacon's programme in the seventeenth century to improve the lot of humankind through technical mastery of nature, and it burst into fullest flower with the Industrial Revolution.

White cites as another powerful factor the 'striking story of creation' in the first chapter of the Book of Genesis, where God makes man in His own image and grants him dominion over the earth and all its creatures. More than a few believers have taken this story as encouraging human beings to exploit nature for their own benefit.[20] This was a major change of attitude from antiquity, when the natural world was animated by the World Soul and there were spirits all over the place. In those days of old,

> Before one cut a tree, mined a mountain, or dammed a brook, it was important to placate the spirit in charge of that particular situation, and to keep it placated. By destroying pagan animism, Christianity made it possible to exploit nature in a mood of indifference to the feelings of natural objects.

Whatever your attitude toward animism (we'll be coming back to it in Chapter 9), White is right to make us think about the effects of powerful technology combined with strong ideas about human superiority. This does appear to have led to increasing devastation of the natural environment *and* to widespread 'conquering, looting, and colonizing' by the greater European powers. Mastery over nature followed by domination of less 'civilized' races can be a lucrative business.

But White also acknowledges the multifaceted nature of Christian belief, and expresses admiration for 'An Alternative Christian View'. He praises Saint Francis of Assisi for his concern 'to depose man from his monarchy over creation and set up a democracy of all God's creatures', and proposes him as 'a patron saint for ecologists'. (More on St. Francis, and Pope Francis, in Chapter 6.) In a similar spirit White mentions the Zen Buddhist understanding of the humans–nature relationship, which he suggests is 'very nearly the mirror image of the mainstream Christian view' – even though he's 'dubious of its viability among us' Westerners.[21]

Some residents of the Bay Area at the time had no doubt about the viability of Zen: the teachings of the Sōtō School impressed people with the basic sanity of the Zen approach to living. You pay more attention to what you're doing *and* to the consequences of your broader interactions. I still occasionally consult my battered copy of a classic from those days, *Tassajara Cooking*, a vegetarian cookbook from the kitchen of the Tassajara Zen Mountain Center. A recently ordained Zen master from the US provided a brief Introduction, in which he celebrates food as 'the countless other creatures that constantly help … the water, sunlight, and turning of the earth.' He cites the great Zen master Dōgen: in the kitchen, 'the pure actions of the cook come forth from his realization of the unity of all things and beings'.[22] (We'll return to Dōgen in the kitchen in Chapter 9.)

People beyond the Zen community were also discovering that eating lower on the food web is good not only for the eater but also for the environment. *Diet for a Small Planet* was an eye-opening book that demonstrated the absurdity of food production in the US: even in 1970 half of the grains produced were being fed to livestock, and it was taking sixteen pounds of grain and soybeans to produce one pound of beef. You could instead ensure an adequate intake of proteins by combining various plant foods in ways that traditional ways of cooking had done for generations. By contrast, the modern global food system was preventing millions from getting adequate nourishment.[23]

The now classic book by the philosopher Peter Singer, *Animal Liberation: A New Ethics for Our Treatment of Animals*, came out in 1975, and further confirmed the wisdom of not eating meat. For me the most powerful chapters were 'Down on the Factory Farm: or what happened to your dinner when it was still an animal', and 'Becoming a Vegetarian: or how to produce less suffering and more food at a reduced cost to the environment'.[24] Being an ethicist, Singer focuses on the morality of meat-eating; but leaving ethics aside, you still have to question the costs of our unnecessarily expensive eating habits not only to other inhabitants of the planet but also to its soil, water and atmosphere. (More on the contribution of meat production to global heating in the final chapter.)

Concerning the broader relations among human beings, economics, and the natural world, E. F. Schumacher's wonderful book *Small is Beautiful: A Study of Economics as if People Mattered* (1973) offered a sane and eloquent treatment that is today more pertinent than ever. For someone who had studied economics and found Thomas Carlyle's label 'the dismal science' to be generous, Schumacher's elegant presentation of economics was a revelation. Because yes, people and nature (and not only goods) surely mattered.

Considering the converse of his dictum 'small is beautiful': Schumacher thought things were turning ugly because economics was looming too large in the modern world, agreeing with his mentor John Maynard Keynes that it would be splendid if 'economists could manage to get themselves thought of as humble, competent people, on a level with dentists'! He was prescient in warning of the tendency of the science of economics 'to usurp the rest', the 'pathological development' whereby it 'absorbs almost the whole of foreign policy . . . the whole of ethics and to take precedence over all other human considerations'. That voracious absorption continues to prevail.

Schumacher gives several reasons for keeping economics in its place and limiting its reach. The main one is that economists forget that they work within 'a "given" framework which lies altogether outside the economic calculus', and operate on the basis of unquestioned assumptions about what makes for a good human life and how the natural world works. For the discipline to function well, 'the aims and objectives' of economics have to come from 'a study of man', and most of its methodology from 'a study of nature'. A major problem is that 'it is inherent in the methodology of modern economics, which is so largely market-oriented, *to ignore man's dependence on the natural world*'.[25] In other words, nature figures in the economic calculus as a given, which we take only for the cost of extracting what we want.

There's a fatal failure to make the fundamental distinction between income and capital, 'the irreplaceable capital which man has not made, but simply found, and without which he can do nothing'. Our relative lack of interest in natural capital derives from our being 'estranged from reality and inclined to treat as valueless everything that we have not made ourselves' – which in turn obscures another crucial distinction, between natural materials and synthetic products.

> Our scientists and technologists have learned to compound substances unknown to nature. Against many of them, nature is virtually defenceless. There are no natural agents to attack and break them down ... which accounts for their dangerous ecological impact.... The long-term consequences of their accumulation are in many cases known to be extremely dangerous, and in other cases totally unpredictable.

Add to the effects of synthetic products the enormous 'quantitative jump in industrial production' after the Second World War, and you begin to encroach upon 'the *tolerance margins* which benign nature always provides' – a very risky business.[26] The study of nature teaches us there are limits.

Schumacher warns again and again of the dangers of pursuing unlimited economic growth, in the light of what we learn from 'the environmental sciences'.

> An attitude to life which seeks fulfilment in the single-minded pursuit of wealth – in short, materialism – does not fit into this world, because it contains within itself no limiting principle, while the environment in which it is placed is strictly limited. Already, *the environment is trying to tell us that certain stresses are be coming excessive.*[27]

As early as 1973 he was remarking on the gross global injustice that 'the "rich" are in the process of stripping the world of its once-for-all endowment of relatively cheap and simple fuels'. Fifty years later, the injustice is compounded by the devastating effect on the poorer countries of the global heating produced by all that plundering.

In order to function as a science, economics has to ignore *quality*, which we appreciate but can't measure, in favour of *quantity*, which does lend itself to calculation. As Robert F. Kennedy aptly remarked, Gross Domestic Product (GDP) measures everything 'except that which makes life worthwhile'. A bigger problem, for Schumacher, is that economics basically ignores the 'goods' that never appear on the market, such as 'air, water, the soil, and in fact the whole framework of living nature'. Insofar as economics fails to account for costs to that whole framework, which is suffering irreparable damage from our economic and industrial activity, 'the entire outlook and methodology of economics is called into question'.[28]

For all these reasons, when it comes to the 'study of man' Schumacher finds the 'western materialism' that undergirds and guides modern economics to be woefully inadequate, because it overlooks everything that makes life worthwhile. Although 'the teachings of Christianity, Islam, or Judaism' or of any of 'the great Eastern traditions' could provide an adequate 'meta-economic' (philosophical) grounding, because of his experience as an economic advisor in South Asia, Schumacher chooses the teachings of Buddhism. A chapter titled 'Buddhist Economics' outlines a saner version of the discipline based on the Buddhist idea that the person is fundamentally connected with other people and the natural environment.

On the Buddhist worldview, *work* gives us an opportunity to develop our abilities while collaborating with others to produce what's needed for a fulfilled life. It values people more highly than goods, and creative activity more than consumption. As 'the Middle Way', Buddhism isn't promoting asceticism but rather *moderation*: 'It is not wealth that stands in the way of liberation but the attachment to wealth; not the enjoyment of pleasurable things but the craving for them.'

Taking 'simplicity and non-violence' as basic principles, the Buddhist economist dismisses 'standard of living' as measured by the amount of consumption (which is a means rather than an end it itself) in favour of 'a maximum of well-being with the minimum of consumption'. A Buddhist economics would reject globalization in favour of 'production from local resources to satisfy local needs', while encouraging respectful and careful treatment of the sentient beings in our natural environment.[29]

Schumacher was afraid that the addictive power of consumerism would make it hard to avoid environmental disaster, which makes it crucial to try and 'develop a new life-style which is compatible with the real needs of human nature, with the health of living nature around us, and with the resource endowment of the world'. What you could call *saner* ways of living. These would involve redirecting technology to 'the real needs of man' – which also means '*to the actual size of man*. Man is small, and, therefore, small is beautiful. To go for giantism is to go for self-destruction.' Yet five decades on, economies of scale continue to make people think that bigger is better.[30]

Schumacher finished writing *Small is Beautiful* in the home of his friend and mentor Leopold Kohr, an Austrian thinker who was a great enemy of gigantism, and who had begun his book *The Breakdown of Nations* (1957) with the bold assertion that *bigness* is the cause of 'all forms of social misery':

> If the body of a people becomes diseased with the fever of aggression, brutality, collectivism, or massive idiocy, it is not because it has fallen victim to bad leadership or mental derangement. It is because human beings, so charming as individuals or in small aggregations, have been welded into overconcentrated social units such as mobs, unions, cartels, or great powers.[31]

I had often been overwhelmed at the bigness of the United States, and sometimes wondered whether it might be a case of too much of a good thing.

At the end of the seventies I moved farther west, to the University of Hawaii, well known for expertise in Eastern philosophy – and where I was to spend most of my career. The more I studied East Asian traditions of thought, the more valuable I found the 'distance' perspective on the Western tradition that such studies provide. As long as you're confined to a set of perspectives rooted in one particular philosophical tradition, it's difficult to appreciate them *as* perspectives and to realise that other ways of thinking may be just as valid as the ways you're accustomed to.

In 1988 the eminent climate scientist James Hansen gave testimony to the US Congress that prompted me to explore further ways of thinking that were new to me. Hansen presented the most compelling evidence to date for what Lynn White had drawn attention to twenty years earlier: human-caused global warming. His warning of the dangers of letting it continue highlighted the importance of understanding the climate sciences. I studied as best I could, and learned enough to begin teaching a course on global warming in addition to the environmental philosophy class I was already offering.

Well, this detour has been a way of introducing the kinds of thinking behind the writing of this book. Wonderment in the face of the wonders of nature led to my pondering our predicament from the perspectives of East Asian as well as Western philosophies, and eventually to thinking about the natural world from the standpoint of the climate sciences as well as philosophy.

To round out the full disclosure I mentioned earlier: because my career was spent teaching at public universities, eventually on three continents, I was able to think and teach free from institutional, financial or political constraints. I have no personal stake in the reality of global heating because I'll be dead and gone by the time the really devastating consequences hit. (Well, not *no* stake, since we have a daughter.) Nor have I received any grants or other kinds of funding that might bias my view – or alleviate the torment of writing this book.

And now the book

A book's appeal depends in part on its tone, and that poses a problem in the present case. Authors who warn of imminent disasters from global warming are often blamed for being alarmist: the audience will be overwhelmed, traumatized, and they'll simply tune out, turn off, and close the book. If your message is too depressing, you lose your readers: most people have enough problems in their lives already. You have to be more upbeat, and show the brighter side of things.

Yes, but what if the reality is sobering to the point of fear, and the potential consequences really dire? Does it help to screen that out in order to get on with our lives, if in the long run this puts those lives at risk? I'm assuming that a blend of both approaches can work: make the perils of the situation clear and show where the obstructions to progress lie; then suggest ways not only to minimize the misery but also to find fulfilment in the more challenging world that's on its way.

Here's the situation: a few people with a big stake in continuing with business as usual – especially in the fossil fuel industries and the global financial system – are prepared to sacrifice the well-being of their fellow human beings and the biosphere in order to maintain the profitable status quo. To this end they've been waging what they themselves call a 'war of ideas' for several decades now – but covertly, pursuing stealthy strategies designed to change the way people think. There are many things these people don't want the general public to know and connections they want to keep concealed. My aim in the first half of the book is to bring those things to light, so that people concerned with doing something about the climate crisis won't be kept in the dark.

(It would be presumptuous to compare my contribution with that of Noam Chomsky, who in his political works has brilliantly exposed myriad injustices by putting disparate narratives together and connecting the dots in illuminating ways. So let me simply acknowledge having been inspired by his example.)

As the ancient thinkers realized: if you're going to do the right thing (in the sense of what's most appropriate), you have to *understand* the situation, the context of your acting. Suppose I'm a philanthropist billionaire who gives a few of his millions to a charity that helps refugees – but which turns out to be a front for a terrorist group dedicated to slaughtering unbelievers. Despite all my good intentions, I end up making the world a worse rather than a better place – because I didn't understand the situation properly. Accordingly, after giving an account of the current situation with the climate, I move on to a consideration of the immediate obstructions to coping with the crisis, together with the history behind them. In my experience, students are not alone in being mostly unaware of this background – and as the philosopher George Santayana once wrote: 'Those who cannot remember the past are condemned to repeat it.'[32]

Acquaintance with the context and history lets us see how we can remove or circumvent the obstructions, and a broader engagement with philosophy in the second half of the book will help us think more fruitfully about what is to be done after that. The enemy in the war of ideas is imposing on us notions of what it means to be human and what the good life consists in. But we can fight back with *better* ideas of who we are as human beings and the kind of society we want to live in.

Commentators have said that since global heating confronts us with a truly 'wicked' problem, we need to go beyond just thinking harder to a complete *reframing* of our thinking. This is surely right; and because the climate crisis is global, it doesn't make sense to approach it, as previous books on the topic have done, with ideas drawn from only one of the world's traditions – especially when it's those Western ways of thinking that got us into the predicament in the first place. So we'll begin the philosophical reflections in the second half of the book with the Chinese tradition, and then come back to comparable ideas in Western thought.

We can't in any case deal adequately with the climate crisis without full cooperation with China, and one way to achieve this is by appreciating the ancient political philosophy that the Xi Jinping regime has been advocating (even if the actual practising has been limited). Some people say we shouldn't be negotiating, far less cooperating, with a regime as abhorrent as the Chinese Communist Party (CCP), because they're authoritarian, repressive, murderous and so forth. Well, you can stand by your ethical principles and refuse to deal with China – and thereby let global heating wreak havoc; or else you can set these principles aside for the time being, and deal with the climate emergency in a fully engaged manner.

To avoid misunderstanding, let me emphasize that when I recommend appreciating the ancient political philosophy that the current Chinese regime has been advocating, the focus is on the *ideas*, and how they might help in our current predicament. The extent to which the regime is enacting these ideas is another matter – a matter of great importance, but not one that's germane to my argument.

Those ideas from Chinese political philosophy turn out to be most apt in our current circumstances – but they also highlight some comparable, but generally overlooked, ideas from the Western tradition that are just as helpful. A meaningful dialogue can enrich our thinking and let each side learn from the other. One thing we can learn from both philosophical traditions is how to flourish in the very different world of reduced consumption that – whether we like it or not – is on its way. This allows me to sound some notes of beauty, and even joy, toward the end of the book, to balance the grimmer beginning.

One thing I'm *not* interested in doing is to preach any kind of morality, and so there aren't any moral 'oughts' in what follows. We don't after all need to engage in ethical discourse in order to ask what kind of society, and world, we want to live in, and how to move toward those. But one thing we *do* need if we're going to slow global heating is meaningful intercultural dialogue, and in my opinion we're more likely to achieve that if we avoid the turbulence that comes from a clash of different moralities. The exception will be an occasional appeal to a basic notion of fairness, or reciprocity, which most cultures appear to share, often formulating it in some version of 'the Golden Rule' ('Do unto others . . .'). This exception allows for considerations of climate justice, which are central to our global predicament.

The UN's Intergovernmental Panel on Climate Change (IPCC) has done excellent work over the past three decades, but I wish their report from 2018 hadn't given so much of the world's media the impression that 'the planet has only till 2030 to stem catastrophic climate change'.[33] The idea that we have only so many years to tackle the climate crisis is misleading: we have to act *now*, and keep on acting until we get to a zero-carbon economy that could stabilise the climate.

The same goes for keeping the global average temperature rise above 'pre-industrial levels' to a certain limit: we can ignore the debates over whether to aim for 2 degrees Celsius or 1.5°C. If the extreme weather and heat we've witnessed in the past several years is an indication of what happens after a rise of 1°C, the further increase to aim for now is clearly *zero* (0°C)! This means, among other things, reducing carbon emissions from burning fossil fuels as rapidly as possible.

People like to use the image of the Titanic to convey the seriousness of our situation, and while the ship metaphor is good (as the population of a globalized world 'we're all in the same boat'), I think the 'bus heading toward a precipice' image is better. We are facing two levels of risk: the nearer we get to the edge of the precipice the more difficult life on earth becomes; but if we reach one of several 'tipping points' that climate scientists are warning us about, the climate spins out of control and the earth gets too hot for humans to survive. Our bus goes over the edge, and it's unlikely that many of us will survive the drop. So we'd better step on the brakes as soon and as hard as we can.

The metaphor is simple, but the process will be complex, because the requisite transformations are profound and involve so many different areas of activity. An often overlooked factor here is the global financial system, which has been co-opted by a group of super-rich operators who use it to produce vast amounts of unregulated credit so that the few can get even richer while the middle classes consume beyond their means. Without this recent feature of capitalism, the fossil fuel industries couldn't keep on searching for even more sources of carbon to profit from. The workings of the economy, government, industry and society are all interconnected with the natural environment that they exploit but otherwise prefer to ignore. Major changes to all these systems will be required.

As I mentioned earlier, it's all interconnecting, and the sooner we begin thinking in terms of interactions the better our chances of tackling the climate crisis successfully. Of course all of us living in the developed world contribute directly to global heating when we use electricity or travel. The PR experts in the fossil fuel industry like to point out that it's our choice to consume their products, and their green-washing departments encourage us all to develop the personal virtues of saving energy. We do indeed need to use less energy, but such collective action on the part of citizens of the developed world won't resolve the climate crisis: for that we need powerful social movements that will bring about robust and swift political action.

I'll be going beyond the question of how to think about the climate crisis to what we might *do* about it later in the book, and especially in the last part. In the meantime let me conclude with an observation by the musician Brian Eno in his Preface to a book about environmental legislation.

> At a certain point in life, if you're a certain kind of person, you find yourself thinking that you could use some of your capabilities to make the world a better place. And if you spend any time thinking about it, you'll probably want your contribution to have as big an effect as possible. You want to apply maximum leverage, so that your efforts can in the end translate into a meaningful result.[34]

Part One

Reality & Alternatives

Insanity in individuals is somewhat rare – but in groups, parties, peoples, ages, it is the rule.

FRIEDRICH NIETZSCHE[1]

The Reality of Global Heating

The situation is so absurd that neither Camus nor Ionesco could have made it up. We're driving the earth's climate to the point where it's already becoming inimical to human life, and our political leaders don't seem to care and remain impotent with respect to changing course. Earlier drafts of this chapter laid out the basic methods and findings of the climate sciences for the benefit of readers who weren't well acquainted with the topics, and showed how we know that human activities, and especially burning fossil fuels, are the main driver of global heating. I doubt whether anyone who seriously doubts this would be reading this book, but there's a reliable literature on the topic, and a fuller account is available in the appendixes (at www.bloomsbury.com/how-to-think-about-the-climate-crisis).

I was thinking that students would find the exposition helpful, especially when it came to trying to persuade conservative grandparents that there's cause for considerable concern. But then I recalled with dismay the research that shows that people who deny the reality of global heating – 'climate deniers' for short – are unmoved by presentations of the actual facts backed up by rational argument. For someone who has devoted a career to philosophy, that's a major disappointment. The power of the fixed ideas that grip the minds of the deniers is capable of making large parts of the real world disappear. Philosophy *can* nonetheless help us with unfixing ideas and opening up new ways of thinking – so don't give up on those stubborn grandparents quite yet.

Along with the ingestion of alcohol, narcotics or hallucinogens, human beings have developed a variety of strategies for ignoring reality when they find it not to their liking. According to an extant fragment from the profoundest among the West's early thinkers, Heraclitus of Ephesus (fifth century BCE): 'People are oblivious of what they do while awake, just as they are forgetful of what they do while asleep.' No wonder philosophers have a reputation for being arrogant: he's saying that people have no idea what their dream lives are like, and don't have much of a clue about their waking lives either. 'Most men do not recognize what they experience, but believe their own opinions.' They just make it up as they go along, 'Absent while present.'[1]

There's a variety of reasons, from psychological to sociological, for people's lack of concern about climate change, but over the years I've been working on this book the general public has become *more* concerned, and so the main thing now is to get our political leaders to do their jobs. The degree of that concern depends on who you think you are. In the US, for example, 57 per cent of respondents in a Pew Research Center poll from mid-2019 thought that climate change is 'a major threat to the well-being of the US'. Among those who identified as Democrats the figure was 84 per cent, while only 27 per cent of Republicans thought climate change is a major threat.[2] Republican beliefs appear to provide a thick shield against the reality of our situation. As George Marshall writes in *Don't Even Think about It: Why Our Brains Are Wired to Ignore Climate Change*: 'Climate change ... exposes the deepest workings of our minds, and shows our extraordinary and innate talent for seeing only what we want to see and disregarding what we would prefer not to know.'[3]

Cultural and psychological biases let us ignore reality, or simply make it up as we see fit – but that doesn't work for long when the reality is the forces of nature. Think of the inexorable power of a hurricane, a tsunami, a flood or drought. Or the non-alternative fact that when the wet-bulb (high humidity) temperature goes over 35°C, the human body overheats – even at rest, and in the shade – and eventually expires from hypothermia.[4] But since we're reluctant to face the reality of our own mortality, we tend to think that death by heat 'couldn't possibly happen to me'. But of course it could.

How we know

Let's think about how we know what's happening in the world, beyond what we perceive of our immediate surroundings. Basically, other people tell you; and if they are reliable reporters and you believe them, you probably do know what you think you know. And if you're asked *how* you know, you cite sources, give justification, or provide evidence – rather than say, 'I just know'. It's a sad sign of the times that the Trump administration dispenses with this convention: they simply say 'This is what's happening', even though it isn't, without even pretending to provide evidence.

In the old days, the task of knowing what was going on seemed simple enough. When I was young, we got our news through the newspapers, *The Glasgow Herald* and *Manchester Guardian*, and radio, the British Broadcasting Corporation. *The Guardian* (its current name) was considered a reliable source because it was old and venerable, and owned by a trust that's dedicated to keep the newspaper free of commercial and political interference (which it still is). You could depend on the BBC in those days because it was a public service broadcaster and similarly non-commercial. In general, news sources that are independent of commercial considerations will be more reliable, less biased by the views of owners eager to make a profit.

Readers of endnotes will notice I rely heavily on the journalism of *The Guardian*, as well as *The New York Times*, in the belief that the reporting in these newspapers is generally trustworthy, and because they're especially good on environmental topics. I always check the studies cited in the articles to ensure that they say what the reporter says they say, and try to consult at least one other reliable source on each topic. I've also made considerable use of the Internet, including consulting the Fox News website and other sites on the right, just to ensure that my media intake stays 'fair and balanced'. But most of what you find over there are alternative facts, and so I've seldom found such sources to be worth citing.

When it comes to discovering what's going on in the physical world, it used to be that research done by scientists at good universities was more reliable than studies by scientists working for industry, who might tend to come up with results that please their employers. When faced with the claim 'Scientific studies have shown . . .', it's always good to ask who funded the research. Support from the National Institutes for Health is relatively unproblematic; but if studies that show smoking isn't so bad for you after all turn out to be funded by the American Tobacco Company, perhaps a little scepticism is called for.[5]

One reason why the general public – and most students I've taught – aren't so well informed about the climate crisis is that some people have a stake in keeping other people in a state of ignorance. A central field in most traditions of philosophy is epistemology, the study of how we come to know what we know – an area that in today's world of alternative facts has become more interesting. And of comparable interest is the new field of 'agnotology', which studies what we *don't* know, and how ignorance comes about.

Ignorance comes in many forms: there's one kind that's a 'native' or 'originary' state, where knowledge hasn't yet happened; and another that's a 'lost realm' or 'selective choice', where knowledge has somehow faded, or attention has moved elsewhere. But there's also an ignorance that's deliberately produced as a 'strategic ploy', and this is the most interesting kind.[6] Why would you want to promote ignorance – unless you had legitimate trade or military secrets to keep? Well, perhaps because you're making a fortune by activities that cause harm to others, and you'd rather nobody knew about it. (We'll encounter some good examples in Part Two.)

If we turn to the climate and ask how we *know* that we're overheating the planet by burning fossil fuels, the answer is that the climate scientists say so (or some 99 per cent of them do). They understand the connections on a basis of sound evidence. The climate deniers deny that the scientists know – but they deny this on the basis of zero evidence. The problem is that many people have come to distrust experts, and the mistrust is spreading. Some experts can of course turn out to be not so expert after all, but in most cases there are reliable ways of gauging expertise in a particular profession or discipline. (It's not, as they say, rocket science.)

The issue of knowledge and understanding in the natural sciences isn't so problematic, thanks to the cooperative, competitive, and self-regulating nature of the enterprise. [1.1] Scientists all over the world are working on various topics in many different areas, and they're constantly communicating and evaluating the results of their research through the medium of peer-reviewed journals, international conferences and so forth. Within what has been called 'the republic of science', it's not hard to gauge levels of expertise: the top scientists tend to win Nobel Prizes and other awards, publish in the best journals in their fields and are usually hired by the most prestigious institutes and universities – while the hacks do none of this, and instead gravitate toward think tanks funded by climate deniers.[7] [1.1]

Scientists (like many philosophers) are contentious types who like to disagree and prove one another wrong. So when seven separate studies between 2004 and 2015 show that around 97 per cent of climate scientists who have published on the topic agree that global heating is caused by human activity, we can no doubt trust them. (Some of the research showed that the nay-saying 3 per cent were mostly in the bottom ranks of the profession.) Even though two of those studies have been downloaded from the Internet more than a million times each, a poll by the Yale Program on Climate Change Communication in 2018 found that most Americans were still unaware of the consensus – which was by then more like 99 per cent.[8]

If you know just a bit about how global heating works, it stands to reason. [1.2] As the French physicist Joseph Fourier discovered back in the 1820s, certain gases in the earth's atmosphere lead to a 'natural greenhouse effect' keeping the earth warmer than it would otherwise be in their absence. Then the Irish scientist John Tyndall discovered that while the nitrogen and oxygen that make up most of the surrounding air have almost no effect on radiant heat, the water vapour, carbon dioxide and methane in the atmosphere absorb, trap and reflect heat back. Heat-trapping gases are distinguished by their selectively absorptive properties: they are transparent to the visible, short-wavelength, heat-imparting light of the sun's incoming radiation, but they partially block and re-radiate the infrared, long-wavelength radiation that's reflected back from the surface of the earth.[9]

The developed countries have been pouring GHGs into the atmosphere since the Industrial Revolution, so that concentrations of those gases are increasing and average global surface temperatures are steadily rising. There are causal connections between these phenomena, yet the deniers deny that we know this, on the basis of objections that turn out to be baseless.

For example: 'The science still *isn't certain.*' We have to wait until there's certainty before we can justify the expense of phasing out fossil fuels. Politicians love to hear this, because it gives them an excuse for their chronic procrastination. But the proposition is nonsense, based on a misunderstanding of how the sciences work. As the theoretical physicist Carlo Rovelli writes, 'Science is not about certainty' – and especially not the climate sciences.[10] These involve disciplines like meteorology and oceanography as well as climatology, which deal with phenomena too vast and changing to yield anything that's certain. They use statistics and calculate probabilities, and employ computer modelling to try to understand and predict patterns of climatic change.

Deniers naturally dispute the validity of the climate models scientists use to predict the risks from global heating, when they estimate how much the temperature will rise in response to how much more GHGs emitted. Computer modelling is of course not the most exact among the sciences, but the research shows that the predictions by climate models since 1970 have actually been fairly accurate.[11] Nonetheless, despite the uncertainties scientists understand a great deal about how the climate works – and more with every passing year. So to say that we should wait because the science isn't yet 'certain' is to miss the point completely. It would be like waiting for Godot, except even more futile.

In the face of uncertainty, scientists recommend following the 'Precautionary Principle', which says that when the evidence gives us good reason to suppose that certain activities will prove harmful in the long run, the burden of proof lies with those proposing to undertake or continue such activities. At the UN Earth Summit in 1992, representatives from 194 nations agreed on this proposal: 'In order to protect the environment, the precautionary approach shall be widely applied by States according to their capabilities'.[12] Sadly, not many states have bothered to comply.

The deniers also object that 'Scientists are *fallible*', and point out that the IPCC has made mistakes. Yes, the thousands of contributory authors, reviewers and consultants who contribute to the Panel's reports (and receive no pay for their labours) are human, and therefore fallible. But the occasional errors that find their way into the reports are negligible by comparison with the enormous amount of responsible research the IPCC has synthesised over the past twenty-five years.[13]

Some people even accuse the Panel of *bias*, but the claim is absurd. Scientists from countries around the world survey and evaluate relevant research on the climate. Since the IPCC is an inter*governmental* panel, politicians have to vet the drafts produced by the researchers who produce the evidence – and everyone has to agree on the language that's used in the final report. Given those parameters, it's a wonder they can agree to anything! This means, as many climate scientists have remarked, that if the conclusions of the IPCC are biased, it's toward being cautious and overly conservative in their estimates. What is more, there's compelling evidence that climate scientists themselves tend to *underestimate* the risks and dangers when they report on climate change.[14]

The deniers claim that 'Global warming could be due to *natural variation* in the climate', and so we don't know that human activity is responsible. It's true that a variety of natural climate 'forcings', as they're called, affect a place's relations with the sun and hence its climate. There's variation in solar output, changes in the axial tilt of the earth, the shape of its orbit (which isn't quite circular), volcanic activity, changes in ocean temperature and currents, and the (slow but massively powerful) movement of tectonic plates. But climate scientists are fully aware of these natural variations and factor them in to their climate models: they are, after all, the ones who discovered natural variation in the first place.

Some deniers insist that '*Colder winters* prove that the planet isn't warming'. Yes, there have been new extremes of cold weather, but the climate is nonetheless warming over the long term. The climate models can account for the cold snaps: scientists say that a warmer Arctic is causing swings in the jet stream that brings colder air to places farther south.[15] Colder weather and global heating are quite compatible: the weather is always 'now', while the heating is a phenomenon of climate, which is like an average of weather over time within a certain region.

Finally, deniers often complain that 'Climate scientists are *corrupt*', because they get paid to come up with results that confirm global heating. Yes, scientists often get paid through large grants from government science foundations, but that's usually instead of rather than in addition to their university salaries. Most of the grant money goes to research assistants, equipment, institutional overheads and so forth, and doesn't enrich the grantees personally.[16] The claim of corruption is absurd, and the deniers have never produced a shred of evidence to back it up. [1.2]

Now, there *are* some scientists who get paid to come up with the desired results: they're employed by think tanks and institutes funded by global warming deniers (as we'll see in Part Two). There are also some independent contrarians with no scientific training who have turned climate denial into a handsome source of income. I had an enlightening encounter with one of them several years ago, when I was roped in to debate Christopher Monckton on the proposition 'Man-made Global Warming is a Global Crisis'. Fortunately I discovered a devastating rebuttal of his views and methods by a group of top climate scientists; but when I outlined their refutations in the debate, Monckton made no attempt to respond, but simply performed his usual well-polished routine – repeating the very claims that I had just shown to have been refuted by the experts! [1.3]

Gaia theory / Earth system science

The situation with the climate is extremely complicated, but we can get some perspective on it by gaining some temporal distance. If the universe started up some 14 billion years ago (Bya), the Earth was formed around 4.5 Bya, life emerged over 3 Bya, and human beings came on the scene only in the last 200,000 years, then the 10,000–15,000 years that we've had of human civilization have been a mere flash in the pan of cosmic time. Most civilizations arose during the Holocene period, beginning around 12,000 years ago – an unusually stable period of the earth's history, which is otherwise punctuated by volcanic explosions, seismic upheavals, asteroid impacts, consequent extreme swings of temperature and other fluctuations.

Looking at the situation in terms of the Earth's energy balance, after energy from the sun arrives, several factors determine how much of it radiates back into space and how much stays in the system. There's the proportion of solar radiation that's reflected off the earth's surface (the 'albedo', which varies mainly with the amount of ice and snow cover), and the capacities of the oceans and the land to absorb and store the sun's heat. Since the beginning, the Earth System has been in dynamic equilibrium, swinging slowly (very slowly) between extremes of cold and heat: between 'Snowball Earth', when the planet is covered with ice, and 'Hothouse Earth', when the earth is completely ice-free.[17] But it has never become permanently frozen like Jupiter, or baked like Venus. After the emergence of life, the Earth System appears to have been self-regulating.

This is remarkable because the sun is getting gradually hotter, and will eventually, in a billion years or so, incinerate the Earth and everything on it. Currently vegetation and other form of life pump down CO_2 from the atmosphere, which keeps the warming in check. But by adding GHGs to the air and subtracting forests, 'we are interfering with temperature regulation by turning up the heat and then simultaneously removing the natural systems that help to regulate it'.[18]

Back in the 1970s the English scientist James Lovelock proposed the 'Gaia hypothesis', which recommended understanding the Earth and biosphere as a huge organism that's capable of self-regulation. (Gaia is the name of the Earth goddess of the ancient Greeks.) After a fruitful collaboration with the American evolutionary biologist Lynn Margulis, Lovelock proposed the 'Gaia theory', which made it clear that 'it is not the biosphere alone that does the regulating but the whole thing, life, the air, the oceans, and the rocks'. The process of 'chemical rock weathering', for example, which keeps temperatures lower by reducing the amount of carbon dioxide in the air, is greatly enhanced by the presence of bacteria and algae on the rock surfaces.[19]

The French thinker Bruno Latour has elaborated the implications of the idea of Gaia in his formidable work *Facing Gaia: Eight Lectures on the New Climatic Regime*, a fascinating and challenging treatment of many themes in the present book. In a chapter on Gaia as 'a (finally secular) figure for nature', Latour shows how Lovelock came to downplay the idea of a huge organism and to highlight ubiquitous interactivity instead: 'waves of action' that 'respect no borders' nor 'any fixed scale'.[20] This view of a world where everything is interacting with everything else, as Latour articulates it, is remarkably reminiscent of ancient Chinese worldviews that we'll consider in the second half of the book.

The scientific community was slow to accept Gaia theory, but after the emergence of Earth System Science (ESS) in the 1980s, more scientists are open to it. The holistic approach of ESS, along with its findings and predictions, overlaps considerably with those of Gaia theory. Earth System scientists investigate the interactions between the several 'spheres' that comprise the system: the lithosphere (the Earth's rocky crust) and pedosphere (the soil layer), the hydrosphere (water) and cryosphere (ice, snow, permafrost), the biosphere (life), the atmosphere (air), and the spheres of human activity (noösphere and technosphere).[21]

The first major international agreement on climate change showed that policymakers already had a good understanding of the Earth System in 1992, when they advocated the Precautionary Principle. Almost all the world's countries signed on to the United Nations Framework Convention on Climate Change (UNFCCC), an international treaty that was approved at the Rio de Janeiro Earth Summit. The language and spirit of the agreement are thoughtful and inspiring: the signers declare themselves 'determined to protect the climate system for present and future generations', and especially against 'human activities' that may 'adversely affect natural ecosystems and humankind'.

The aim of the agreement concerned 'the climate system' understood as 'the totality of the atmosphere, hydrosphere, biosphere and geosphere and their interactions'; and the commitment was to 'stabilize greenhouse gas concentrations in the atmosphere at a level that would *prevent dangerous anthropogenic interference with the climate system*'. That's the right way to frame the problem and the right outcome to aim for – and later we'll see what the signers thought is the right way to achieve *fairness* in the light of 'differentiated responsibilities' of the various signatories.[22]

By the beginning of the new century the science had become more sophisticated, and more comfortable with the inevitable uncertainties.

The 2001 Amsterdam Declaration on Earth System Science stressed the importance of understanding the interactions among the sub-systems:

> The Earth System behaves as a single, self-regulating system comprised of physical, chemical, biological and human components. The interactions and feedbacks between the component parts are complex and exhibit multi-scale temporal and spatial variability.

Earth System scientists are especially concerned with how the effects of global heating interact with the many other changes that human beings are inflicting on the system.

> Human-driven changes cause multiple effects that cascade through the Earth System in complex ways. These effects interact with each other and with local- and regional-scale changes in multidimensional patterns that are difficult to understand and even more difficult to predict. Surprises abound.

– and some of them could be quite unpleasant.

The stability of the Holocene, which was so congenial to the development of human civilization, is by no means the normal condition of the Earth System. This is something to be grateful for – and that should make us wary of overly forceful interventions.

> Human activities could inadvertently trigger such changes with severe consequences for Earth's environment and inhabitants. . . . They have the potential to switch the Earth System to alternative modes of operation that may prove irreversible and less hospitable to humans and other life.[23]

The changes we're bringing about are having such an impact on the Earth System that many scientists think the new situation deserves a new name: the 'Anthropocene'. We could be proud of having a geological epoch named after us humans – except that its markers are things like radioactive fallout from nuclear weapons, widespread heavy metals and ubiquitous layers of plastics. Not to mention the jump in concentrations of carbon dioxide, which will be measurable in ice cores as long as there's any ice left. Some of us may be proud that human activities have become 'equal to some of the great forces of nature in their extent and impact'; but they do well to recall that 'Pride goeth before destruction, and an haughty spirit before a fall'.[24]

The Anthropocene marks a major change in the Earth System, from a long history of countless species arising and perishing, the fruits of symbiosis often wiped out by eruptions or other violent acts of nature, to a situation where one particular species is forcing the climate into a new regime. In Lovelock's language, we are responsible for 'Earth's disease, a fever brought on by a plague of people'. We are raising Earth's temperature – and do well to note that a fever's function is to help the immune system eliminate invaders. Gaia is already 'ageing', Lovelock reminds us, not as able to fight off disease as when she was young and vigorous. So now, 'like an old lady who has to share her house with a growing and destructive group of teenagers, Gaia grows angry, and if they do not mend their ways she will evict them.'[25] And since there's no life outside Gaia, 'evict' here means 'kill off' – and 'they' are us. This is *The Revenge of Gaia* referred to by the title of Lovelock's book from 2006.

The most significant message from the findings of ESS is that changes in the system can happen on much shorter timescales than scientists used to think. Climate scientists appear until recently to have misunderstood the workings of the system – but in the opposite direction from what the deniers claim: changes in the various spheres are happening *faster* than previously envisaged. We are now in what Bruno Latour aptly calls a 'New Climatic Regime', and it's challenging already.[26] In the three decades since the nations of the world signed on to the UNFCCC, acknowledging the validity of scientific insights into the climate system and the consequent need to take care of it, Earth System science has come into its own and confirmed the increasing magnitude of the risks. And yet, for reasons to be explored (in Part Two), all the good ideas presented in the UN Framework Convention, and the binding commitments for taking action that the developing nations and the European Union recommended, have come to nothing.

Consequences of global heating

Coping with global heating is the greatest challenge we face as a species, mainly because it's what the US military calls a 'threat multiplier'.[27] As the climate breaks down and the temperature goes up, all our other problems – world poverty, food and water security, terrorism, migrants and refugees, environmental pollution, species extinction – become far more challenging.

For example, extreme weather events forced over 7 million people to leave their homes during the first half of 2019, a record mid-year number since the Internal Displacement Monitoring Centre began estimating such displacements in 2003. An analysis of these data from the past decade by researchers at Oxfam shows 'a five-fold increase in the reported number of extreme weather disasters that resulted in people being displaced' – at an average of 'over 20 million people a year'.[28] Most of these people lived in poorer countries that have contributed minimal emissions to global heating.

One of the factors behind the Syrian Civil War – which began in 2011 and eight years later had generated 5.6 million refugees, with another 6 million people internally displaced – was an anomalous three-year drought that lasted until 2010, devastating crops and forcing much of the rural population to move to the cities. Several studies have shown that the drought was made more likely by global warming.[29] Another factor was the chaos brought about in the Middle East by the Iraq War, which George W. Bush launched because God told him to.[30] And yet the US has been happy to let other countries take in the refugees.

Similar droughts in Central America contributed to the 'migrant caravan' of 2018, again linked to global heating, to which the US has been historically the greatest contributor. People were also fleeing endemic drug violence – another problem 'made in the USA'. But instead of welcoming them, in accordance with the American way, Trump wants to build electrified walls with spikes on top, or moats full of alligators or snakes, patrolled by soldiers who would shoot migrants in the legs to slow them down.[31] Xenophobia turned genocidal.

Next up will be millions of migrants from coastal areas around the world, suffering from too much water rather than too little, fleeing inland as the sea rises and inundates. As Jeff Goodell shows vividly in his nicely titled book, *The Water Will Come: Rising Seas, Sinking Cities, and the Remaking of the Civilized World*, the changes will be challenging.[32]

Looked at another way, global heating confronts us with 'the largest collective action problem that humanity has ever faced' – or, rather, 'multiple collective action problems' that transcend not only national boundaries but also generations.[33] Our climate predicament is global, and can't be resolved by action on the part of only some individuals or countries; but our leaders are dragging their feet because they're profiting from the status quo, or are in thrall to rich people who are making fortunes from it.

The gravity of the situation became inescapably clear in 2018, with the publication by the IPCC of a report, *Global warming of 1.5°C*, commissioned by the nations adopting the Paris Agreement on climate change two years earlier. The subtitle advocates '*strengthening the global response to the threat of climate change, sustainable development, and efforts to eradicate poverty*'. The authors warn that unless we manage a 50 per cent reduction of our carbon emissions by 2030, we'll overshoot the 1.5°C limit and end up with 2° or more – and disastrous consequences. This would be a major shock to the system: not just some adjustments here and there, bur rather 'rapid and far-reaching transitions in energy, land, urban and infrastructure (including transport and buildings), and industrial systems'. The required changes will be 'unprecedented in terms of scale': we need 'deep emissions reductions in all sectors' and 'significant investments' in clean energy.[34] Major changes, then, in the way we in the developed world have been living.

On top of that, remember climate scientists tend to underestimate the risks from climate change. A 2019 study that explores 'the workings of scientific assessments for policy' determined that 'previous estimates of overall global warming have been too low', and that 'scientists tend to underestimate the severity of threats and the rapidity with which they might unfold'.[35] Add to this the extremely conservative nature of the IPCC's conclusions, and you see why it makes no sense to think in terms of having, say, ten years to come up with a technological 'fix'. In particular, climate scientists have warned that the *Global warming of 1.5°C* report understates the perils of reaching a variety of tipping points.[36]

The situation is that we haven't been able to slow the bus down – and now have to step on the brakes as quickly as possible. If we can avoid going over the edge it still won't be very pleasant, which gives us reason to change our ways, in energy policy especially, as soon as we can.

For readers with strong constitutions, a good way to find out what's in store is to read *The Uninhabitable Earth* by David Wallace-Wells. With sections titled 'Heat Death', 'Hunger', 'Drowning', 'Wildfire', 'Disasters No Longer Natural', 'Freshwater Drain', 'Dying Oceans', 'Unbreathable Air', 'Plagues of Warming', 'Economic Collapse' and 'Climate Conflict', the narrative is sober and sobering, and grounded in a good understanding of the science.[37] As those titles suggest, it's not a pretty picture: in fact it's a horror show. And yet the author doesn't depict our situation as irremediable, as the original subtitle *Life After Warming* suggests.

One of the saddest aspects of the situation is that the health of *children* is especially vulnerable to the effects of global heating. A 2019 report by the Lancet Countdown on Health and Climate Change, a massive international and multidisciplinary research project, focuses on children and warns that climate change will affect the health of children born today 'from infancy and adolescence to adulthood and old age'. Around the world, the authors say, 'children are among the worst affected by climate change'. This is because their physiology and immune systems are still developing and are thus more susceptible to environmental changes. The report concludes by urging governments to take action to reduce GHG emissions as rapidly as possible.[38]

The problem is that our problems are many and interconnected. We've already made such great progress in killing off the other species with whom we share the planet that scientists have called it the Sixth Mass Extinction. Since a single species is responsible (Homo sapiens), and the destruction is for the most part deliberate, 'First Mass Extermination' would be a more fitting name.[39] A report from 2018 authored by a group containing fifty of the world's top environmental researchers shows that 'Humanity has wiped out 60% of mammals, birds, fish and reptiles since 1970'. We've been eating them, destroying their habitats and poisoning their environment with pollutants.[40] We're a rogue species.

The next year saw the results of 'the most thorough planetary health check ever undertaken' – by the Intergovernmental Science-Policy Platform on Biodiversity and Ecosystem Services, which shows that we're losing even more biodiversity and 'natural resources' with every passing year.[41] Now, some people don't care much for animals, and especially not for insects, but the fact is that we depend on the planet's wildlife for our own survival. Those other species are embedded in the Earth System: if we continue with business as usual and let it all collapse, we won't have enough to eat, or any medicines to cure our ills. It will be the end of civilization as we know it.

Most people prefer pandas and polar bears to plecoptera and other insects, but we depend more on the insects – and yet we're eliminating them fast: over 40 per cent of insect species are threatened with extinction. The major factors are habitat loss through urbanization and intensive agriculture with its pesticides and fertilisers. As one professor of biology put it: 'Love them or loathe them, we humans cannot survive without insects.'[42] This is another example of overlooked interactivity: these factors directly threaten the world's food supply and at the same time make other effects of climate change worse – which in turn reduces biodiversity.[43] And so on and so forth: enough to make the head spin from the sheer amount of destruction.

The perils of tipping points

In 2005 James Hansen gave a presentation to the American Geophysical Union with the title 'Is There Still Time to Avoid "Dangerous Anthropogenic Interference" with Global Climate?' (An allusion to the UNFCCC warning from 1992 about the risk to the climate system.) He concluded that yes, there was still time, but we'd need to act fast, and somehow 'override the influence of special interests' (fossil fuel companies) which have been 'a roadblock wielding undue influence over policymakers'. But on the way, Hansen delivered this grim warning: 'We are on the precipice of *climate system tipping points* beyond which there is no redemption.'[44]

A few years later, the environmental journalist Fred Pearce published a disconcerting book titled *With Speed and Violence: Why Scientists Fear Tipping Points in Climate Change*.[45] This justified fear is taking a long time to grip the general public. These tipping points are limits to how much warming the planet can take before positive feedback loops kick in that amplify the warming and keep on amplifying it. Here are three examples.

Because the world's oceans are getting warmer, the polar ice caps are melting – and faster than the climate models predicted. Less ice reflecting sunlight back into space (lower 'albedo') means more heat in the atmosphere – which in turn increases sea temperatures, which leads to more melting of ice, and so on.

With warmer temperatures, the tundra and the permafrost on which it sits begin to melt, which releases methane (CH_4), a GHG that warms the atmosphere far more effectively than carbon dioxide (around thirty-four times stronger over 100 years, and even more so in the shorter term).[46] This generates another dangerous feedback loop. And as the oceans heat up, especially at the poles, vast deposits of methane hydrates on the sea floor will begin to release methane in gas form – which in turn will warm the atmosphere even further.

Third, climate scientists have been concerned, after three severe droughts in the Amazon basin between 2005 and 2015, that more frequent droughts there (which the climate models say are likely) could radically alter the role that the rainforest plays in the earth system. Global heating could bring us to a tipping point where the 'lungs of the earth', which usually breathe in more carbon than they exhale, turn into a steady *source* of carbon emissions rather than an absorbing sink.[47]

Brazil is hugely important for the future of global heating because of the size of its population and economy – and because it's home to 60 per cent of the Amazon rainforest. The Amazon is a crucial component of the biosphere, but since the election of Jair Bolsonaro as president of Brazil at the end of 2018 the outlook has been bleak. Bolsonaro wants to *develop* the rainforest for the sake of illegal opportunists and to the detriment of the remaining indigenous peoples who, inconveniently, have lived there for ages.

Like Trump he has surrounded himself with global warming deniers and advocates of environmental deregulation, so that six months into his presidency the monthly deforestation had increased significantly.[48] If Bolsonaro succeeds in further developing the forest for profit, the loss of that huge 'carbon sink' will exacerbate global warming even further. The unprecedented fires in the Amazon in the summer of 2019 suggest that this tipping point, which seemed relatively unlikely ten years earlier, may now be the most urgent one to avoid.

In all three cases, to push the climate beyond the tipping points can lead to runaway global heating, with the climate changing rapidly and irreversibly in ways that are impossible to control. The paths toward these tipping points overlap, and the forces driving the warming interact and feed each other, increasing the likelihood that we'll go over one edge or another. What the scientists call 'cascading effects' are to be expected.

If this weren't unsettling enough, there's a key uncertainty here that makes it difficult to tell how close we are to tipping points, and this concerns the amount of particulate air pollutants, or aerosols, in the atmosphere as a result of our burning fossil fuels. These particles, by blocking and reflecting incoming sunlight, are keeping the earth cooler and 'masking' the warming effect of increased carbon dioxide.

Air pollution is a huge public health issue worldwide, and many governments are committed to reducing it. China is in the forefront because of its many densely populated megacities. As China, India and other countries reduce emissions of particulate air pollutants, public health will improve 'on the ground' – but the rate of global warming will also increase. The problem is that climate scientists don't know by how much. Here's James Hansen again:

> If aerosols have been masking most of the greenhouse warming and humanity reduces particulate pollution by even half, the net climate forcing would double. *That increased forcing, combined with a continued greenhouse gas increase, might push the planet beyond tipping points with disastrous consequences.*[49]

Alarming, yes – but this warning comes from one of the world's top climate scientists.

The most sobering assessment so far is a study from the end of 2019 authored by some of the world's best experts on the science of tipping points, 'Climate tipping points – too risky to bet against', who declare 'we are in a climate emergency'. The latest data on ice collapse, deforestation in the Amazon and elsewhere, and other biosphere tipping points suggest that we may already have emitted enough carbon to produce a temperature rise of 1.5°C. What makes the situation more precarious is the possibility, because of interaction among different systems close to their tipping points, of 'a global cascade of tipping points leading to a new, less habitable, "hothouse" climate state' – something we need to avoid at all costs.

The implications of their research lead these sober scientists to issue a remarkably stark warning: 'This is an existential threat to civilisation.' And to add pointedly: 'No amount of economic cost–benefit analysis is going to help us. We need to change our approach to the climate problem.' Their prognosis is surely on the mark – we need to change our approach. No need for any more cost–benefit analyses: the risks are too high.[50]

Also in late 2019 a group of scientists published a 'Warning of a Climate Emergency' which was endorsed by more than 11,000 scientists from 153 countries. Because we're destroying so much of the natural world, and pushing against so many boundaries within the Earth System, they warn that 'an immense increase of scale in endeavors to conserve our biosphere is needed to avoid untold suffering due to the climate crisis'.[51]

As the author of an especially moving book on the consequences of our new climate regime succinctly put it: 'We're fucked. The only questions are how soon and how badly.'[52] If we want it to be not so soon and less badly, we need to take immediate and decisive action. Regardless of the uncertainties involved, the stakes are so high that it makes sense to do whatever we can, as soon as we can, if we want to limit the damage and minimise the misery. But most of the people driving the warming don't care: they are insulating themselves from the damage and have no interest in stepping on the brakes. So we need to get them out of the driver's seat, because if the bus goes over the edge . . .

To end the chapter on a more positive note, let's turn to James Hansen again. In an interview on the last day of the Paris climate conference in 2015, Hansen dismissed the event as 'a fraud': 'It's just worthless words. There is no action, just promises.' Sadly he was right about that. But then the conversation took a brighter tone when 'the father of climate change awareness' said he believes 'China, the world's largest emitter, will now step up to provide the leadership lacking from the US'. In a rare access of optimism Hansen added: 'I think we will get there because China is rational. Their leaders are mostly trained in engineering and such things, they don't deny climate change, and they have a huge incentive, which is air pollution. . . . *But they will need cooperation.*'[53]

I've added emphasis to that last sentence because it anticipates the main topic of Part Three of this book. One reason to regard the Chinese regime as more rational than the US government is that it's free of libertarian lunatics and fundamentalist fanatics. That country is governed by a group of technocrats who would never dream of doubting the reality of global heating. The question is whether we can persuade them to step up, now that the US has left the leadership field pretty vacant.

2

Specious Promethean Solutions

There's an *attitude* that's helping us ignore the reality of our situation, and which I'll call 'Promethean'. If this brings to mind the spectacular Ridley Scott film from 2012 (*Prometheus*) that's fine, because connections between high-tech hubris and punishment – not to mention the demise of the human race – are all relevant.

At the beginning of the previous chapter we saw Heraclitus draw attention to the human inclination to ignore reality, or make it up as we go along. Heraclitus has a close counterpart in ancient China, the Daoist philosopher Zhuangzi (fourth century BCE), who reveals the basis for our becoming too clever for our own good.

> The flow of my life is bound by its limits; the mind bent on knowledge, however, never is. If forced to follow something limited by no bounds, the bounded current of life is put in danger. And to meet this danger by enhancing knowledge even further – that merely exacerbates the danger.[1]

Our lives are limited by our bodies and their capacities, but the farther our knowledge reaches the more we come to feel as if we're beyond limitations, because we can envisage possibilities that transcend our physical capabilities. But this is a risky business, and if we respond to the riskiness by employing cleverer strategies, we can end up making things worse rather than better.

In the modern context we keep on burning fossil fuels, and imagine that we can always develop more sophisticated technologies to fix the problems this activity causes. There's no need to give up business as usual because we'll always find clever ways of keeping it going – except for the inconvenient fact that not one of these ways works. There's only space to list them here; amplifications and justifications can be found in the Appendix [2.1]. Then we'll consider the Promethean attitude that's driving this self-destructive behaviour, before a realistic assessment of how to respond to the limits that the climate crisis reveals.

Poor alternatives

In the beginning was Coal – a particularly Promethean product not just because it produces fire, but also because we get it by *mining*, another typically Promethean technology. It was coal that fuelled the Industrial Revolution, and it's still going strong – despite widespread agreement that it has to be stopped if we're to deal with the climate crisis. Because, for all the benefits it has brought us, coal is *a killer*, and not just of miners. Owners of coal-fired power plants don't live close to them: the pollution damages the health and shortens the lives of the poor people in the neighbourhood instead. The effects of coal burning on the atmosphere and biosphere and atmosphere are so awful that if it were a new discovery or invention, nobody except the most ruthless capitalist would advocate using it, and no rational government concerned about the welfare of its people would permit it.

A quick first step would be to *stop* the enormous subsidies that the fossil fuel industries have been enjoying for decades. The leaders of the G20 nations *and* the Asia-Pacific Economic Cooperation forum (APEC) – both are groups concerned with international financial stability – agreed to phase out subsidies back in 2009, when the world total was only around $550 billion. But instead of going down, the amount has been increasing ever since, no doubt because the fossil fuel beneficiaries keep paying off the politicians. If only the policymakers could muster the courage to defy their moneyed masters, they could put an end to fossil fuel subsidies *tomorrow* – and everyone else, indeed the entire biosphere, would benefit.

Fossil fuel enthusiasts say that we can attain salvation through developing more clever technologies. In the face of dangerous risks we ingenious humans *can* do something after all. There are ways for us to continue with the fossil fuel burning business *and* at the same time reduce our emissions of GHGs. Because we need to meet our 'energy needs' somehow, don't we? Or should we focus on what now has to be the first priority, which is *reducing* our energy needs.

They propose a variety of technological solutions: carbon capture and storage (CCS), hydraulic fracturing for natural gas, expanded nuclear power. There are also biofuels, such as ethanol, but in many cases these consume as much energy to produce as they ultimately deliver; and where arable land is converted from needed food crops to biofuel production, the glaring social injustice renders this option difficult to promote. Then there's geo-engineering, and especially carbon *extraction* and storage. But when you examine the viability of these approaches, they all turn out to be unviable. If you want 'clean coal' technology, for example, it's now more expensive than clean and renewable alternatives.

Geo-engineering: ever since the Romans invented and deployed the siege engine (*ingenium* in Latin – whence our word 'ingenuity'), engines have been the driving force behind our conquest of the earth. The Industrial Revolution depended on the steam engine, and the internal combustion engine has revolutionised agriculture and transportation.[2] We have already engineered some gigantic projects – so why not the whole earth *and* its climate?[3] Despite the risks, we are driven to persist. But geo-engineering is actually the most insidious proposition: it lets industry continue to emit and politicians to procrastinate, with the hope that we'll find a way to cool the climate, while its effects on the Earth System are impossible to predict and would probably make the situation worse rather than better.

Enthusiasts of technology have long enjoyed exercising control over the natural world. How long will it take before they acknowledge that the outcome of all their efforts is that natural forces are becoming less and less controllable?

Many people will tell you that more *nuclear power* provides the best way to reduce our GHG emissions, but new power plants are prohibitively expensive to build, and when you take the entire nuclear-fuel cycle into account – from planning to decommissioning – it turns out that the GHG emissions are *higher* than average-fuel-cycle GHG emissions from natural-gas-fired plants.'[4] There is good reason to keep on running the nuclear power plants that are operating until they need to be decommissioned, but any future plants would have to be seriously questioned about their overall costs and carbon emissions to ensure that they really are closer to zero carbon than their clean and renewable competition. [2.2]

The Promethean spirit

The situation is insane. We are Homo *sapiens* for heaven's sake, the only species of the genus Homo to have survived, so at least we must be clever – if not as 'wise', 'judicious', or 'knowing' as the *sapiens* suggests. We've known for decades that burning fossil fuels and destroying forests are overheating the planet. Some political leaders deny this: perhaps they're ignorant, but probably they're lying. Don't the deniers understand that to persist in going beyond the natural limits imposed on life by the resources of a finite planet is a very risky business? Part of the problem is that we're being driven by forces of which we're unaware.

If we look behind the push for geo-engineering and similar invasive procedures, it's impossible to ignore a towering figure from ancient Greek myth: the Titan Prometheus. Let's be guided here by what a Neo-Platonist philosopher wrote about one ancient story (though referring to them all): '*These things never happened, but always are.*'[5] The events in the myths of Prometheus never happened – but are always going on behind or beneath what humans do. From this perspective, patterns of behaviour we've been enacting without realising their consequences may become more evident.[6]

Prometheus is best known for his defiance of Zeus, king of the gods and keeper of the order of the world, by stealing fire from the gods and giving it to humans. Zeus had withheld fire on the grounds of justice: he denied human beings fire so that they would continue to work hard in order to make a living, which was their role in the appointed scheme of things.[7] As protector of the world order, Zeus had good reason to set limits to human endeavour. We can see this if we consider our profligate burning of fossil fuels in the context of the history of our using fire.

Fire is a relatively recent phenomenon on earth, dating from some 400 million years ago: for the first four billion years of Earth's existence, there wasn't sufficient oxygen in the atmosphere or enough of the right kind of biomass for fuel. At first, natural fires were ignited mostly by lightning, though also by falling rocks, volcanic eruptions and extra-terrestrial impacts. Then hominids developed techniques of kindling fire and keeping it going.[8]

The vegetation covering the earth's surface incorporates energy from the sun through photosynthesis, over time spans ranging from seasonal grasses to long-living trees. When that energy is incorporated in edible plants, we can use it by ingesting them; when it's in other vegetation, we can draw on the energy by burning them. The uses and range of fire were greatly expanded with the advent of agriculture, which can produce biomass to serve as fuel. But extracting energy from vegetation wasn't enough: we then moved on to coal – in China long before Europe – but since mining was confined to surface deposits, world consumption was limited in scale.

In the run-up to the Industrial Revolution, however, Europeans found a way of combining the art of using fire with another Promethean technique, mining – and then took them deep within the earth so as to greatly increase the opportunities for transgressing the limits imposed by nature. The invention of the steam engine, most efficiently fuelled by coal, and especially of the steam pump, enabled the development of 'deep shaft' coal mining. This combination of technologies allowed human beings to delve deeper into the earth than ever before, reaching back in geological time to extract fossil biomass that was deposited during the Carboniferous Period – well over 300 million years ago.

The problem is that the natural limits on the use of fire have *not* disappeared: rather, as we push ever deeper into the earth beneath our feet, they simply shift to the sky above our heads. A prominent fire historian has described the consequences of our move from agricultural to 'industrial fire' as follows: 'The limitations on fire reside no longer in its sources – ignition and fuel – but in the sinks such as the atmosphere that must receive combustion's unbounded by-products.'[9] It is precisely these limitations that our Promethean hyperactivity refuses to acknowledge, as we continue with oil, coal and agri-business as usual. You would think that the relentless increase in wildfires worldwide would make us rethink our determination to keep on burning fossil fuels, but as usual we remain blind to the interconnections.

Some versions of the myth have Prometheus creating human beings, by mixing together 'new-made earth with fresh rainwater'. And in addition to the comforts of fire (heat and cooking), the Titan gave us various arts and crafts to help with survival: house-building, agriculture and animal husbandry, and then ship-building (which involves deforestation), mining for iron and gold, and the art of medicine. These arts – the Greek word is *technai*, the root of our 'technology' – make life more comfortable by affording some protection against injury, illness and premature death. Prometheus boasts of also preventing mortals from foreseeing their fate – death – by filling them with 'blind hopes'.[10] However, becoming so comfortably secure may actually prevent you from living life to the full. And having blind hopes is a sickness if we're so bedazzled by the Promethean spirit, and so narcotized by the high tech conveniences of modern life, that we fail to foresee an avoidable catastrophe with the climate.

Ancient authors such as Ovid and Pliny the Elder deplored mining because its products promoted decadence: gold was used for ostentatious luxury, and iron for weapons to fight wars – usually to get your hands on other people's gold. Pliny, the great Roman historian of natural science, warned of unforeseen consequences from mining – an encroachment on the body of Mother Earth – and deplored it for its sacrilegious aspects.

> We trace out all the veins of the earth, and yet, living upon it, undermined as it is beneath our feet, are astonished that it should occasionally cleave asunder or tremble: as though in truth these signs could be any other than expressions of the indignation felt by our sacred parent! We penetrate into her entrails, and seek for treasures in the abodes of the spirits of the dead, as though each spot we tread upon were not sufficiently bounteous and fertile for us![11]

Natural science now tells us that geothermal projects, fracking and the relentless extraction and combustion of fossil fuels, together with the consequent global warming, promise over the long term to occasion more frequent convulsions of the earth that bring tsunamis and volcanic eruptions in their train.[12]

We might in any case want to heed Pliny's warning that delving into the bowels of the earth is an affront to 'our sacred parent', because it anticipates Lovelock's warnings of 'the revenge of Gaia'.[13] The respect of ancient peoples for 'Mother Earth' is hardly misplaced, since we depend on the Earth and its bounty for our survival. To benefit the living is an unobjectionable goal – except perhaps when it involves such rude incursions into 'the abodes of the spirits of the dead'.

Plato's treatment of the Prometheus myth suggests significant limitations to the gifts that Prometheus bestowed upon humanity. The protagonist of his dialogue *Protagoras* notes that while Prometheus was able to steal 'artful wisdom' from the gods, 'humanity got the survival wisdom but did not get the political, for that was in the keeping of Zeus'.[14] This account speaks clearly to our current predicament, in which our understanding proves to be incomplete. Inspired by the spirit of Prometheus, humanity has become skilled in the technical arts of survival and comfort creation (while forgetting that these skills are gifts *and* stolen goods), but it lacks the political arts that would integrate technological expertise with the art of living well together in diverse communities. This shortcoming is all the more evident now that humans have to live in a community that is also global.

And let's not forget that Prometheus, whose sacrilegious theft set in train so much technical ingenuity, suffered dreadful punishment for his crime. According to Hesiod:

> With painful fetters Zeus bound shifty-planning Prometheus, with distressful bonds, driving them through the middle of a pillar; and he set upon him a long-winged eagle which ate his immortal liver, but this grew again on all sides at night just as much as the long-winged bird would eat during the whole day.[15]

In antiquity the liver, as the most powerful and blood-rich organ in the body, was highly regarded as 'the seat of life', and so this punishment strikes at the core of the transgressor's existence. And as we moderns persist in transgressing natural limits with the aid of clever technologies, we may likewise find the source of our very vitality being depleted on a daily basis.

Prometheus Bound by the ancient Greek tragedian Aeschylus highlights from the beginning the protagonist's *immobility*. Hephaestus nails Prometheus to the rock with fetters and wedges that 'leave it loose nowhere', and drives 'the obstinate jaw of the adamantine wedge right through his breast'.[16] This physical immobility, which lasts throughout the play, mirrors a psychological fixation: the protagonist's pride, stubbornness and utter inflexibility. For one so obstinate in the assertion of self-will against higher powers, the punishment of complete immobilization is grimly fitting.

At the end of the play, Prometheus remains just where he was at the beginning, having suffered physical torment but no change of mind or heart, intractable in his defiance of the most powerful of the Gods. In thrall to Prometheus's gifts of technology, we display a similar intransigence. In our determination to persist in heating up Earth's atmosphere – despite warnings from floods, droughts, hurricanes, tornadoes and other manifestations of extreme weather – we are enacting this ancient drama once again, blithely oblivious to the punishment in store.

These myths attest to Prometheus's part in making us who we are: moulded from clay by his hands, instructed by his arts and techniques and fortunate beneficiaries of his igneous gift. In drawing attention to the power of the Promethean drive in human nature, they warn of the perils of arrogant overreach, and of our failure to be grateful for what the earth provides. We refuse to see that the drama's ending is anything but happy, which is why they call it a tragedy.

Our predicament doesn't stem from our use of fire and practice of the Promethean arts per se: it would be possible to use and practise them sustainably. But our compulsion to burn fossil fuels knows no bounds, and we drive our agriculture and animal husbandry to extremes of productivity by advanced technologies that result in impoverishment of soil as well as humans over the long term. We appear to have lost that other capacity of Prometheus – namely, foresight.

Economics and carbon budgets

For well over two decades environmental economists have been comparing the costs of mitigating climate change 'now' with the probable costs of dealing with the effects of higher temperatures 'later'. Eminent figures like Sir Nicholas Stern, William Nordhaus and Paul Krugman (the last two are Nobel Prize winners) have been saying for years that it will be cheaper to invest now in mitigating global heating than to wait and pay the costs of repairing whatever damage ensues. (Although there's no way to repair the lives of people who die in climate disasters.) Nordhaus has described his earlier work as showing that 'policies to slow global warming would have *net economic benefits, in the trillion of dollars* of present value', and that a carbon tax is the best way to attack the issue'.[17] He later developed a tendency to underestimate the risks of global heating, for which his models have come in for severe criticism.[18]

A statement from 1997 signed by 2,600 American economists refutes the excuse for inaction (later given by presidents from Bush the Younger to Trump) that moving to clean and renewable energy sources will 'hurt the economy'. On the contrary: 'sound economic analysis shows that there are policy options that would slow climate change without harming American living standards, and these measures may in fact improve U.S. productivity in the longer run.' A decade later, Nicholas Stern presented the conclusions of the Stern Review, among which were these:

The scientific evidence is now overwhelming: climate change is a serious global threat, and it demands an urgent global response. . . . If we don't act, the overall costs and risks of climate change will be equivalent to losing at least 5% of global GDP each year, now and forever.

Or perhaps, he added, it could be even as much as 20 per cent of GDP. By contrast,

> the costs of taking action – by reducing greenhouse gas emissions to avoid the worst impacts of climate change – can be limited to around 1% of global GDP each year. . . . The costs of stabilising the climate are significant but manageable; delay would be dangerous and much more costly.[19]

In subsequent books Stern continued to show, more positively each time through promise of greater prosperity, the economic benefits of acting now rather than later.[20] Nordhaus (among others) has criticized the Stern Review especially with respect to discount rates, and others have criticized Nordhaus's work – but the details needn't worry us here because the main theme is echoed by another Nobel Prize-winning economist.

In 2010 Paul Krugman wrote an excellent essay titled 'Building a Green Economy', which contains illuminating discussions of negative externalities and the kinds of 'Pigovian taxes' that could compensate for them. Near the beginning he writes:

> The casual reader might have the impression that there are real doubts about whether emissions can be reduced without inflicting severe damage on the economy. In fact, once you filter out the noise generated by special-interest groups, you discover that there is widespread agreement among environmental economists that a market-based program to deal with the threat of climate change – one that limits carbon emissions by putting a price on them – can achieve large results at modest, though not trivial, cost.

Krugman argues that immediate economic action to reduce GHG emissions is crucial, and would cost the world economy little by comparison with the price we'll have to pay if we delay. Comparing the costs of reducing emissions and mitigating greater damage later, he writes: 'Climate change will lower gross global product 5 percent, stopping it will cost 2 percent.' He acknowledges the extreme complexity of the issue, which renders all predictions uncertain – but observes that in any case the significant risk of utter catastrophe must override simple cost-benefit calculations, and that strong climate policy to reduce emissions is urgently needed.[21]

If these arguments haven't had any purchase, it's because William Nordhaus isn't the only economist to underestimate the costs that climate change will bring, as sea levels rise and extreme weather becomes more extreme. A collaborative study from 2019 by some of the top economists and scientists in the US and Europe demonstrates the extent to which most economists are consistently 'missing risks' and failing to appreciate their magnitude.[22] They're ignoring what ESS is telling us about the likelihood of our reaching tipping points and cascade effects. Don't forget, in this crisis situation, 'no amount of economic cost-benefit analysis is going to help us'.

With every passing year since these economists began issuing recommendations, as the prices of renewable energy steadily fall, the costs of mitigating the crisis come down. And with ever more extreme weather events wreaking havoc, the bills for fixing the damage after the fact go steadily up. And yet our political leaders continue to chant the misleading 'It will hurt the economy' mantra instead of heeding the advice of the economic experts. We'll consider the reasons for this despicable failure shortly.

There's been a great deal of discussion over the past decade of the global *carbon budget*, the proportion of the world's 'recoverable' fossil fuel reserves that we can burn without running the risk of climate catastrophe. Some three-quarters of these reserves are owned by governments through state-owned enterprises (China, Iran, Iraq, Russia, Saudi Arabia, Venezuela, etc.), and most of the rest by investor-owned companies like Peabody, Exxon Mobil and BP. Since some countries with substantial reserves lack the capital, infrastructure and technology to bring them to market in the short term, there may still be time to persuade their political leaders to leave most of them in the ground; but the investor-owned companies persist in searching for more fossil fuels to profit from.[23]

Global carbon budget studies calculate risks by asking: How much more fossil fuel can we burn, how many additional gigatons (billion metric tons) of carbon can we put into the atmosphere, up to such and such a year – and still stand a so-many percent chance of keeping the temperature rise under so-many °C?[24]

A landmark study from 2009 concluded that 'less than half' the world's fossil fuel reserves could be burned if we're to stand a decent chance of staying below a 2°C rise. The researchers emphasized that 2°C is by no means 'a safe level', noting that small island states and least developed countries had been calling for a limit of 1.5°C.[25] In fact, many of the top climate scientists warned that the 2°C limit was recklessly high and lacked scientific justification: it was a figure regarded as useful only because it was politically realistic.[26]

In an eloquent essay in *Rolling Stone*, Bill McKibben put the results of that 2009 study together with some numbers from the world of finance.[27] On the basis of the latest evidence, he reckoned that as much as four-fifths of fossil fuel reserves would have to stay in the ground unless we wanted to run the serious risk of (in Nicholas Stern's well-turned phrase) 'frying the planet'. A comprehensive report from 2013 by James Hansen and seventeen co-authors (including such luminaries as Jeffrey Sachs and Johan Rockström), 'Assessing "Dangerous Climate Change"', estimated that almost three-quarters of proven fossil fuel reserves would have to stay in the ground if we wanted to restore the planet's energy balance.[28]

As McKibben's essay made clear, the carbon budget confronts the fossil fuel industries with two major sources of loss: *sunk costs* and *stranded assets*.[29] When the world eventually shifts to a zero-carbon economy, the current fossil fuel infrastructure will be obsolete. This vast system – from oil wells and super-tankers to power plants and petrol stations – is said to be worth 'around ten trillion dollars'. And assuming some of it has to be retired before the capital costs are paid off, the owners will find themselves writing off 'hundreds of billions of dollars in lost value'.[30] We can rest assured that these owners, as good capitalists, will do their utmost to pass on these 'sunk costs' to anyone other than their shareholders. And with trillions of dollars at stake it's worth their while to spend vast sums of money on keeping the capital infrastructure going for as long as they can – even if that involves disseminating lies about the effects of their doing business.

The 'stranded assets' would be the proportion of the world's known fossil fuel reserves that can't be brought to market because enough people have decided it's too dangerous to burn them. A Citigroup study from 2015 estimated that 'around $100 trillion of assets could be "carbon stranded", if not already economically so' – and this was based on the very modest goal of 'a 50% chance of reaching a 2°C' temperature increase, which we now know would be disastrous.[31] No wonder the industry is prepared to sink to the lowest depths of deceit in order to avoid such a scenario.

When this situation first became apparent there was a lot of talk about a 'carbon bubble' in the economy, and the danger it posed to investors. Several thousand gigatons of fossil fuels were valued on the world's stock markets as if they were going to be sold, and if only a portion of them can be burned without frying the planet, fossil fuel portfolios are actually worth only a fraction of their declared value. In spite of this, the financial markets in fossil fuels haven't undergone any major transformation in the intervening years, which suggests that investors are confident that we'll continue to fail to do anything substantial about reducing carbon emissions.

Their confidence appears to be justified. At the end of 2019 the United Nations Environment Programme issued its tenth annual 'Emissions Gap Report', which studies different scenarios between 'where we are likely to be' if we continue business as usual and 'where we need to be' if we're to avoid dangerous degrees of global heating. Considering the 'nationally determined contributions' that countries agreed to at the UN climate meeting in Paris (2015), the report says: 'The summary findings are bleak. Countries collectively failed to stop the growth in global GHG emissions, meaning that deeper and faster cuts are now required.' This means that most countries are going to have to increase their commitments fivefold to keep the temperature rise below 1.5°C – meaning annual emissions reductions of 7.6 per cent from 2020 to 2030. It's hard to imagine how this can be done.[32]

It's especially hard to imagine because instead of trying to reduce the costs they've already sunk into fossil fuel infrastructure, the captains of the industry, with generous help from the big banks, persist in *expanding* the system – committing us to an even more damaging overshoot of the carbon budget. In fact 'the world's 50 biggest oil companies are poised to flood markets with an additional seven million barrels per day over the next decade'.[33] This is a generous contribution to what's called the *production gap*: 'the discrepancy between countries' planned fossil fuel production and global production levels consistent with limiting warming to 1.5°C or 2°C'. Through this gap we can see the charade that is being played around the Paris Agreement: in spite of their woefully inadequate climate pledges, ten of the top fossil fuel-producing countries plan to produce enough by 2030 produce in turn some 39 billion tons of

CO_2 – which is '120% more than would be consistent with a 1.5°C pathway.[34] Well over twice the amount that can be safely burned.

So, with several tipping points on the horizon, we might as well stop fooling ourselves and admit that our carbon budget is *zero*. The sooner we cut down, the less likely we are to push the climate over the edge. But there are some people on the bus who have a vested interested in keeping our feet away from the brake pedal for as long as they can. With so many trillions of dollars at stake, the fossil fuel industry is prepared to spend whatever it takes to keep on with business as usual.

Let's now take a closer look at the hidden sources of the money that's flooding our politics, and then at the three immediate obstructions to taking appropriate action on the climate crisis.

Part Two

Covert Operations, Outrageous Obstructions

One can do good only if one knows how things are and what their situation is. . . . So-called 'good intentions' and 'meaning well' are by no means sufficient. Actualisation of the good presupposes that our activity is appropriate to the real situation—to the concrete actualities that are the 'environment' of a concrete human action— and that we take these concrete actualities seriously and with clear-eyed dispassion.

JOSEF PIEPER[1]

The Rise of the Libertarians

On my gradual way out from university teaching, aiming for a graceful exit, I offer the occasional seminar at the University of Vienna. On the way to the Department of Philosophy, I walk through the main university building, whose courtyard has statues and busts of famous professors arrayed in the elegant arcade that runs around three sides. Sigmund Freud is there, in an suitably shadowy corner. Fifteen Nobel Prize laureates are celebrated in the vestibule, among them the economist Friedrich von Hayek. I pay my respects on the way through, but in pausing in front of Hayek, and then the philosopher Karl Popper in the arcade, a frown tends to furrow the brow.

The reason for the frown is that in 1947 Hayek and Popper co-founded with several others (including the economists Ludwig von Mises and Milton Friedman) the Mont Pelerin Society, with Hayek serving as the first president. Concerned about the precarious 'position of the individual' in society, along with 'a decline of belief in private property and the competitive market', the founders resolved to deploy 'intellectual argument and the reassertion of valid ideals' in order to secure the freedom of the market and the individual.[1]

Hayek and Mises (whose PhD was from Vienna) were major figures in the 'Austrian School' of economics, and their political thought was (like Popper's) an understandable reaction to the horrors of totalitarianism that they had witnessed in the 1930s and during the Second World War. However, their ideas were weaponized by later luminaries in the Mont Pelerin Society like the American economists James M. Buchanan and F. A. Harper, who waged a 'war of ideas' to get neoliberal ideology into the US government – and as many other governments as possible. And they've been winning that war: their ideology now conditions the thinking of many of the governed as well.

Concerning 'the ideology that now governs our lives', the activist writer George Monbiot observes: 'Not only is it seldom challenged; it is seldom even identified. As a result ... it has no standard or widely recognised name.'[2] He usually calls it neoliberalism, but I'm going to opt for (right-wing) 'libertarianism' in recognition of its effects beyond the sphere of economics.

Libertarianism as a political philosophy takes many forms, from right to left, from capitalist to socialist and even anarchist. As its name suggests, *liberty* or freedom is the paramount value, and the sovereignty of the individual is to be maintained by minimizing the size and power of government and letting the 'free market' rule the economy. Libertarians derive many of their ideas from what in Europe is called 'neoliberalism', as first elaborated by the Austrian School of economics, and then developed in the US by economists like Milton Friedman. Friedman's ideas were put into practice by Ronald Reagan in the US and Margaret Thatcher in the UK, to devastating effect.[3]

For the sake of convenience, I'll ignore the ambiguities of the term and its overlap with 'neoliberal', and use the term 'libertarian' to refer to someone who advocates freedom from government regulation and taxation, insists on property rights and the free market, and opposes any kind of welfare state or other socialist arrangements. What we have now is a number of libertarian billionaires who are waging a covert 'war of ideas' (their term) against the rest of us. Once their campaign is exposed, we can draw on philosophy for better ideas to counter theirs.

The influence of libertarian ideology has been growing steadily since 1945, and by the end of 2019 it was steering the government of the Brexiting UK as well as the Trump administration. GHG emissions have also been growing over the same period. This is no mere coincidence: emissions are a natural consequence of this ideology, which supports the first major obstruction to vigorous engagement with the climate crisis: the financial clout of the fossil fuel industries. The next chapter gives an account of this clout, and Chapter 5 deals with the second major obstruction, which is the political power of the Religious Right, especially in the US.

Extremes of inequality

In the 'good old days' of the Gilded Age in the late nineteenth century, when the gap in the US between rich and poor yawned wider than ever before, millionaires were accustomed to having the government do their bidding when it came to helping private enterprise. Infusions of money into politics prevented taxes from becoming too high and regulations too burdensome. The super-rich deflected attention from the bribery and corruption they engaged in by founding private philanthropic organizations, which made them appear generous while saving them a fortune in tax relief.[4]

After the First World War, however, Roosevelt's New Deal and the rise of labour unions led to less corrupt government and more equitable social and political arrangements. This state of affairs lasted until the 1970s, but since then there has been a reversion to a new Gilded Age. In 2014 a 700-page book by a world expert on economic inequality, Thomas Piketty, became an unexpected best-seller. It's called *Capital in the Twenty-First Century* because one of the main arguments is that the current growth of wealth depends more on inherited capital than earned income. Piketty warns of 'the emergence of a new patrimonial capitalism', whereby inherited wealth concentrated in the hands a few is increasing economic inequality and making those few ever more powerful.[5]

Paul Krugman began a review of the book by calling it 'a magnificent, sweeping meditation on inequality'. The 'big idea' of Piketty's big book is that we're reverting to a situation where 'the commanding heights of the economy are controlled not by talented individuals but by family dynasties'.[6] (Think Coors, Scaifes and Kochs rather than Trump. Not meritocracy, but rather plutocracy or, at the extreme, kleptocracy.) Of course, the controllers are clever and keep their influence concealed: as Piketty writes, 'no hypocrisy is too great when economic and financial elites are obliged to defend their interests'. Five years after his warning that 'the risk of a drift toward oligarchy is real and gives little reason for optimism about where the United States is headed', the drift became an increasingly powerful current.[7]

Robert Reich, who was Secretary of Labor in the Clinton administration, is optimistic that capitalism can be reformed and the economic inequality gap closed – but only if we go beyond the simplistic opposition between the 'free market' and 'government intervention'. This opposition is a smokescreen hiding the real problem, which is that the rich have successfully manipulated the rules of the market to their own advantage. He shows many ways in which the economic system can be made more equitable, 'for the many, not the few'.[8]

Bruno Latour's great little book *Down to Earth: Politics in the New Climatic Regime* brings together 'three phenomena that commentators have already noted but without always seeing their connection': the 'deregulation' that the darker side of globalization has loosed upon the world; a 'vertiginous explosion of inequalities' (economic especially); and the 'systematic effort to deny the existence of climate change'.[9] With respect to the first phenomenon, Latour makes this helpful distinction:

> For 50 years, what is called globalization has in fact consisted in *two opposing phenomena* that have been systematically confused.
>
> Shifting from a local to a global viewpoint ought to mean *multiplying* viewpoints, *registering* a greater number of varieties, *taking into account* a larger number of beings, cultures, phenomena, organisms, and people.

That was what many people hoped for when the phenomenon first gathered momentum.

> Yet it seems as though what is meant by globalization today is the exact opposite of such an increase. The term is used to mean that *a single vision*, entirely provincial, proposed by a few individuals, representing a very small number of interests . . . has been imposed on everyone and spread everywhere.[10]

For obvious reasons, Latour calls the first kind 'globalization plus' and the second 'globalization minus'.

Neoliberal deregulation, increasing inequality, and climate denial are indeed connected, and so I'll begin this part of the book, on the major obstructions to our tackling the climate crisis, with a survey of the extreme state of economic inequality at the end of 2019.

Two studies of 'carbon inequality' that appeared in 2015 highlight the grossness of the injustice involved in the climate crisis.[11] The previous year around *one half* of the 'global carbon emissions attributed to consumption' by individuals were produced by the richest 10 per cent of the world's population, while the poorest half (around 3.5 billion) emitted only 10 per cent of the total. Most of these poorer people live in 'the countries most vulnerable to climate change'.

Apparently 'the top 1% richest Americans, Luxemburgers, Singaporeans, and Saudi Arabians are the highest individual emitters in the world, with annual per capita emissions above $200tCO_2e$': that's two hundred tons per year – two *thousand* times the emissions of the poor people in 'Honduras, Mozambique, Rwanda and Malawi'. And when you consider the most affluent residents of all countries (some of whom live in the so-called 'developing' world, usually as kleptocrats), it turns out that 'the average footprint of the richest 1% of people globally could be 175 times that of the poorest 10%.'[12] That may not seem quite fair – but it gets worse.

Between the fruitless United Nations climate conference in Copenhagen in 2009 and the more successful one in Paris in 2015, 'the number of billionaires on the Forbes list with interests in fossil fuel activities rose from 54 to 88, while the size of their combined personal fortunes expanded by around 50% from over $200bn to more than $300bn'.[13] Well, it's one thing for these billionaires to be spending fortunes on their lifestyles and enjoying their burgeoning wealth; but when they're making a killing from products that are overheating the planet, that's another and more unfair thing. Through their carbon emissions from all those mansions and limousines and super-yachts and private jets, this economic elite is making a major contribution to ruining the lives of the poorest people on the planet and making things harder for the rest of us.

It gets worse still. Every year researchers at Oxfam publish a report timed to coincide with the annual meeting of the World Economic Forum in Davos, Switzerland, where leaders in economics, politics, business and entertainment come together to discuss what they see as the world's most pressing problems. The reports draw attention to the problem of growing economic inequality, and every year the inequality increases. In 2016, for example, the eight richest people in the world owned *more wealth* than the 3.6 billion people comprising the poorer half of the world's population.[14] The reports warn that this increasing concentration of the world's wealth in the hands of a few is unsustainable, just as experts at the World Economic Forum had warned that economic inequality and social polarization constituted major risks for the world economy.[15]

Yet every year the rich get even richer and the poor get poorer.[16] In the last decade the wealth of the world's 2200 or so billionaires (the 0.001%) rose 'much faster than global GDP'. Exact figures are hard to come by because so much money is sheltered in tax havens: in 2014 that amounted to almost one tenth of households' wealth in the world – some $7.6 trillion – and is surely a much larger figure by the time you read this.[17] One reason the wealth of the richest grows so fast is the size and power of 'Secrecy World' or 'Moneyland', the underbelly of economic globalization, a dark internetwork of ingenious institutions (some of them merely virtual) for making capital appreciate and 'growing' your money – and of course keeping it hidden so you can avoid taxes.[18]

In addition to all this, and a major factor behind global warming, is that an economic elite hijacked the global financial system in the 1970s and now control it for their own good, and to the detriment of the rest of us and the planet. In opposition to everything the nations of the world agreed when they signed the Paris Agreement in 2016, the financiers continue to finance fossil fuel extraction to the tune of billions. By issuing 'millions of dollars of unregulated credit to fund supposedly limitless consumption', these people are wrecking the climate – and paying the politicians handsomely to look the other way and leave them to their antisocial devices.[19]

A war of ideas

The first campaign on the British front in the libertarian war of ideas was led by a wealthy English dairy farmer by the name of Antony Fisher. At the end of the Second World War, Fisher happened to read a condensed version of Hayek's *The Road to Serfdom* in *The Reader's Digest*. This prompted him to visit Hayek at the London School of Economics to ask him how to protect the freedoms that the War had been fought for, in the face of increasing government 'collectivism'.

> Hayek explained his view that the decisive influence in *the great battle of ideas and policy* was wielded by intellectuals. . . . His counsel was that I should join with others in forming a scholarly research organisation to supply intellectuals in universities, schools, journalism and broadcasting with authoritative studies of the economic theory of markets and its application to practical affairs.[20]

The strategy was to provide better weaponry to the intellectuals already working in the system, so that they could provide stronger support in the coming war of ideas. Hayek continued to engage in 'the great struggle of ideas' against socialism, Marxism, and any kind of state intervention in the 'free market' for the rest of his long career.[21] [3.2]

In the early 1950s Antony Fisher got to know the libertarian economist F. A. Harper (of the Mont Pelerin Society), who impressed him with his right-wing libertarian ideas. Harper believed that social security programmes – which take from people 'against their will some of the product of their labors' (in the form of taxes) as well as 'some of the free choice of how and when their incomes will be spent' – are 'the exact equivalent of theft'. And if we don't protect 'rights of private property' against government enthusiasm for 'public utilities', then 'collective theft becomes validated'. So what is to be done? 'Ideas must be met by ideas, on the battleground of belief.'[22] Yes indeed they must (and will be, in Parts Three and Four).

On a more practical plane, Harper taught Fisher the latest 'factory' techniques for raising broiler chickens for slaughter, and encouraged him to put the subsequent profits to establish a libertarian think tank, the Institute of Economic Affairs (IEA). Founded in 1955, the IEA was the first free-market think tank in the UK, and since Fisher and friends already knew 'the truth' of the free market's supremacy, 'their task was to evangelize'.[23] The IEA was still going strong almost seventy years later, as we'll see in the next chapter. Fitting, perhaps, that it should have been funded by the profits from cruel and inhumane exploitation of another species by means of new technology.

In the early 1970s Fisher went to Wichita, Kansas, to visit Charles Koch 'to sell him on the idea that think tanks can play a critical role in promoting freedom' – including freedom to change the climate, with sad consequences for the planet.[24] The hard sell worked well, as we'll see shortly. Then in 1981 Fisher founded the Atlas Network, with the aim of coordinating the activities of libertarian think tanks worldwide: thirty years later, Atlas claimed (plausibly) to have created or connected 'more than 275 free-market think tanks in 70 countries'.[25] Free market – 1; Earth's climate – 0.

A major advance on the American front of the Fight for Freedom was the founding in 1957 of the Thomas Jefferson Center for Political Economy and Social Philosophy at the University of Virginia by James McGill Buchanan, a political economist from Tennessee. Buchanan took up Hayek's call to arms with his promise that the Jefferson Center, as 'a community of scholars who wish to preserve a social order based on individual liberty', would train 'a new line of thinkers who could effectively oppose the 'increasing role of government in economic and social life'. The historian Nancy MacLean has given a comprehensive account of Buchanan's ideas and their far-reaching influence in her book *Democracy in Chains*. 'He could win this war', she writes of Buchanan's launch of the Jefferson Center, 'and he would do it with ideas'.[26]

Like F. A. Harper, Buchanan wanted to combat 'the seemingly unfettered ability of an increasingly more powerful federal government to force individuals with wealth to pay for an increasing number of public goods and social programs they had had no personal say in approving'. For Buchanan, tax-funded social programmes to help the unfortunate and disadvantaged at the expense of the rich, who have earned their money by working hard, were 'a form of legally sanctioned gangsterism'. All talk of doing things for the common good is nothing more than 'a smoke screen for "takers" to exploit "makers"'.[27] Like F. A. Harper's, Buchanan's ideas are important because of their enormous influence on Charles Koch and the development of the Koch Brothers' Network – which by 2017 had succeeded in buying the Republican Party and the Trump administration.

This kind of libertarianism is the perfect ideology for men in positions of power who are fans of Ayn Rand – a woman not so well known outside the US, but whose ideas continue to exert a strong influence there. The year Buchanan founded the Jefferson Center, Rand published *Atlas Shrugged*, a 1,200-page monster of a novel – so turgid and melodramatic as to be unreadable (at least for me). And yet it has probably been more effective than any other book in spreading right-wing libertarian ideas, even though Rand liked to think that her own 'Objectivism' was a far superior philosophy. (Just as she fancied that she was a superior thinker to Nietzsche, who was an early influence). One of Rand's great admirers was Alan Greenspan, whose neoliberal economics brought us the horrors of the Reagan and Thatcher years, and thereby changed the world.

When the ultra-conservative Tea Party movement was launched in 2009, it was fuelled by Rand's ideas. Some influential Rand fans nowadays are Ron Paul (and son *Rand*), Justice Clarence Thomas, Paul Ryan, Glenn Beck, Rush Limbaugh, Rex Tillerson, Mike Pompeo and Donald Trump.[28] Of course! As Rand once wrote in her journal: 'One puts oneself above all and crushes everything in one's way to get the best for oneself. Fine!'[29] And in Silicon Valley there's the late Steve Jobs, Travis Kalanick, Peter Thiel and others; and in the UK Sajid Javid and Daniel Hannan ('the intellectual architect of Brexit').

Rand's philosophy, if you can call it that, is like libertarianism in promoting a worldview that's convenient if you inherited or earned great wealth, and as long as good fortune stays with you. But if you happen to fall on hard times, the ideas lose their lustre. Rand promoted free-market capitalism her whole career and derided 'humanitarian' government programmes like Medicare. But when she and her husband became infirm in later years, and she realized how expensive health services were, she left her principles to one side and enrolled in Medicare.[30]

But if we just consider the theory rather than the practice, the individualist and libertarian idea is that we should be free to live as we choose, and if the free market means that following our business model disadvantages other people – well, that's life. When there are winners, there have to be losers. The opposing school of thought says that's not fair, that it's not all right that your business activity disadvantages other people who aren't even involved in the business. You can see this economically in terms of negative externalities, or of the basic fairness of the 'polluter pays' principle.

This principle is at the basis of most environmental law, and says that if, for example, a factory produces pollution that harms environing ecosystems and human health, its owner is responsible for cleaning the pollution up and disposing of it safely. Here's the 'Rio Declaration' from the UN Earth Summit of 1992: 'National authorities should endeavour to promote the internalization of environmental costs and the use of economic instruments, taking into account the approach that the polluter should, in principle, bear the cost of pollution.'[31]

The problem for the national authorities was that the fossil fuel industries claimed that carbon dioxide emissions can't be regarded as pollution because it's a naturally occurring gas that promotes plant growth. But then in 2007 the British economist Nicholas Stern highlighted the crucial role of 'externalities' in his influential book *The Economics of Climate Change*:

> In common with many other environmental problems, human-induced climate change is at its most basic level an *externality*. Those who produce greenhouse gas emissions are bringing about climate change, thereby imposing costs on the world and on future generations, but they do not face directly, neither via markets nor in other ways, the full consequences of the costs of their actions.

The free market is unable to 'correct' this kind of externality: you have to have policy intervene. All in all, Stern concludes, climate change exposes '*market failure on the greatest scale the world has seen*'.[32] Because if you insist on the sanctity of the free market in the realm of climate economics, you end up by 'frying the planet'.

Naomi Klein laid out the internal contradictions in the ideas of 'free market fundamentalism' and economic 'extractivism' ('a nonreciprocal, dominance-based relationship with the earth') in her comprehensive book *This Changes Everything: Capitalism vs. the Climate* (2014).[33] She shows how climate change deeply unsettles the market fundamentalism that underlies hard-core conservatism, especially in the US. Libertarians *have* to deny the reality of global warming, because 'as soon as they admit that climate change is real, they will lose the central ideological battle of our time over whether we need to plan and manage our societies to reflect our goals and values, or whether that task can be left to the magic of the market'. After the global financial crisis of 2008, this reliance on the market looks like their weakest point in their ideological armour.

Klein demonstrates the utter impotence of free market ideology when confronted with a problem like global heating, which 'demands collective action on an unprecedented scale and a dramatic reining in of the market forces that are largely responsible for creating and deepening the crisis.'[34] The sooner that ideology is discredited the better: but taking it down is difficult because there's so much money propping it up.

Jane Mayer has 'followed the money' in great detail in her excellent exposé *Dark Money: How a Secretive Group of Billionaires is Trying to Buy Political Control in the US* (2016). (A revised edition would have to change the subtitle to *Billionaires Managed to Buy Total Political Control*.) She finds the immediate source a few decades back:

> During the 1970s, a handful of the nation's wealthiest corporate captains felt overtaxed and overregulated and decided to fight back. Disenchanted with the direction of modern America, they launched an ambitious, privately financed war of ideas to radically change the country. They didn't want to merely win elections; they wanted to change how Americans thought.

An ambitious undertaking indeed, which they would pursue by building a network of private foundations and think tanks whose 'overarching purpose was to use philanthropy to support a war of ideas' – with the aim of making Americans *think libertarian*.[35]

If you think that think tanks are containers in which you watch thoughts and ideas floating around and fish out the best ones as needed, that's the old style. The new, neo-conservative think tanks bulldoze the old ideas and blast their way into public awareness with the massive firepower of their ideology: they call themselves 'the artillery' in the war of ideas. The rich libertarians found a trove of effective weaponry in the writings of Harper and Buchanan. And since the economists were eager to put their ideas into practice and transform the nature of political economy in the US, the alliance was a boon for them as well as for the billionaires.[36][3.1]

Libertarian largesse rules

In 2004 the environmental lawyer Robert F. Kennedy, Jr. warned of the dangers from 'an unholy marriage between polluting industries and the radical right' in an impassioned book titled *Crimes against Nature: How George W. Bush and His Corporate Pals Are Plundering the Country and Hijacking Our Democracy*. Kennedy recounts how, beginning in the 1970s, a libertarian 'Gang of Five' – 'right-wing foundations established by major corporate polluters' – funded a variety of think tanks with the aim of 'strangling the environmental movement' and denying global warming.[37] The gang members are: the John M. Olin Foundation, the Sarah Scaife Foundation (funded by the Mellon fortune), the Castle Rock Foundation (endowed by the Adolph Coors Foundation), the Bradley Foundation and the Charles G. Koch Charitable Foundation. [3.3]

The origins and motivations of the Olin Foundation are exemplary here. You make a fortune through business operations whose by-products allegedly harm workers and people living near your factories by poisoning the surrounding water, air and soil. On the basis of the 'polluter pays' principle, government regulations punish you for causing such harms and require you to clean up your mess. You respond by using your vast profits to get rid of regulations and change any laws you find inconvenient. And when it comes to harmful emissions of carbon dioxide, you'll fight to the bitter end to make sure nobody is going to tax or regulate.

A later entrant to what has been called 'the climate change counter-movement' was the Mercer Family Foundation, founded by the billionaire hedge fund manager Robert Mercer and directed by his daughter Rebekah.[38] (More on the Mercers in the next two chapters.) But the greatest benefactor of climate denial organizations is the 'donor-advised fund' Donors Trust/Donors Capital (founded 1999), which is a kind of broker that can grant donors anonymity and passes on their contributions to organizations of their choosing.[39] A useful thing to have if you're fighting a covert war of ideas. Among major donors are apparently – and unsurprisingly – the Olin, Bradley and Koch Foundations. And of course you'll also want to have control over as wide a swathe of media as you can manage.

This is why some say that the most powerful person in the climate denial industry is another of those libertarian billionaires, the media mogul Rupert Murdoch. Murdoch has used his huge media empire effectively to obstruct progress on climate change on several continents.[40] Mainly thanks to his efforts, Australia has been the only developed nation that has actually managed to regress by *repealing* a tax on carbon. Add the contribution from the climate-denying mining magnate Gina Rinehart, the country's richest person, and you see why the Australian government's attitude toward the climate crisis is so incredibly retarded.[41]

But whereas Murdoch's machinations are fairly well known, an obstructer who has been arguably more effective has worked mostly under cover. Charles D. Koch is a major general in the covert war of ideas being waged by the libertarians. (The name is pronounced 'Coke', as in petroleum coke: a big product for Koch Industries, and especially rich in carbon. The co-owner, David H. Koch, who died in 2019, was also a major figure.) Jane Mayer and others have told the story well, so I can treat it briefly: it's basically a case of using your vast profits to buy the political influence that will ensure that you continue to make vast profits – regardless of the harm done to the rest of the world.[42]

The story of Koch Industries and Foundations recapitulates what we saw with the Olin Foundation: libertarian capitalism at its most ruthless.[43] You make a fortune doing things that harm other people and the environment, and to retain the freedom to do so, you arrange to have politicians and policymakers change the laws in your favour. The Koch Brothers' aim was to cut the government down to size and ensure that what's left of it would be good for their business (like those subsidies for fossil fuel production).[44] They invested heavily in election campaigns for the judiciary, to get friendly laws onto the books for as long as they needed. By 1990 '*more than two out of every five* sitting federal judges' had participated, all expenses paid, in a law school programme at George Mason University supported by the Koch Brothers.[45]

They also provided lavish support for the American Legislative Exchange Council (ALEC), a barely legal organization well funded by corporations and trade associations that specialises in getting state legislatures to adopt the right laws and shun restrictive regulations. In particular it provides 'direct assistance to state legislators and firms eager to minimize any state government engagement in environmental protection'.[46] ALEC has been especially successful at preventing states from adopting legislation that would encourage the development of clean and renewable sources of energy.[47] Almost *one-third* of state legislators are members – a sad indication of the huge influence of big business on the laws of the Land of the Free. That's how it goes in US politics: by injecting large amounts of money into the system, you can align its doings with your desires.

For the longer term war of ideas to make society more libertarian, the Koch Bros have been conducting a 'full spectrum' of operations on three related fronts. First, they've been getting libertarian ideas into the universities by funding faculty positions, fellowships and research centres.[48] The second front involves libertarian think tanks, whose purpose is to turn the ideas produced by the academics into 'a more practical or usable form'. There's the Charles Koch Foundation (founded 1974), which later became the Cato Institute, whose aim is to promote 'Individual Liberty, Free Markets, and Peace'. In 1980 their protégé Rich Fink (real name) founded the Mercatus Center at George Mason University, with generous funding from the Kochs.[49] The Cato Institute later organized the first major conference of global warming deniers, which became a model for subsequent meetings of this kind, such as the annual International Conferences on Climate Change arranged by the Heartland Institute.[50]

On the third front of operations, 'citizen activist or implementation groups' translate the policy ideas into 'proposals that citizens can understand', and then 'press for the implementation of policy change'. The libertarian backers set them up as grassroots citizens groups, but they're actually 'AstroTurf' organizations (nothing natural about them), and they register them as non-profit educational bodies so that donations can remain secret. The Koch Bros led the way with Citizens for a Sound Economy (1984), which later became Americans for Prosperity.[51] Both organizations, as the enactors of ideas issuing from the universities and think tanks, have paid dividends on the millions funnelled through them. They've succeeded in blocking numerous proposals to reduce global warming through environmental regulations that would have damaged Koch Industries.

The success of Koch Industries' political activities has inspired other fossil fuel concerns to adopt the full-spectrum approach. The industry has managed what has been called 'the invisible colonization of academia', by injecting increasing amounts of largesse into top-tier institutions.[52] Funding from companies like Shell, Chevron, BP and ExxonMobil flows into research centres at Harvard, MIT, Stanford, UC Berkeley, the University of Texas, etc. and helps keep them afloat. Would it be cynical to suppose that this situation, which neither the institutions nor the corporations advertise, is kept covert because it harbours a morass of conflicts of interest? And that the last thing the results of that well-funded research would imply is a reduction in fossil fuel burning? [3.2]

We'll be in a better position to answer such questions when we understand the history of the relevant relations between government, the sciences and the fossil fuel industry. And this brings us to the first of (what the Chinese would capitalize as) the Three Obstructions.

The Financial Clout of Fossil Fuels

If you're in the business of the extractive industries, the natural sciences can get in the way of your making a profit when their findings serve as a basis for inconvenient government regulations. So you need to make friends with cooperative politicians like the Republicans in the US, who are prepared to put the scientists in their place when they come up with unhelpful findings. Republican legislators have been supporting the war of ideas for several decades by waging a 'war on science' for the benefit of the fossil fuel industries, and with spectacular success.[1] In the meantime they have inspired similar wars in other countries, above all in Brazil.

They conduct campaigns on two major fronts: on one hand they try to suppress any inconvenient findings from real scientists, and dismiss any that manage to surface as 'junk science'; and on the other they cultivate a contrarian fringe of outlier scientists whose findings are more congenial, and promote these mediocrities as the only ones engaged in 'sound science'. The ploy comes from the Tobacco Institute's response to a finding by the US Environmental Protection Agency (EPA) in 1992 that second-hand smoke is carcinogenic: well, for Big Tobacco that's just 'another step in a long process characterized by a preference for political correctness over sound science'![2]

The first major battle in the modern science wars was triggered by the publication in 1962 of Rachel Carson's *Silent Spring*, a pioneering exposé of the dangers of synthetic pesticides like DDT, which lent more momentum to the environmental movement in the US. The captains of the chemical industry realized that Carson's warnings about the dangers their products posed for animal and human life were going to be bad for business. Even worse, *Silent Spring* accused the industry of playing down or denying the existence of 'chemical residues on the food we eat', supporting research programmes where outlier entomologists find that chemical control of insects is a good thing, and trying to conceal the inconvenient fact that many species were developing resistance to their products.[3] [4.1]

The chemical industry initiated a smear campaign and threatened lawsuits to prevent publication, which gave the book additional publicity and the number one slot on the *New York Times* best-seller list.[4] All this exposed the general public to something new: conflict between opposing groups of researchers, civil war within the Republic of Science. A decade or so later, the fossil fuel industries institutionalized such conflicts by funding think tanks that would pay their scientists to disagree with 'mainstream' scientists when necessary – which allowed lay people to say 'I don't believe what the scientists say'. The science became increasingly politicized as conservative politicians endorsed the evidence of think-tank scientists while rejecting the findings of scientists from national institutes and universities. It's another instance of the strategic generation of ignorance – which often takes the form of insisting that experts don't know what they're supposed to know.

Opting for ignorance

The year 1957 gave us not only Buchanan's Jefferson Center and Rand's *Atlas Shrugged*, but also a landmark study of climate science by two scientists at the prestigious Scripps Institution for Oceanography who investigated the exchange of carbon dioxide between the atmosphere and the oceans. The results led them to warn of the risks of increasing carbon emissions:

> Human beings are now carrying out a large scale geophysical experiment.... Within a few centuries we are returning to the atmosphere and oceans the concentrated organic carbon stored in sedimentary rocks over hundreds of millions of years.[5]

In other words, burning that amount of ancient fossil fuels – containing energy from the sun that came in so long ago – threatens to throw off Earth's energy balance.

Later that year, scientists from the research division of the Humble Oil and Refining Co. (later to become Exxon) published a paper on the same topic, in which they disagreed with the Scripps scientists on just how much CO_2 the oceans were absorbing.[6] Further studies and testimony to Congress made it clear that 'climate change had arrived in Washington'.[7]

As early as the 1960s, then, scientists working for the fossil fuel industries had every reason to suppose that use of their products causes harmful air pollution and smog, and raises concentrations of atmospheric CO_2 to levels that could change the climate in adverse ways.[8]

The Union of Concerned Scientists has published two reports that tell the subsequent, sordid story of feigned ignorance in depressing detail: *Smoke, Mirrors & Hot Air: How ExxonMobil Uses Big Tobacco's Tactics to Manufacture Uncertainty about Climate Change* (2007), and *The Climate Deception Dossiers* (2015) which exposes a 'coordinated campaign of deception underwritten by ExxonMobil, Chevron, ConocoPhillips, BP, Shell, Peabody Energy, and other members of the fossil fuel industry'.[9] It's a wonderful case study for epistemology, or agnotology: the fossil fuel companies have known for decades how dangerous for the planet their products are – but for the sake of greater profits they have feigned ignorance. What is more, they continue to channel their profits into *spreading* ignorance throughout the public sphere.

You would think that all this compelling evidence would have prompted the fossil fuel concerns to remake themselves into 'energy companies' long ago. They could have ensured long-term profits by shifting to more sustainable sources of energy. But instead they decided to continue with business as usual, and to protect themselves by investing a good proportion of their vast profits in underhand dealings that would maintain the status quo – invoking the very 'contrarian theories' that their own scientists had already declared discredited![10]

Over thirty years after James Hansen testified about the dangers of global warming to the US Senate Committee on Energy and Natural Resources during the summer heatwave of 1988, and warned that it would 'affect the probability of occurrence of extreme events such as summer heat waves', Big Oil is still spending millions on obstructing progress.[11] In 2019 the State of Washington tried to do the right thing by instituting a tax on carbon (something that will soon be normal), but BP and Chevron poured millions into a campaign that succeeded in defeating the measure. The same year we learned that the largest five stock market-listed oil and gas companies – BP, Shell, ExxonMobil, Chevron and Total – 'spend nearly $200m a year lobbying to delay, control or block policies to tackle climate change'. I seldom use the word 'disgraceful', but it seems unavoidable here.

To add insult to injury, these fossil fuel giants now profess to be very concerned about the global warming that their products have produced –

even while continuing to deny responsibility. The hypocrisy is as gigantic as their operations: 'while publicly endorsing the need to act, they are massively increasing investment in a huge expansion of oil and gas extraction. In 2019 their spending will increase to \$115bn, with a mere 3% of that directed at low carbon projects.'[12] This is an even greater disgrace: after so many decades of knowing the harm done by their products, the world's top twenty polluting companies (accounting for one-third of global emissions) are investing almost nothing in renewable energy projects.[13]

To fully understand the success of the fossil fuel industries' promotion of ignorance and the efficacy of their deceptions, we need to see how the libertarian billionaires established the required disinformation infrastructure.

Disseminating doubt

The year 1984 saw the creation not only of the Kochs' Citizens for a Sound Economy but also of three other think tanks that became formidable forces in the denial of global warming: the George C. Marshall Institute, the Heartland Institute and the Competitive Enterprise Institute. (The avalanche of Newspeak and Doublethink that year must have set George Orwell spinning in his grave.) These set-ups hire highly visible and audible contrarians who don't do original research of their own, but simply pick holes, or fasten on anomalies, in the research of genuine experts in the field to demonstrate the foregone conclusion that either global warming isn't taking place or else it can't be attributed to human activity. Their real area of expertise is 'merchandising doubt', as the historians of science Naomi Oreskes and Erik Conway have termed it, who give a comprehensive account in their book *Merchants of Doubt*. The subtitle sums up the story perfectly: *How a handful of scientists obscured the truth on issues from tobacco smoke to global warming.*[14]

The signing of the UN climate change agreement at the Rio Earth Summit in 1992 made it clear that global warming was becoming a major international issue. The commitment to reduce GHG emissions posed an unprecedented threat to the profits of the fossil fuel industries.[15] In view of the need to cast doubt on this danger, the libertarian billionaires poured more money than ever into right-wing think tanks and AstroTurf groups devoted to misleading the public about the risks to the climate system.

In 1993 the Clinton administration proposed doing what needed to be done to combat global warming: putting *a tax on fossil fuel use* (a 'BTU' tax) that would have exempted renewable sources of energy. Because Koch Industries have always emitted enormous amounts of GHGs – the figure for 2015 was over 28 million metric tons – this tax would have cost them a fortune. As Rich Fink put it, 'over time, it could have destroyed our business'.[16] The tax proposal was approved by the House, but then the Kochs' heavy investment in Citizens for a Sound Economy (which is also supported by companies like Philip Morris, General Electric and Exxon) paid off handsomely. The group's energetic propaganda efforts made people think the tax would cost them a fortune, and senators that they'd be unpopular if they supported it – and so the proposal failed to pass the Senate. If that energy tax had gone through the country would have taken a different direction, and the planet would today be a much cooler place.

In those days the libertarians had to fight harder to get what they wanted because the government had an effective defence against bogus science in the form of the Office of Technology Assessment (OTA), whose expert staff produced reports on science and technology for the benefit of members of Congress and their committees. The OTA published significant studies concerning mitigation of global warming and adaptation to climate change over a range of the country's environments. But when the Republicans took over Congress in 1995, one of their first triumphs was to 'de-fund' the OTA and replace it with a 'free market' approach to science and politics.[17] Liberated from an independent source of information and judgment, politicians in the pockets of the fossil fuel industries were free to choose their own scientists and 'expert' witnesses for their committees. This freedom would soon open up a brave new world of alternative facts.

It was easy for the fossil fuel industries to get their message across because most of the mainstream media were weak in reporting what was happening with global warming. Just a few months after the signing of the Kyoto Protocol at the end of 1997, the American Petroleum Institute swung into secretive action with its (wonderfully named) 'Global Climate Science Communications' plan. A key component was the 'Media Relations Program', which aimed to ensure that 'media recognizes the uncertainties in climate science' and that 'media coverage reflects *balance* on climate science and recognition of the validity of viewpoints that challenge the current "conventional wisdom".'[18]

The Program worked wonders. The mainstream media took responsibility for 'fair and balanced' reporting, by presenting both sides of the question – as if the sides on global warming were comparable. This gives the impression of a debate that hasn't yet been resolved: just what the *Wall Street Journal*, for example, wants you to believe, reflecting as it does the prejudices of its owner, Rupert Murdoch.[19]

The actual balance between climate scientists on the issue of human-caused global warming was at that time overwhelmingly 'Yes'. Even after the scientific consensus that global heating is human-caused reached 99 per cent, the American general public remained oblivious. A CBS News poll in the autumn of 2019 showed that almost half of the American people believed, falsely, that 'scientists disagree that human activity is a main cause of climate change'. Unsurprisingly, almost three-quarters of Democrats polled knew that it is, while only just over a quarter of Republican voters thought so.[20]

The remarkable thing about media coverage of climate change in the US is how little there was of it until the late 2010s. Although 2015 saw an unprecedented number of landmark climate studies published and climate events take place – record high temperatures, Pope Francis's climate change encyclical, the Paris Climate Agreement, etc. – television coverage of climate issues that year actually shrank. For example, ABC News reduced its coverage of climate change to thirteen minutes (!) for the entire year.[21]

When we move from mainstream media to non-professional digital sources and social media, which is apparently where most young people get their information about the world from, it gets even worse. A comparison of the visibility of some four hundred expert climate scientists and the same number of prominent climate contrarians over the first sixteen years of the present century showed the contrarians to be 50 per cent *more visible*. And almost half of the contrarians (some of whom, like Monckton, aren't even scientists) didn't have a single peer-reviewed publication in a scientific journal.[22] No wonder people don't know what's happening with climate change.

If mainstream media have been too quiet on global warming, the far-right media are hyperactive – and hypereffective. The most popular shows on talk-radio have a powerful influence on a sizeable audience: Rush Limbaugh, for example, has 'the most listened-to talk-radio program in the US', and in 2011 he was reaching 15 million listeners.[23] His view of the world is skewed by a conspiracy-oriented mindset. Despite having no background in the natural sciences, he dismisses 'manmade global warming' saying 'This is a hoax, this is BS'. And he claims that some people (climate scientists) are getting well paid through grants that they get only 'if they come up with the right result'.[24] He gives no evidence for this outlandish claim, but just growls loudly and often enough, and the faithful believe what he says.

If you're inclined to believe, please read *The Most Dangerous Man in America: Rush Limbaugh's Assault on Reason*, in which John K. Wilson meticulously debunks the BS. He shows that Limbaugh, in his 'non-fiction' books as well as his radio shows, spouts falsehoods that he doesn't retract when they're shown to be false, peddles outrageous conspiracy theories, and consistently denies the findings of the sciences. 'My views on the environment,' Limbaugh tells us, 'are rooted in my belief in Creation.'[25] He believes that God made Creation indestructible, so that 'we couldn't destroy the earth if we wanted to'. (We'll see this argument again in the next chapter.)

Then there's the power of Murdoch's Fox News Channel, which in 2015 was reaching almost 95 million viewers. Fox News is graced by popular luminaries like Glenn Beck, Bill O'Reilly and Sean Hannity – a friend of Trump's whose audience is almost as large as Limbaugh's. Hannity thinks that 'climate change hysteria has been politically motivated' and that 'global warming is a hoax'. He trots out the tired 'natural variation' objection, insinuating that climate scientists are stupid for not having thought of it. Another conspiracy theory, with again zero evidence.[26]

So what is it like for the millions of workers who are the major audience for Limbaugh and Hannity? Joe Bageant interviewed some of them for his terrific book, *Deer Hunting with Jesus: Dispatches from America's Class War.*

> It is safe to say that radio supplies the workers with most of their knowledge of things political. Most do not subscribe to a newspaper. . . . If you've ever done 'eight straight' cutting tabs off molded plastic or stacking pallets, you know how powerful the sound of the relentless 'one voice speaking to the many' is to those working in headphone radio space, that bubble of radio reality within the roaring of machines. For eight hours it is a voice inside your head that sounds like your own voice. Ask any assembly-line worker, night janitor, or house painter.[27]

It's probably safe to say that for several of those hours the voices belong to Limbaugh (whose show is from noon to 3:00 pm) and Hannity (from

3:00 to 6:00 pm). Bageant's account helps to explain how so many people could buy into their 'assault on reason' and rejection of the reality presented by the sciences.

Lastly there's the Breitbart News Network, which Steve Bannon made into a megaphone for the Trump 2016 campaign and a 'platform for the alt-right'. The network is co-owned by the Mercer family and is another organization keen on spreading conspiracy theories and denying global heating. Self-described 'libertarian conservative' climate deniers publish inaccurate and misleading articles claiming that global warming isn't happening, and colluding Republicans like Representative Lamar Smith, Chair of the House Committee on Science, gleefully tweet the relevant links, and refuse to retract even when climate scientists refute the article.[28]

What real climate scientists say, mostly in professional journals, about the climate crisis has a minimal impact on public opinion by comparison with mainstream media and the power of the denial machine: the billionaire backers, beachheads in universities and colleges, the conservative think-tank network, the front groups and AstroTurf organizations – and all of it amplified by the echo chambers of the Internet!

Buying the right politicians

Toward the end of the twentieth century, people began to wonder whether campaign contributions and lobbying in Congress were giving outside money too much influence on the country's policies and laws. Honourable legislators tried to reduce the impact of cash through measures like the Campaign Finance Reform Act of 2002, sponsored by senators John McCain and Russ Feingold. This was a small step forward – but the Koch Bros soon made sure that it was followed by a large step back. They were ramping up their donations to organizations dedicated to climate denial to the tens of millions, while vigorously promoting state legislation to *prevent* or limit incentives for renewable sources of energy. From 2006 to 2010 Koch Industries spent some $50 million on political lobbying, while the Koch Political Action Committee outspent all other oil companies on contributions to federal candidates.[29]

At the end of the Preface to his book *Requiem for a Species: Why We Resist the Truth about Climate Change*, Clive Hamilton nailed the major source of the resistance nicely: 'The most immediate reason for "our" failure to act on global warming has been the sustained and often ruthless exercise of political power by the corporations who stand to lose from a shift to low- and zero-carbon energy systems.'[30] That was in 2010, and since then the ruthlessness has only intensified. [4.1] By this time the Kochs' top-secret biannual 'summit' meetings of fellow investors in the Koch Network (also known as the Kochtopus) had grown in size and money power in response to an urgent new aim: to neutralize the new government. There was a Democratic majority in Congress and a black man in the White House. Being extremely rich and (mostly) involved in finance, the participants naturally shared a good libertarian antipathy toward government regulation and taxation. Also a fondness for insider trading, tax avoidance, abuse of employees, bribery, and environmental and workplace safety violations. It's hard to resist the thought that many of these Koch Network investors are so rich *because* they're criminals, and want to prevent the government from punishing their kind of criminal behaviour. And since the extractive industries were well represented, there was a special concern to forestall governmental action on global warming.[31]

Another aim of the secret meetings was to reverse Campaign Finance Reform, and all those Koch Network millions helped achieve it. In 2010 a lamentable decision by the US Supreme Court in the *Citizens United* case struck down key components of the Act, basically affirming the right of the very rich to buy the politicians and policies they want. A Court of Appeals decision two months later in the *SpeechNOW* case made it even easier for the billionaires to buy the kind of government they wanted.[32]

The 'Super PACs' and other monstrosities that proliferated in the wake of these victories turned the US into a full-on plutocracy, where the 0.1 per cent can rule the rest as they see fit. The Global Commission on Elections, Democracy and Security, a distinguished international body headed by Kofi Annan, roundly condemned this degradation of the democratic process. They warned that the *Citizens United* decision had 'undermined political equality, weakened transparency of the electoral process and shaken citizen confidence in America's political institutions and elections'.[33]

During the 113th US Congress (2013–14) fossil fuel campaign contributions were over $40 million, and the amount spent on oil and gas lobbying alone was over seven times as much, for a total of over $326 million. A generous expenditure – but then look at what the big spenders gained: *subsidies* for federal production and exploration totalling $33.7 *billion*.[34] At more than 10,000 per cent, this is a better return than most investments yield.

By 2016 'outside spending' in US elections was up from $204 million to $1.4 *billion*, with campaign contributions from the fossil fuel industries reaching new records every two years. According to the Center for Responsive Politics:

> More money was spent in the 2012 election than any other in U.S. history. The final cost of this presidential-year election totalled more than $6 billion – including more than $300 million in dark money spent by politically active 501(c) groups that don't disclose their donors.[35]

The Supreme Court's decision basically allowed government policies to be bought by very rich people whose identities remained hidden.

By this time the billionaires in the Koch Network – or 'Freedom Partners', as they prefer to call themselves – had pretty much stopped collaborating with the Republican Party, since they had at their disposal not only more money but also more data on consumers and their preferences. This made them more efficient at targeting and persuading voters. The Freedom Partners now included such stellar billionaires as Sheldon Adelson and Robert Mercer. Two years later, the Koch network 'had a bigger payroll than the Republican National Committee' – though sponsored by only 'four hundred or so of the richest people in the country'.[36] That's a lot of influence by a very few people.

Having joined forces with the Koch Bros in 2011, Robert Mercer outspent them three years later with his two-and-a-half million dollar donation to the Freedom Partners' Action Fund. He was also quicker to support the Trump campaign in 2016, and thereby gained more influence on the new and inexperienced administration. He got Steve Bannon to connect the Trump campaign with Cambridge Analytica, a British company part-owned by Mercer and his daughter Rebekah, which develops psychological profiles of voters and was also influential, under murky conditions, in the Brexit vote and a scandal over data from some 87 million Facebook users.[37]

Rebekah Mercer helped have Bannon chosen as the campaign's CEO, and was repaid after the election with a place on Trump's transition team. She also managed to get such powerful movers as Michael Flynn and, eventually, John Bolton, appointed to high positions, though neither lasted very long.[38] In any case the Mercers' project to buy the kind of politics they wanted was paying off handsomely.

Although the Kochs were slower to get behind the Trump campaign, their influence had already pervaded so much of the Republican Party that their clout in the government became stronger than ever. A Public Citizen report, 'The Koch Government: How the Koch Brothers' Agenda Has Infiltrated the Trump Administration', counted *forty-four* Trump administration officials with close ties to the Kochs and their political groups. There was Vice President Mike Pence, Secretary of State Mike Pompeo, 'the single largest recipient of Koch campaign funds in Congress', White House Legislative Affairs Director Marc Short, who later became Pence's Chief of Staff, former EPA Administrator Scott Pruitt, and White House budget director Mick Mulvaney, who was later appointed Acting White House Chief of Staff.

In the lower echelons, there was plenty of work to be done and just the right staff to do it.

> Koch allies are also staffing jobs at the Environmental Protection Agency, Interior Department, Energy Department and the Treasury Department. The positions they are advocating overlap with the Kochs' economic interests, in weakening regulatory enforcement, lowering corporate taxes, loosening environmental regulations and opening up public land to oil and gas extraction.

Many of these people came from Koch Industries and other polluters, and so they knew how to do the right thing.[39]

When Trump took office, Freedom Partners put out 'A Roadmap to Repeal: Removing Regulatory Barriers to Opportunity', beginning with 'Step 1: What Can Be Repealed in the First 100 Days'. The document provided a bullet-pointed list of things for Trump to rescind, including 'new federal coal leases', the 'Paris Climate Agreement requiring greenhouse gas emissions reductions' and 'proposed EPA programs incidental to the Clean Power Plan'. This is followed by a list for Congress to 'prioritize', which includes: 'coal mine permitting', the 'Bureau of Land Management federal lands Methane Rule', the 'Renewable Fuel Standard obligations' and the 'EPA Greenhouse Gas Emissions Standards' for motor vehicles.[40] A recipe for disaster as far as global heating is concerned.

At the end of the first 100 days, the Koch Network issued a progress report whose authors were especially delighted with 'the Tax Cuts and

Jobs Act' of 2017, because 'the Network made an eight-figure commitment to this initiative' – and got a splendid return on its investment.[41] In the meantime, the brazen lies trumpeted by the Republicans and the Trump administration – this Act will benefit workers and the middle class – have been exposed as such. The tax cut turned out to be a bonanza for corporations: instead of directing 70 per cent of their tax savings into better pay for workers or new investments, as the proponents of the Act had promised, they enriched themselves by buying back their own stocks. No surprise that 90 per cent of the American people were soon less well off.[42]

A section of the report called 'Removing Regulatory Burdens' concerns 'unnecessary and harmful regulations imposed during the Obama Administration' and commends the progress that's been made: 'In the first eleven months of President Trump's Administration, *the White House and Congress have closely followed the Network's Roadmap to Repeal*' (emphasis added). Yes, Congress took special care to follow the roadmap closely, in gratitude for all those millions in contributions. There's a checklist of over a dozen environmental regulations that the polluting industries found burdensome, but that have now been neutralized, prime among which is 'Withdraw the U.S. from the Paris Climate Agreement – *Withdrawn*'. This last was the Koch Network's biggest coup – especially since a majority of the American people and big business leaders wanted the country to stay in.[43]

The Koch Brothers not only spent a fortune promoting things that are good for them and harm the rest of us, but they also managed to prevent things that would be good for us but bad for them. In 2013 they collaborated with the ALEC to get state legislatures to adopt surtaxes to make solar energy unattractive, and funded ads in several states to mislead consumers about relative costs and benefits. So why doesn't Florida – the sunniest state with the 'best solarity' in the Union – lead the country in solar power installation? Because the Kochs generously funded successful efforts to prevent it. They have also poured millions into combatting movements to improve the quality of life in American cities, and reduce GHG emissions, by providing more public transport.[44] (Who needs public transport if you're a billionaire?)

In 2018 it turned out that ALEC and Koch Bros money was behind the successful push to roll back standards for car emissions in the US. If Trump's plans to relax regulations on fuel efficiency are put into effect, by 2035 GHG emissions from American cars and trucks would increase by up to a billion metric tons.[45] This is significant: transportation accounts for a third of US carbon emissions, and the amount is increasing every year. Very bad news for the whole world's climate.

This comes on top of the Trump administration's 'Affordable Clean Energy Plan', which keeps energy dirty by letting power plants emit more PM2.5 particles and ozone. The administration's very own EPA conducted an analysis that predicts an additional 14,000 premature deaths by the year 2030 as a result, and 48,000 more cases of exacerbated asthma. A Harvard study from 2018 suggests that the fatalities would more likely be around 80,000 per decade.[46] By mid-2019 the Trump administration had reversed, or was reversing, no fewer than *ninety-five* environmental regulations designed to protect the health of citizens and the environment.[47]

Let's think about this for a moment. A government makes legislation that will financially benefit its leaders and their rich donors from industry, while admitting that it will shorten the lives and damage the livelihoods of thousands of less fortunate citizens.[48] Trump doesn't care – but how is it that the fans that make up his 'base' don't realize he's deliberately putting their livelihoods at risk?

Well, it's because the Trump team has won the Mother of All Victories in the Republican war on science. They have done everything in their power to neutralize the scientists, keep science out of policymaking, and silence anyone who might let the public know what is being done against their interests.[49] And when it comes to climate denial, the US government has also declared war on other nations, using carbon emissions as its main weapon. Enacting policies that accelerate global heating gratuitously damages the lives of millions in the developing world.

The Trump team has also been victorious in the war of ideas more generally by reducing the size and the competence of the federal government – by denying it the competent staff and financial resources that it needs in order to function properly.[50] Then they could say, 'See! Government just doesn't work'. That's what the billionaire donors have been paying for, diminished and ineffectual governance, and they're certainly getting their money's worth.

Oligarchs have been just as successful in buying political influence in the UK, whose government by 2019 was behaving like a fifty-first state – or, more accurately, an unincorporated territory of the US like Puerto Rico. You'd think the Johnson government would be unsettled by the American neglect of that territory after Hurricane Maria. But remember

Antony (caged chickens) Fisher and his Institute for Economic Affairs? Well, over six decades later the IEA continued to flourish: by 2018 it had moved into what its director called 'the Brexit influencing game' of providing donors in the US access to government ministers in the UK. If American firms give the IEA money, it will produce research that demonstrates the effectiveness of free-trade deals – which could open the doors for farming operations in the US to export 'beef from cattle treated with growth hormones and chlorine-washed chicken' to the UK. You might almost think you hear the flutter of 'chickens coming home to roost' – except they're imprisoned in cages, now on both sides of the ocean.[51]

The IEA can well boast of its major role in precipitating Brexit, and more. When Boris Johnson became prime minister in 2019, the IEA Weekend Newsletter began with a burst of joyful tidings for 'liberty lovers' concerning 'the most liberal, free-market oriented cabinet since the days of Margaret Thatcher':

> The IEA is delighted to note that no less [sic.] than 14 cabinet members and cabinet attendees are alumni of IEA initiatives … designed to champion ideas of free enterprise and social freedom. They now make up three of the four great offices of state, including Chancellor of the Exchequer Sajid Javid, Foreign Secretary Dominic Raab, and Home Secretary Priti Patel.[52]

Among other alumni luminaries is Jacob Rees-Mogg, Leader of the House of Commons and a climate ignoramus whose superficial views on 'carbon emissions and climate change' would embarrass any science-literate schoolboy.[53] So now the UK government is a minor image of the US government, with key positions filled by politicians who have imbibed the right ideas at libertarian think tanks well funded by American billionaires.[54] No wonder Johnson's Britain looks more and more like Trump's America.

Since the Conservatives won the general election at the end of 2019, Brexit – a dream of libertarians on both sides of the Atlantic – will take place in early 2020. To the delight of the faithful, the European Union, source of so much inconvenient regulation, will suffer, and the UK will be free again. But for most of the British population, Brexit will bring misery: in the words of Chris Patten (a former Conservative Party Chairman), it is 'the most calamitous example of national self-harm'.[55] And that misery will be made worse by extreme weather – because it's unlikely that Britain Unleashed will perform much better than America First in response to the climate crisis.

So: rich libertarians have been fighting a covert ideological war against the rest of us, ensuring that economic inequality will grow, and not caring if they burn the planet as long as they get richer. In the face of this outrage, it's hard not to feel enraged. Rage against the Machine seems a perfectly appropriate emotion. Not moral indignation, nor righteous or mindless anger – but a clear rage that sees what's wrong here. We need a rage that says 'No, this isn't how we want things to go on', a psychical energy that can help us *change* the way things are going. It's the kind of anger against injustice that Plato valued for its power to change things for the better, in the psyche as well as politics. Then it's a matter of channelling it in the right directions.[56] If we can do this, it *is* possible to take the power back from the plutocrats.

But first we need to understand some further aspects of the situation and the various stories being played out within it – and especially around the second of the Three Obstructions, which derives from a peculiar form of Christianity that developed in the United States.

The Political Power of the Religious Right

The Republican war on science is a Holy War, and this is especially true of the war on climate science. The problem isn't the prevalence of evangelical Christianity in the population: it's when conservative politicians make policy on the basis of fundamentalist faith – because this renders government incompetent when it comes to environmental issues and the public good. Religious influence on politics comes primarily from what Harold Bloom called 'the American Religion', the peculiar blend of Christian sects and individualist beliefs that developed in the New World.[1]

The American Religion at its extreme understands the drama of salvation as an individual affair acted out by the immortal soul in its direct relation to the Almighty – bypassing the body, family, society and the Creation. If all that ultimately matters is the salvation of one's unique soul, the devastation of the earth and the misery of one's fellow human beings isn't going to mean so much. Indeed if you believe in 'the Rapture', as many conservative evangelicals seem to, you'll be too busy looking forward to being 'caught up into the clouds, to meet the Lord in the air' than to worry about what's happening to the Earth, on which we actually live.[2]

A Holy War for 'wise use'

'Who can doubt but that in the wise operations of God's Providence, the immense oil resources of the country have been developed at this particular time, to aid in the solution of the mighty problem of the nation's destiny?' The time of this particular question was the American Civil War, which broke out shortly after oil was first discovered, and its author the Reverend S. J. M. Eaton. In those days, few could doubt that the resource that would make America great (once recovered from the ravages of the Civil War) was a gift from the Almighty. There's an enlightening account of the connections between American petroleum and the American religion in the recent book by Darren Dochuk, *Anointed with Oil: How Christianity and Crude Made Modern America*.[3]

In modern American politics the first figure to marshal the forces of religion against science was Ronald Reagan, when he was governor of California in the late 1960s. Reagan drew on the power of religious conservatism to push for prayer in public schools, and spread the doctrine of creationism as 'a valid alternative to the theory of evolution' – which after all is 'only a theory'.[4] He encouraged conservative evangelicals by telling them 'Religious America is awakening', and thanks to his efforts over two terms as president, the American Religion became a powerful and vehemently anti-scientific force in US politics.

The influence of Religious America grew stronger when Joseph Coors, heir to the Coors Beer fortune and an enthusiastic Christian, began using his millions to promote a right-wing libertarian political agenda. Because the mass production of beer was a polluting as well as a lucrative business, the Adolph Coors Company – which was also involved in coal mining, oil drilling and cattle grazing – chafed against environmental protection regulations and set out to have them eliminated.[5] In 1973 Coors co-founded the Heritage Foundation with Paul Weyrich, another religious conservative who went on to co-found the Moral Majority with Jerry Falwell, which would make the Christian Right a more powerful force in American politics. Weyrich also co-founded ALEC, some of whose activities were discussed in the previous chapter.

About his activism Weyrich said, 'It is a war of ideology, it's a war of ideas, it's a war about our way of life', and the mission of the Heritage Foundation was to produce 'the intellectual shock troops of the conservative revolution'. He and Coors, who was the Foundation's primary funder for many years, were fighting for a way of life that was free from worries about climate change: since its inception the Heritage Foundation has been a major force in promoting climate denial.[6]

In 1977 Coors funded the launch of the Mountain States Legal Foundation, a 'public interest legal foundation dedicated to individual liberty, the right to own and use property, limited and ethical government, and the free enterprise system'.[7] With generous support from fossil fuel concerns like Phillips Petroleum, Exxon, Texaco, Amoco, Shell and Chevron, the Foundation's aim was to counter any environmental regulations that might eat into corporate profits. Another thoroughly libertarian enterprise.

Coors money also fuelled the cleverly named 'Wise Use [of natural resources] Movement', an AstroTurf organization that came together at the end of the 1980s. The movement gained further momentum from joining forces with the Christian Coalition founded by the religious broadcaster Pat Robertson – 'whose special contribution to right-wing theology was to substitute environmentalists for communists as the new threat to democracy and Christianity'. The fossil fuel industries were happy to finance the campaigns of candidates from the Christian right, because they would get rid of environmental laws that reduced the industries' profits.[8]

One of the first initiatives launched by the Republican Congress after their 'Contract with America' put them in charge at the end of 1994 was Project Relief, a joint project between politicians and 350 lobbyists to relieve industry of burdensome federal regulations. (Among the big donors were the Adolph Coors Co., Amoco, Ashland Oil and Chevron.) In exchange for lavish campaign contributions, the Republicans gave the captains of industry a seat at the table where they would together craft a moratorium on environmental regulations that would 'freeze future environmental and public health protections' and 'nullify safeguards already in place'. It would be 'open season' on the natural world – and thanks to a handsome communications budget, Project Relief got the legislation passed in the House by a comfortable margin.[9] These cosy discussions were the model for the Bush Junior administration in 2001 and Trump in 2017.

An especially effective holy warrior is Fred Palmer, who was general manager of the Western Fuels Association (WFA), a consortium of coal suppliers and coal-burning utilities, in the mid-1980s. He then became chairman of the board of the 'Information Council on the Environment', an AstroTurf organization whose purpose was to 'reposition global warming as theory (not fact)' by using 'spokesmen from the scientific community'. (Those Western Fuels are fossil fuels.) Rush Limbaugh would do a radio advertisement assuring listeners that 'the facts simply don't jibe with the theory that catastrophic global warming is taking place'.[10]

A decade later the WFA founded the 'Greening Earth Society' with Palmer as president, which bought the services of climate-sceptical scientists to counter 'global warming alarmism' and proclaim the benefits of having a warmer planet swathed in higher concentrations of carbon dioxide.[11] A conservative Roman Catholic with a winning smile, Palmer was able to persuade people that more carbon dioxide would result in a greener earth because he had faith. He *believed* in fossil fuels, as 'among God's greatest gifts to the human community'. He once told the audience at a coal industry conference: 'It is easy to conclude that, under a preordained plan, coal and oil lay in wait for exploitation by humans to permit our creation of an environment on earth conducive to the spectacular success of our species.'[12] It's the good Reverend Eaton all over again: an America 'anointed with oil'.

A documentary from this time shows Palmer explaining how to get with the divine plan: 'You're doing God's work. Every time you turn your car on, and you burn fossil fuels, and you put CO_2 in the air, you're doing the work of the Lord. Absolutely. That's the system. That's the ecological system we live in.'[13] You have to wonder what this unusual understanding of ecology is based on. The Genesis story (1:26) has God giving man dominion 'over all the earth, and over every creeping thing that creepeth upon the earth' – but it says nothing about what lies beneath the surface.

Palmer went on to do more good works at Peabody Energy, the largest privately owned coal company in the world, which promoted the myth that burning coal is the best way to lift people in the developing countries out of poverty. Peabody lavishly funded climate denial groups, and filed for bankruptcy in 2015.[14] Palmer went on to the Heartland Institute, where he became Senior Fellow in Energy and Climate in 2017, and continued to profess his faith in coal as something from which 'more people live better and longer'.[15] Except coal miners and people who die from the pollution.

To base one's sense of reality on faith, and see the world as the manifestation of divine providence, is common among followers of the American Religion. But the factor that leads people to deny human-caused global heating appears to be the degree of the believer's conservatism rather than the particular denomination. For example, the Southern Baptists (the largest Protestant denomination in the US) expressed deep concern about environmental damage in the early 1970s, condemning 'endangerment of the earth by pollution, human extravagance and wastefulness . . . and general misuse of creation', and encouraging people to be 'faithful stewards' of God's creation instead. But by 2005 they had turned ultra-conservative, claiming without evidence that 'tens of thousands of scientists agree that there is no conclusive evidence for the man-made global warming theory'.[16]

The next year, the National Association of Evangelicals suffered a deep rift when a group of Christian leaders formed the Evangelical Climate Initiative and issued 'An Evangelical Call to Action on Climate Change'. The Call is based on four claims: 'human-induced climate change is real';

the bad consequences will 'hit the poor the hardest'; 'Christian moral convictions' demand a response'; 'governments, businesses, churches, and individuals' all need to take immediate action on climate change.[17] This reasonable and compassionate call provoked a furious reaction from conservative Evangelicals and Southern Baptists, who managed to browbeat the National Association of Evangelicals into declining to take a position on global warming.

[5.1] A major force behind this conservative backlash was E. Calvin Beisner, PhD, who is the national spokesman for the Cornwall Alliance for the Stewardship of Creation, which he founded in 2005. Beisner claims that 'Earth's climate system', sustained as it is by God's 'faithful providence', is 'robust, resilient, self-regulating, and self-correcting'; and since God said it's going to stay that way, there *can be no* adverse effects from global warming.[18] Earlier evangelical views of Christian stewardship of the Earth reminded us that the Creation 'belongs to God, and we are to exercise our dominion over these things not as though entitled to exploit them, but as things borrowed or held in trust'. Beisner by contrast highlights our freedom to exercise full-on dominion over the earth, which includes 'mining for precious metals and fossil fuels' and so may require, he says archly, a little bit of '*forceful rule*'.[19] [5.1]

The main problem here is that Beisner's basic premise concerning the climate has been shown by the past few decades of Earth System science to be false: the System *was* resilient and self-regulating until recently, but now human activities have compromised Earth's ability to be self-correcting. Nevertheless, Beisner's theological views are worth knowing because the same ideas motivate the most prominent Christian soldier on the climate front in the Republicans' Holy War on science, Senator James Mountain Inhofe.

Inhofe, 'Facts and Science'

Before getting into politics Inhofe was in the business of property development, and he chafed under environmental regulations that cramped his style and reduced his profits. Early in his political career he compared the EPA to a 'Gestapo bureaucracy' (a puzzling slur, given that the Gestapo was the secret police whereas the workings of the EPA are almost all on the public record). After 2003 Inhofe was able to gloat over turned tables when he became head of the committee that regulates the EPA: payback time.[20] We saw it with the Coors, Olins and Kochs: their resentment over being punished by the government drives them to get rid of regulations resigned to protect people from environmental harms. [5.2]

Inhofe has had a long career as a senator from Oklahoma, a state rich in oil and natural gas, and as a champion in raising money from oil companies. From 1989 to 2019, he pulled in over $2 million from the oil and gas industries – no surprise that Koch Industries has been his single largest contributor.[21] Widely regarded as the most conservative member of Congress, he is a vocal climate denier and vehement opponent of environmental regulations. Because he was Chair of the Senate Environment Committee for two four-year terms, his destructive influence on environmental legislation has been enormous.

For reasons that are at first unclear, he rejects the evidence of the climate scientists and the reports of the IPCC as politically motivated and bogus. Like Christopher Monckton, he cites cherry-picked facts and figures, and might appear – to someone unfamiliar with the climate sciences – to know what he's talking about. But he doesn't, and the scientists he cites are among the 1 per cent of outlier deniers and happen to receive funding from the fossil fuel industries, either directly or through organizations like the Marshall Institute. Even if the planet *is* getting warmer, Inhofe argues, it's due to 'natural variability'. And even if we humans are responsible, more carbon dioxide is a good thing because it helps plants grow.

This is a typical pattern of argument for the contrarians, and reminiscent of what Sigmund Freud called 'kettle logic'. When a man accuses his neighbour of returning a borrowed kettle in damaged condition, the neighbour protests: 'I gave the kettle back in perfect condition. Anyway it was already damaged when you lent it to me. And in fact I never borrowed your damned kettle in the first place!'[22]

When Inhofe became Chair of the Environment Committee the first time, he delivered a two-hour speech that was a farrago of errors, doublespeak, misrepresentations and selected evidence. A revised version, 'The Facts and Science of Climate Change', was available on his official website for many years. Climate scientists have been sharply critical.[23] He began the speech by acknowledging the 'profound responsibility' that comes with his new position, 'because the decisions of the committee have wide-reaching impacts, influencing the health and security of every

American'. In retrospect, he was being overly modest, since the decisions of his committee during his chairmanship had a distinctly adverse impact on the health and security of many people in *other*, poorer, countries as well as in the US.

Most of the studies Inhofe cites have been discredited by top climate scientists, but he keeps on citing them all the same, and his misleading claims remain up on his website. Occasionally he cites real climate scientists but misinterprets their findings; and when they complain about this misuse of their work he simply ignores them. As he pulls in huge donations from the fossil fuel industries, he accuses proponents of 'global warming alarmism' of 'raking in million of dollars . . . to fuel their ever-growing fundraising machines, part of which are financed by federal taxpayers.' And then the speech's rousing finale: 'With all of the hysteria, all of the fear, all of the phony science, could it be that man-made global warming is *the greatest hoax* ever perpetrated on the American people? It sure sounds like it.'[24] Yes it sounds very much like one of those darned conspiracies to me.

Inhofe's first term as Chair of the Senate Environment Committee fell squarely with the Younger Bush presidency, and no doubt received much inspiration concerning the nature of reality from that higher office. The reality-denying inclinations of the Religious Right were hugely boosted during those eight long years, thanks to George W's reliance on his religious instincts, on what God 'told him' to do. As a self-described 'libertarian Republican' explained it at the time, the reason Bush 'dispenses with people who confront him with inconvenient facts' is this: 'He truly believes he's on a mission from God. Absolute faith like that overwhelms a need for analysis.'[25] Inhofe has faith like that, which precludes any need to base his decisions on the reality of the situation.

Indeed, 'the reality-based community' is a term of contempt used by a senior advisor to Bush the Younger, referring to those who lack political power or money, and who are naive enough to believe in some kind of objective reality. In an interview with a Pulitzer Prize-winning journalist in 2004, this man was admirably candid about what the Bush administration was up to. In response to the old-fashioned idea that the press should report what actually happened, what politicians actually decided and did, he said: 'That's not the way the world really works any more. We're an empire now, and when we act, we create our own reality. . . . We're history's actors, and you, all of you, will be left to just study what we do.'[26]

To put it another way: we in the government do whatever we like because we have the power, and we lie whenever it's to our advantage, impressing the appropriate falsehoods upon the public through the most effective means at our disposal. Just like the Soviets. This became the new American way long before the 'post-truth' politics of the Trump team and their 'alternative facts'.

Inhofe often used his power as a member of the Environment Committee to harass climate scientists, and notably after the incident of the emails stolen from the server of the Climatic Research Unit at the University of East Anglia ('Climategate'). The news media inflated the contents of the hacked messages into a huge scandal, and the global warming denial community proclaimed that they confirmed a conspiracy on the part of unscrupulous scientists. Inhofe immediately launched a vigorous campaign of intimidation of seventeen researchers whose emails had been hacked, claiming in a Minority Staff report that 'the scientists involved in the CRU controversy violated fundamental ethical principles governing taxpayer-funded research and, in some cases, may have violated federal laws'.[27] No attempt here to reserve judgment until the situation is properly understood.

Subsequently, no fewer than *seven* independent investigations, four in the US and three in the UK, by institutions from the National Science Foundation to the House of Commons, found no evidence of wrongdoing whatsoever on the part of the 'Inhofe Seventeen'. But of course this had no effect on the senator's persistent insinuations that Michael Mann and his colleagues were criminals: in reality as created by Inhofe, they remain guilty of violations.[28] This fantasy has unpleasant consequences: several of the Inhofe Seventeen, as well as climate scientists in other countries, have been subject to threats of violence and death.[29] The war on science does produce casualties.

Inhofe's Minority Report accuses climate scientists of harassment because they presume to question the credentials of the deniers' contrarian collaborators. Mann and his colleagues, it says, 'launched a campaign of petty invective against scientists who dared question their findings and methods … casting their opponents as industry shills masquerading as scientists, savaging their reputations'.[30] But they *were* industry shills – well paid – and for the most part *not* climate scientists, which is why they drew criticism from experts in the field. A prime example is Willie Soon, whose discredited study with Sallie Baliunas was loudly touted by Inhofe and the Bush administration.[31] [5.3]

God, climate and national security

Inhofe revealed the religious motivation behind his crusade against climate science in a book that appeared in 2012, *The Greatest Hoax: How the Global Warming Conspiracy Threatens Your Future*. In a radio interview he gave in order to promote the book, he said: 'My point is, God's still up there. The arrogance of people to think that we, human beings, would be able to change what He is doing in the climate is to me outrageous.'[32] The humility is admirable – we human beings do need to be put in our place sometimes – but since Inhofe espouses the same conservative evangelical position as Beisner, that humility is probably false.

The convenient anti-scientific conclusion still holds: if we human beings can't change what God is doing in the climate, we might as well continue burning fossil fuels because it can't possibly affect the rate of global heating.

Once *The Greatest Hoax* gains momentum, the author moves into a confessional mode.

> I take my religion seriously – I always say I'm a Jesus guy.... Many times during my global warming fight, I turned to ... one of my favorite Bible verses, Genesis 8:22:
>
>> As long as the earth remains
>> There will be springtime and harvest,
>> Cold and heat, winter and summer,
>> Day and night.
>
> And this is what a lot of alarmists forget: God is still up there, and He promised to maintain the seasons and that cold and heat would never cease as long as the earth remains.[33]

Beisner also refers to this verse, a favourite of Christian climate deniers everywhere. We shouldn't be alarmed by global warming because God promised to maintain a regular climate on earth, in perpetuity. Even if human activities are warming the atmosphere, it won't affect the regularity of the seasons – and so we can safely ignore the alarmists and continue the business of burning as usual.

Inhofe may well take his religion seriously, but his reading of this passage is overly optimistic. The sentence comes before God establishes His covenant with Noah, and is something He says 'in his heart'. He isn't promising Noah anything – but is simply talking to Himself, thinking that He won't go the way of total destruction again. The subsequent covenant is broad in extension, but its intention is narrower. The Lord is talking about refraining from destroying everything 'by the waters of a flood'. But the Old Testament God is perfectly capable of saying, in the face of repeated human wickedness: 'I said not by the waters of a flood: destruction by heatwave, drought, wildfire, or hurricane-force gales may yet be visited upon you.' A possibility that Inhofe and colleagues discount out of hand.

Inhofe once admitted in an interview to being 'guilty of two things', saying: 'I'm a Jesus guy, and I have a heart for Africa'.[34] He has made some twenty trips there, at taxpayers' expense, on a mission he calls 'a Jesus thing'. But if Inhofe really had a heart for Africa, he would consider how many places on that vast continent are being ravaged by the effects of global warming, and how much his years of working as the Environment Committee Chair to deny the human contribution have increased climate change misery. A study from 2019 confirms that Africa is one of the most vulnerable parts of the world when it comes to climate change, because both rainfall and droughts will become more extreme and thereby disrupt food production in lethal ways.[35]

If Inhofe were the only congressman driven by religious zeal to deny global heating and persecute climate scientists, it would be bad enough. But several of his colleagues likewise believe that 'God controls the climate'—rendering climate science irrelevant. It wouldn't be a problem if they simply checked their personal beliefs at the door, but they insist on conducting government business on the basis of their faith, which means they do considerable damage – to Congress's reputation as well as to their constituents – through the power they wield on science-related committees.

Some fellow travellers in recent years are Representative Joe Barton from Texas, former Chair of the Energy and Commerce Committee; Paul Broun from Georgia, at one time on the Subcommittee on Energy and Environment; John Shimkus from Illinois, a previous ranking member of the Subcommittee on Environment and Economy; Ralph Hall from Texas, once Chair of the Science Committee; Lamar Smith, again from Texas, and Hall's successor as Chair of the Science Committee. Like his colleagues, Rep. Hall said, 'I don't think we can control what God controls' (the climate), and was unusually candid about his view of climate scientists.

Because he believed – like former Texas governor and later Secretary of Energy Rick Perry – that climate scientists are getting paid to come up with results that confirm global warming, Hall said this: 'I don't believe 'em. I still want to listen to 'em and believe what I believe I ought to believe.' Nonetheless, since listening to the testimony of scientists is a major part of the Science Committee's job, while Chair Hall also believed that those pesky experts on the climate should be given a hearing.

> I think we ought to have an honest ear to science. They can come before my committee. I always put someone to come and testify when they're testifying against it to give them the other side. I think we oughta listen to 'em. *I just don't think we oughta mind 'em.*[36]

It's the 'fair and balanced' approach: if you're obliged to listen to some real scientists, better bring in some other kind as well and pay them handsomely to present the contrarian, climate sceptical side.

But it's only for show anyway, for while the Chair may have listened to the scientists who testify before his Committee, he wouldn't pay attention to a thing they say (mind 'em) because his mind was already made up, because he *believed*. That might have qualified him to be Chair of a House Committee on Christian Fundamentalism, but the Committee on Science and Technology needed leadership from someone who knows something about the natural sciences, was open to the evidence they provide, and capable of reasonable judgment.

Lacking space for the discussion of Hall's like-minded colleagues, I refer the interested reader to the Appendix [5.4]. Overall, two things are striking about these true believers: their utter lack of expertise in areas they have political power over, and a reckless arrogance that's harmful to others. You have to wonder how such incompetents keep getting re-elected year after year, given how obviously unqualified they are, and that their fundamentalist dogmatism inflicts harm on distant populations as well as their own constituents.

It's significant that many of these incompetents also believe that *national security* must be a priority, and should be supported by maximum military might. But are they so ignorant of the military establishment that they don't know its leaders take one of the greatest threats to national security to be – climate change? Inhofe certainly can't be that ignorant: he was the ranking Republican on the Senate Armed Services Committee (SASC) for years before becoming its Chair in 2018. Whereas politicians can usually get away with neglecting long-range planning, the military has a major stake in being prepared, and so is required to think ahead.

Every four years the Department of Defense issues a *Quadrennial Defense Review Report*, which in recent times has warned of the dangers of climate change. As a senior member of the SASC, Inhofe must have read the 'Global Trends' section of the 'Future Security Environments' chapter of the report from 2014, which is clearer than ever about the threat.

The pressures caused by climate change will influence resource competition ... around the world. These effects are *threat multipliers* that will aggravate stressors abroad such as poverty, environmental degradation, political instability, and social tensions – conditions that can enable terrorist activity and other forms of violence.[37]

So did the senator ever rebuke the Joint Chiefs of Staff for being global warming alarmists? After becoming Chair of the SASC, did Inhofe not do his duty and upbraid the US military for reckless expenditure of taxpayers' money on a mere hoax? (I can find no evidence that he did.) And if he refuses to understand what to the leaders of the armed services is crystal clear – that national security is closely connected to climate change – you have to question his qualifications for even being on that committee, let alone chairing it.

Climate change now changes so many games that its impact on national security is greater than ever: global heating is the Mother of all Threat Multipliers. And yet in 2014 the House of Representatives passed an amendment to the National Defense Authorization bill that prohibited the Department of Defense from using its funding 'to assess climate change and its implications for national security'. More enforced ignorance. The Republican sponsor explained his motivation by asking a question: 'With all the unrest around the world, why should Congress divert funds from the mission of our military and national security to support a political ideology?'[38] Uh? Well, because we're overheating the planet and the effects are increasingly threatening national security. Just ask the Joint Chiefs of Staff.

Inhofe ignores the *Quadrennial Defense Review Reports* and refuses on religious grounds to acknowledge that 'we need to take radical action', while keeping those grounds concealed and branding environmentalism as a 'religion'. After years of railing against 'climate alarmists' as a member of the Environment Committee, he quietly acquiesces in the Armed Services' acknowledgement of the climate crisis. Difficult to avoid seeing an element of hypocrisy here – and gratifying to note that Inhofe celebrated Global Climate Week in 2019 by instituting the Inhofe Climate Hypocrite Awards.[39]

A former member of Inhofe's staff for the Environment Committee once said of climate scientists who were warning of the dangers of global warming, 'They deserve to be publicly flogged.'[40] In several European countries Holocaust denial is a crime; global warming denial has the potential to jeopardize many more lives and livelihoods than six million.

I used to think the world should be grateful that Inhofe didn't have an even more influential position, such as secretary of state, in which case foreign policy would be conducted based on the basis of conservative faith rather than informed understanding. But then someone almost as dangerous was appointed secretary of state in 2018: Mike Pompeo. As the single largest recipient of Koch campaign funds in Congress, Pompeo is opposed to doing anything about the climate crisis. But on top of that he sees Islamic jihadism as an 'evil that's all around us', and politics as 'a never ending struggle' against it – 'until the Rapture'.[41] Wow.

I also used to think that the syndrome of using religious faith to deny reality and render government ineffectual was mainly a North American problem, but we saw in the Introduction how Brazil's Bolsonaro is threatening the world's climate by encouraging destruction (sorry, 'development') of the rainforest, while at the same time denying that deforestation is taking place. Baptized as an evangelical early in his campaign for the presidency, he claims to be 'fulfilling a mission from God'.[42] It's no surprise, then, to learn that 'much of Bolsonaro's political support comes from agribusiness, the arms industry, and the Religious Right, a nexus of power referred to as the Three "B"s – beef, bullets, and Bibles.'[43]

But let me end on a gentler note, addressed to Inhofe and his staff, Bolsonaro and global warming deniers everywhere (and borrowed from an 'ordinary layman of the Church of England'):

> Laying down your arms, surrendering, saying you are sorry, realising that you have been on the wrong track and getting ready to start life over again from the ground floor – that is the only way out of our 'hole'. This process of surrender – this movement full speed astern – is what Christians call repentance.[44]

The problem here is not mainstream Christianity, which knows the value of repentance, but the evangelical and fundamentalist perversions of it that have flourished in the US and are on the way to becoming All American. In the next chapter we'll see how, by contrast, mainstream Christianity is aligned with other major religions in having a constructive role to play in taking care of the climate crisis.

TRANSITION:

From The Third Obstruction
To Philosophy and China

Along with the fossil fuel industries and the Religious Right a third factor is obstructing progress on dealing with the climate crisis, though it works in different ways: the Titans of Silicon Valley (Amazon, Apple, Facebook, Google, YouTube, etc.). There isn't space here to do more than outline this additional Obstruction, but I hope that my ideas on the topic will appear before too long in a slim volume titled *Being Here: There's No App for That*. There are two sides to the Third Obstruction: the enormous carbon emissions generated by the Internet, and the art mastered by the Tech Titans of diverting people's attention away from what's happening around them. By colonizing their customers' attention for commercial gain, they're preventing meaningful engagement with the climate crisis – and many other things in life.

It's another libertarian thing, insofar as the Tech Titans have become rich and powerful through strict adherence to the tenet of avoiding taxes and regulation. And in the case of Silicon Valley billionaires, the drive to dominate is ramped up by Ayn Rand. Among the enthusiasts are Jeff Bezos (Amazon), Jack Dorsey (Twitter), Travis Kalanick (Uber), Evan Spiegel (Snapchat), Kevin Systrom (Instagram) and Peter Thiel (PayPal and Facebook). The late Steve Jobs (Apple) was also a Rand fan.[1]

We tend to be unaware of it because our attention to the hardware usually stops at the surface of the screen or gadget, but our use of information and communications technology (ICT) increases global heating because the production and maintenance of the gigantic infrastructure that underlies our consumption of Internet content depend largely on energy generated by fossil fuels.

Enormous amounts of electricity are required to power the four major components of the Internet, which has become 'the central nervous system of the modern global economy': the end-user devices (from smartphones to television screens), the communication networks, the data centres, and the manufacturing required to produce all of those. In 2012, the ICT sector consumed more electricity than any country in the world except the US and China. As more people gain Internet access and the world economy becomes more digitalized, the industry is projected to consume 20 per cent of the world's electricity and contribute more than 5 per cent of carbon emissions by 2025.[2]

The total amount of energy consumed and carbon emitted by the Internet is growing so rapidly that one expert at the beginning of 2016 predicted a three-fold increase over the following decade – clearly more than the planet can bear, unless some miraculous technological innovation takes place in the meantime. A comprehensive study by the Shift Project ('The Carbon Transition Think Tank') suggests that the time has come for some 'digital sobriety' and a shift to 'lean ICT'.[3]

The term 'cloud storage' suggests to many users that the cute cat videos they upload to the Internet then hover around benignly somewhere over the digital rainbow. The reality is that they're stored on huge servers on the ground, which generate so much heat that the fans required to keep them cool also consume vast amounts of energy. Are binge-watchers of Netflix aware of their carbon footprint? Or viewers of videos on YouTube? Lots of people thought the music video for the song 'Despacito' was hot, as evidenced by the record 5 billion views it received in 2018. The not so cool part is that 'it burned as much energy as 40,000 U.S. homes use in a year' – and those American homes use more than most.[4]

As for other 'content', it appears that the majority of YouTube videos about climate change in 2019 *opposed* the scientific consensus that global warming is human-caused.[5] That's a distinctly unhelpful situation when we're facing a serious crisis, but contributing to the public good doesn't figure in Tech Titan business models. Google (which owns YouTube) has made generous donations to climate denial organizations like the Competitive Enterprise Institute and other conservative think tanks discussed in previous chapters. The company claims to support political action on the climate crisis, but its actions belie its words: it promotes opposition to the scientific consensus on climate change, and funds climate denial, in order to keep the favour of conservative legislators who will protect the laws that protect companies like Google from libel suits and other nuisances.[6]

But more important than the message, as Marshall McLuhan pointed out long ago, is the medium.[7] ICT has the effect of capturing so much of our attention that we no longer have time to reflect on what and how we're doing. As the media theorist Sherry Turkle observes: 'We have created a communications culture that has decreased the time available for us to sit and think uninterrupted.' She points out how this heavy investment in ICT devices inclines us toward regarding people (ourselves included) as objects rather than persons – leading to a decrease in human *empathy*, especially among younger people.[8]

Many studies have pointed to this decrease in empathy in users of ICT, and without time to think – and to feel empathy for less fortunate people in Bangladesh or sub-Saharan Africa whose livelihoods are being jeopardized by our high-consumption lifestyles, let alone for the plight of future generations – we're hardly going to be motivated to do anything about the climate crisis.

The tech distractions are effective because they're part of a much larger phenomenon, a full-spectrum performance by a huge cast of players in late capitalism and high consumerism, which the French philosopher Guy Debord aptly called 'the Spectacle'.[9] It's an all-encompassing play in which almost all of us are already acting a role – whether we know it, or like it, or not. The value we assign to the distractions provided by the Tech Titans depend in part on who we think we are, which in turn depends on who *they* think we are – on the basis of the vast amounts of data they've collected regarding our desires, and likes, and needs. ICT is nicely aligned with the libertarian war of ideas, insofar as electronic media bring with them a message about what it means to be a human being. It's basically a complement to the neoliberal conception of people as competitive beings focused on their own profit: we are free individuals freely spending our time and money for the fulfilment of our desires.

Of course the Internet and social media could also be enormously helpful in galvanizing people into action on the climate crisis, but many of us are first going to have to reclaim our time and attention from the vampires of Silicon Valley.

Time now for a transition to the second half of the book and more philosophy. With a better understanding of the situation – with the climate, and the billionaires' war of ideas, and the Three Obstructions – we can entertain some *better* ideas to counter the libertarian credo. What's pushing us to the brink of self-destruction isn't just greed and lust for power: the opponents of action on the climate have been making effective use of a broader ideology. However, under closer examination their story about who we are, as one species among many on a finite planet, turns out to be petty and flawed.

We saw how the American Religion promotes a narrow view of who we are, especially in relation to the world of nature: virtuous souls who do 'the work of the Lord' by exploiting natural resources for our own advantage. Philosophically, or theologically, we are immortal souls whose salvation lies entirely in a direct relation with the Creator – rendering the body and the natural world irrelevant, and our relations with family and society inconsequential for the drama of salvation. Fortunately this is a rare variant of Christianity, one that isn't found much in other countries.

Many religions and interpretations of religion have a more 'this-worldly' and communitarian orientation that values nature and the body, regarding them as part of divine creation or else as noble and creative in themselves. The world's religions can generally be forces for the good in our response to the climate crisis. The message of Pope Francis's 2015 encyclical letter 'on care for our common home', with its emphasis on 'the interconnectedness among all things', is exemplary. His reading of Holy Scripture is in remarkable harmony with nontheistic ideas from Daoism and Chinese Buddhism, and together they afford a nobler and more comprehensive vision of who we are as human beings than we find in individualism.

There's no denying that our geopolitics have failed, massively, to rise to the challenge of global heating. The first United Nations Climate Change Conference took place in Berlin in 1995. After the third conference, in Kyoto in 1997, most industrialized countries signed on to the Kyoto Protocol, which legally bound them to reduce their GHG emissions over specified periods of time. Although Bill Clinton signed the Protocol, the US Congress declined to ratify it, and George W. Bush rejected it altogether in 2001, which effectively rendered it moribund. A black mark to the US for that one. After the twenty-first UN conference in 2015, nearly 200 countries signed on to the Paris Agreement. And then in 2017 Trump announced that the US was pulling out of that one too: America First.

In any case the 'success' of the Paris Agreement is merely symbolic: because it doesn't legally bind, the countries that signed are in most cases ignoring the commitments they made and continuing with business as usual. There's no indication that the world's democracies are serious about coping with the climate crisis in spite of all the hand-wringing rhetoric spouted by their leaders. People say the climate crisis is so huge, such a 'wicked' problem, that we have to *reframe* our thinking in order to tackle it. They're right: we need to think about how to reform our political and economic systems, and how to revision ourselves and our place in the larger context of the geosphere, in order to manage the global scope of the crisis.

We can fix some immediate problems, such as removing the Three Obstructions, within the framework of the democratic systems we currently have. Assuming that public opinion, energized by the younger generation, turns against the libertarians, and that our democracies can prove robust enough to get the money out of politics and take the power back from the oligarchs – even so, we can't possibly slow global heating adequately without full and enthusiastic cooperation from the Chinese. Of course we also have to engage India, and Brazil, and other large countries; but since China is the greatest contributor to carbon emissions (gross contributions, not historical, nor per capita), cooperation with the Chinese is the most urgent priority.

Given the need to think about the climate crisis differently, why not think in terms of a worldview far removed from our current one – namely, ancient Chinese philosophy? And since traditional Chinese ideas are a core component of the philosophy advocated by the Chinese government, an acquaintance with them is likely to facilitate dialogue with China on how to slow global heating. An engagement with Chinese philosophy not only offers a liberating alternative to modern Western worldviews, but also highlights equally helpful ideas from earlier in our own tradition that have for the most part been marginalized. Drawn from two different traditions, these older and overlooked ideas can provide a ground for fruitful intercultural dialogue as well as a more fulfilling and life-affirming understanding of who we are as human beings.

Part Three

Finer Philosophies
& Fairer Politics

The true philosophers teach through their deeds, by working on the very changeable views of human beings.

Whoever cannot obey himself will be commanded. That is the way of the living.

FRIEDRICH NIETZSCHE[1]

Libertarian Limitations, Religion's Contributions

Having seen how successful the libertarians have been in their war of ideas, and how effectively the obstructions set up by the Fossil Fuelers, the Religious Right, and the Tech Titans have prevented progress on tackling the climate crisis, it's time to look more closely at the philosophy underlying all this regressive activity.

Libertarian ideology is often infused by religious fervour: witness the 'free-market fundamentalist' faith in the invisible hand that Adam Smith wrote about, which is sometimes worshipped almost as the right hand of God himself. And yet, as E. F. Schumacher pointed out in *Small Is Beautiful*: 'to the extent that economic thinking is based on the market' – which works by reducing all values to prices – '*it takes the sacredness out of life*'. But perhaps the faithful don't mind that, because the apotheosis of the individual is what's most important. Schumacher again: 'The market is the *institutionalisation of individualism* and non-responsibility. Neither buyer nor seller is responsible for anything but himself.'[1] Whether we're regarded as consumers, worshippers or internetworked minds, we are above all, and fundamentally, *individuals*.

Happily the hyper-individualism of the American Religion turns out to be an aberration when considered in the context of mainstream Christianity and other religions, which are for the most part oriented toward *community*. Insofar as they have better ideas and tell more realistic stories about who we are as a species, they can make significant contributions toward dealing with the climate crisis.

The incoherence of individualism

The idea of taking the individual to be central is relatively recent, even in the Western tradition. It isn't to be found in Plato, nor in his student

Aristotle, who famously maintained – on the basis of a good understanding of social animals such as bees and ants – that human beings are basically social and also *political* animals. But then individualism does underlie most ethics, political theory and social science since the European Enlightenment of the eighteenth century, and informs modern democratic as well as libertarian ideology.

This view of human beings regards us as fundamentally free, independent and autonomous selves; and in the realm of politics and economics, these selves are understood to be equal, and rational in pursuing their self-interest. If you grew up in a Western society this surely seems reasonable, and perhaps evidently right. To the extent that we're members of a polity of some kind, we have chosen that condition freely. (I'll use the usefully neutral term 'polity' to refer to a 'political entity' in general, whether the ancient Athenian *polis*, or 'city-state', the Chinese empire or the federal republic of the United States.)

Societies come into being, on this Western view, through individuals' freely choosing to associate with others under some kind of 'social contract'. The political philosophies of Thomas Hobbes and John Locke systematized these ideas, and explained the rationale behind a move from an imagined 'state of nature' to an artificial, political state: people are willing to give up some of their freedoms for the benefits of a situation where the state protects their persons and property against injury and theft.[2]

Locke, whose ideas greatly influenced Thomas Jefferson and other Founding Fathers, made the notion of *rights* to life, liberty and property central to his political philosophy. And since rights pertain primarily to people as individuals, they too are based on individualism. We need to distinguish between so-called 'first generation' civil and political rights, such as those promulgated in the US Bill of Rights (1789), and 'second generation' social, economic and cultural rights, as enshrined in the Universal Declaration of Human Rights adopted by the United Nations in 1948.[3]

The former concern the rights of citizens to be free from undue interference by the government – including freedom of religion, speech, the press, peaceful assembly and security 'in their persons, houses, papers, and effects, against unreasonable searches and seizures' by the state (Fourth Amendment). I'm at liberty to do what I want, as long as it doesn't encroach on other people's freedom to exercise *their* rights. Libertarians love this idea, but dislike second generation rights, which are more positive and include the right to employment, shelter, food and food security, health care and education.

As the late Henry Rosemont, Jr., a distinguished scholar of Confucian philosophy, has shown, these two sets of rights are *incompatible* as long as they're 'grounded in foundational individualism'. This is because securing the rights of everyone in society to employment, shelter, etc. is going to impose costs (such as paying taxes) on those who already enjoy such things.

> To whatever extent we may be morally and thus politically responsible for assisting others in the creation and obtaining of those goods which accrue to them by virtue of having social and economic rights, to just that extent we *cannot* be altogether autonomous individuals, enjoying full civil and political rights, free to rationally decide upon and pursue our own projects rather than having to assist the less fortunate with theirs.[4]

This is, as we saw, the complaint of the right-wing libertarians: it curtails our freedom when the government forces us to pay taxes without giving us a say in how those revenues are spent. They might use the money to provide education for poor people, and minorities, and – worst of all – *immigrants*. The economic libertarian movement spearheaded by James Buchanan began in the southern states of the US, where a major motivation was to oppose desegregation of the public schools, which were increasing their spending on black students.[5]

Rosemont goes on to show how the prioritizing of first-generation rights in a democracy leads not only to the undermining of social, economic and cultural rights, but also to its own perpetuation.

> When individual freedom is weighted more heavily than social justice – defined broadly as a fair allocation of resources for everyone – the political, legal, and moral instruments employed by the rich and powerful in defending and enhancing that freedom virtually ensure that social justice will not be achieved, and hence poverty not alleviated. Such being the case, an unequal and unfair status quo will be able to perpetuate itself indefinitely.[6]

And this is just what has been happening: having bought the Republican Party in the US, the rich libertarians have ensured that laws are made, and courts are stacked, in such a way that will make them even richer and more powerful. And since the capitalist ethos becomes more libertarian as it takes over more of the world, the gap between rich and poor yawns wider not only in the US but also in China and other capitalist-friendly countries as well.

Libertarians insist on first-generation rights while rejecting second-generation ones. They imagine the individual self not only as autonomous and independent, but also as free from bonds to custom and culture, tradition and history, and even from relations to other people, from casual acquaintances to the closest kin. But when abstracted from its relationships, the self seems too empty to give us an adequate sense of who we are. And if you actually take the individual out of society by putting it in solitary confinement, the ill effects confirm Aristotle's idea that we are basically social animals. Deprived of interaction with our fellow human beings, all but the strongest among us fall prey to a variety of mental disorders. The effects are so damaging that United Nations special rapporteurs on torture have recommended that solitary confinement be outlawed as 'cruel and unusual punishment'.[7]

In a chapter on libertarianism aptly titled 'The Apotheosis of the Individual Self', Rosemont shows how the ideology takes 'the concept of the free, rational individual self to its logical limit'. He presents the libertarian arguments – and especially for 'the inherent freedom of individuals to freely pursue their own projects so long as they respect the similar freedom of all other individuals to do the same' – and shows how difficult they are to refute as long as you subscribe to individualism (which most liberal and conservative critics also do).[8]

Individualism has tended to dominate the American mind, and especially when it comes to political philosophy, but in course of the twentieth century it elicited a counter-movement toward 'communitarianism', as exemplified by the pragmatist thinker John Dewey who advocated democracy as 'communicative community'. The striking parallels between Dewey's pragmatism and Confucian thought have led some scholars to recommend, sensibly, that we draw on American pragmatism for terms and ideas to facilitate conversations with the Chinese on political matters.[9]

More recently the liberalism of John Rawls and libertarianism of Robert Nozick elicited a backlash from more communitarian thinkers. In an essay from 1979, Charles Taylor argued against what he calls 'political atomism', a view that sees society 'as constituted by individuals for the fulfilment of ends which are primarily individual'. Such individuals are imagined to be 'self-sufficient', by contrast with Aristotle's view of the human being as 'not self-sufficient outside a *polis*'. Thinkers like Alasdair MacIntyre, Michael Walzer and Michael Sandel (nowadays a superstar in China) have similarly advocated communitarian over liberal ideas.[10]

Nor do you have to be a professional philosopher to see the irrelevance of individualism in today's world. Brian Eno laid it out nicely in a recent Preface:

> We should be thinking of ourselves as a global community with attendant responsibilities, not as a collection of individuals engaged in a Darwinian struggle at any cost to the planet. What does 'individual' mean anyway, when almost everything we do – like taking a train or buying the groceries – involves us in the accumulated brainpower of thousands of other people who've set these systems up and maintain them?[11]

By insisting on rights we try to evade our responsibilities, while ignoring our radical interdependence. If we only compete, and never cooperate, our humanity suffers.

The rich libertarians in their splendid independence have to ignore that they (or their parents) made their money on the basis of an infrastructure (city amenities, transportation, central banks, etc.) that was paid for by millions of people paying their taxes. And they continue to make money, and avoid taxes in most cases, on the basis of infrastructure that's maintained through other people paying their fair share. Libertarianism is basically a philosophy of *selfishness* – and tailor-made for the very rich and fortunate.

But overall, they tell us, the economic payoff from not burdening the super-talented rich with taxes is grand: a rising tide lifts all boats, and a bigger pie of GDP means a bigger slice for everyone. But as Piketty demonstrated in *Capital in the Twenty-First Century*, that claim is all trumped up. More and more studies show how economic inequality – which is growing globally with every passing year – is *not* a good thing for any society, insofar as it increases violence, alienation, and other undesirable conditions in addition to poverty.[12]

The incoherence of understanding ourselves as independent selves becomes evident when we consider the nature of our experience. Insofar as we find ourselves 'projected' onto the world, we can say that everyday, unmediated sensory experience always puts us *outside* our bodies and into the places around them. I see the table over there against the wall, the tree against the clouds, the distant peak against the blue of the sky. These things are out there and *public* in the sense of being accessible to all experiencers in the relevant place. Hearing, as much as sight, takes place outside ourselves and in the distance. I hear the music coming from the pub across the street, the roar of the waves breaking on the shore below, the car approaching from behind. And you would, too, if you were there. It doesn't make any sense to insist that it's only *my* experience and not shared with others.

There is of course a sense in which my experience is 'mine', but it's an illusion to think that my mind is really my 'own'. The mind is always projecting a world, on the basis of prior experience of external entities. And it's constantly filled with impressions of other people and things, images and voices and sounds, ideas and concepts and above all *language* – and who knows what else that is 'not-me'. And as for the 'I' in the middle of all these mental processes, which is supposed to be in control of the whole show, many great thinkers from Plato to Nietzsche held it to be complex, multiple, a synthesis of elements from 'outside'.[13]

Interdependence with the world is even more evident when you consider our *embodiment*, and what it takes for us to stay alive – and we're all of us embodied all the time, even when asleep and unconscious. To be active at all, the body has to engage in numerous *inter*actions: a constant exchange of the air in the lungs with the atmosphere; a regular intake of water and discharge of fluids, as well as evaporation of moisture through the skin; the ingestion of food that incorporates energy from the sun by way of nutrients drawn from the earth. Physical activity would be impossible if our bodies weren't adapted to the mass of the planet and its gravitational pull: except when totally relaxed on our backs, we're engaged in a constant musculoskeletal negotiation with the force of gravity. Nothing is independent here: it's all interconnecting.

Nor can I declare independence by pointing to my chest and insisting *this* is me. When I do that, I'm pointing mostly to water: around two-thirds of the human body by weight is H_2O. Next in terms of weight are the organelles, components of our bodies' cells known as *mitochondria*.[14] Mitochondria reside within all cells in the human body and generate the energy necessary for their functioning and the body's life. There are some 10 million billion of them in the body of the average adult (!), making up almost half its 'dry weight' (what remains after all the water is extracted). But the really remarkable thing about them is that their DNA is *different* from the DNA of the body's own cells – and quite similar to the DNA of the mitochondria that power the cells of all multicellular organisms, whether animals or plants. So if I try to assert my physical identity by invoking my 'own' cells, that fails too because almost half *their* bulk is not me, and they can't even live without the energy supplied by those 'resident alien' mitochondria.

What with all those mitochondria and water molecules, we're up to around 84 per cent of the body that's *not* us, and we can't even claim the remaining 16 per cent because of the human *microbiome*. Just as the mitochondria energize our cells, we wouldn't be able to live without all the bacteria in our intestines and elsewhere. Research by the Human Microbiome Project suggests that the human body is home to *trillions* of microorganisms, 'outnumbering human cells by 10 to 1'. Since they're so small, these microorganisms comprise only around 2 per cent of the body's mass, but that still brings our 'own' stake in the body, the part that's really *mine*, down to below 15 per cent – hardly a definitive proportion.[15]

When Walt Whitman wrote 'I contain multitudes', he didn't know by how much he was right. If, as good libertarians, we were to declare independence from these multitudes of resident aliens, and to follow through by having them taken out of our bodies, we'd be dead on removal. We depend on them for our survival: life is always *inter*life, symbiosis. Recent discoveries in microbiology show that the notion of the 'biological individual', which is central in the 'studies of genetics, immunology, evolution, development, anatomy, and physiology', is ultimately incoherent. A landmark study by two top biologists and an eminent philosopher of science bears the title, 'A Symbiotic View of Life: We Have Never Been Individuals' (the subtitle an echo of a title by Bruno Latour).[16]

If the fantasy of independence makes no sense in the case of the human body, where all those microorganisms and organelles live in harmony with our own cells, it's no surprise that it should fail when extended to the macrocosm of the society and then humanity as a whole. If the human body thrives on diversity, interaction and cooperation, why not the body politic as well? Yet the prevailing political philosophies see us as individuals competitively pursuing our own self-interest, which is, as Schumacher pointed out, a woefully superficial view: 'The market represents only the surface of society.'[17] Moving up to the level where nation states have to interact, if they behave like autonomous individuals, it's no surprise that the 'the international community' is impotent when confronted by the climate crisis.

But before we look at the positive contributions religions can make in this area, let's recall how much harm the US Religious Right inflicts when it gains political power and interferes with science – and counter it by considering the optimal power relations between religion and philosophy, which imply the separation of church from state.

The role of religions

As philosophers from Plato to Nietzsche have acknowledged, religion is an integral factor in many, if not most, human lives – but one that in its organized form can cause troubles. Aside from the horror of religious wars, where even within the same faith people kill each other for belonging to the wrong sect, there's a tendency for religion to meddle in politics and natural science – fields in which its categories are inapplicable and its interferences harmful. It's interesting that John Tyndall, whom we met in Chapter 1 as the discoverer of the mechanisms behind the natural greenhouse effect, was also an early champion of the autonomy of the natural sciences with respect to religion and theology.

In his presidential address to the British Association for the Advancement of Science in Belfast in 1874, Tyndall argued that religion should no longer be permitted to trespass on the domain of science. But unlike the fundamentalist atheists of today, who gleefully attack all forms of religiosity, Tyndall warns against deriding the religious sentiment, on the grounds that it enjoys 'an immovable basis in the nature of man'. The most pressing problem of the present, he says, is how 'to yield this sentiment reasonable satisfaction'. He presents his prescient solution in a sentence of remarkable length and eloquence.

> Grotesque in relation to scientific culture as many of the religions of the world have been and are – dangerous, nay destructive, to the dearest privileges of freemen as some of them undoubtedly have been, and would, if they could, be again – it will be wise to recognize them as the forms of a force, mischievous, if permitted to intrude on the region of *knowledge*, over which it holds no command, but capable of being guided to noble issues in the region of *emotion*, which is its proper and elevated sphere.[18]

There is a proper place for the formidable force of religious feeling, a region of noble issues; but when religion infringes on natural science it leads to mischief and mayhem – not only burnings of books regarded as heretical, but also burnings of their authors at the stake. Tyndall several times praises the ideas of the great Giordano Bruno (a figure otherwise unheard of in modern scientific associations), who fell victim to the wrath of the Roman Inquisition.

Tyndall's campaign for the autonomy of science was in part a reaction to the rejection of Darwin's theory of evolution by believers in the literal truth of the creation stories in the Book of Genesis. Such campaigns have had only a limited effect in the US, where belief in 'scientific creationism' or 'creation science' is widespread. A Gallup survey from 2012 suggests that for the previous thirty years the percentage of Americans who subscribe to a creationist view of human origins had remained constant at around 45 per cent. (The figure among declared Republican voters in 2012 was 58 per cent.) The percentage who believe that 'God created human beings pretty much in their present form at one time in the last 10,000 years or so' had sunk to 40 per cent by 2019 – but that's still a good proportion of people whose view of who we are contradicts the consensus on evolution from the natural sciences.[19] So why should they believe the scientists when they warn of a climate crisis?

Not long after Tyndall delivered his speech in Belfast, a more trenchant critic of Christianity, Friedrich Nietzsche, similarly stressed the need to keep religion from encroaching on science. Like Tyndall, Nietzsche acknowledges religion's prevalence in human societies and the benefits of many of its functions, and agrees that it has to be kept in check.

> It always costs dearly and terribly when religions reign *not* as means of cultivation and education in the hands of the philosopher, but reign for themselves and as *sovereign*, when they want to be ultimate ends and not mere means among other means.[20]

There's nothing wrong with religions as long as they don't become tyrannical – something you can prevent by letting them be guided by philosophy. Being a different enterprise from religion, philosophy can survey the world's religions disinterestedly with a view to highlighting those features of them that benefit humankind rather than just the faithful. In particular, philosophy can help direct religious forces toward protecting the earth rather than destroying it

Christian and Muslim theologians have shown how many of the pertinent passages in the scriptures can be interpreted less anthropocentrically than adherents of the American Religion take them, emphasizing the responsibility of believers to take the best possible care of God's Creation. If you pay attention to those passages that praise the goodness and beauty of the earth as created by God – of which there are many in the Qur'an as well as the Bible – and consider that He consistently found it all beautiful and good, you have every reason to treat it with reverence and respect.[21]

The idea that the Creator finds the entirety of Creation 'very good' constitutes a powerful justification of the inherent worth of natural phenomena, as opposed to their merely extrinsic usefulness to humans, which we take as licence to exploit them for our own ends. So if we 'consider the lilies of the field, how they grow', we discover that God has arrayed them in such a way that they surpass 'even Solomon in all his glory'. It would thus be prudent to ensure that we're not gratuitously destroying them.[22]

Nor do you have to be a believer to experience awe in the face of the majesty of the natural world. You may understand nature (as the Chinese traditionally do) as continuously *self-creating* rather than created by an external deity, and spontaneously unfolding in an equally awe-inspiring way. Or as Nietzsche does, when he celebrates the divine play of the natural world along with nature's 'extravagant and indifferent magnificence, which appals but is also *noble*'.[23] Whereas the monotheisms revere nature as God's creation, religions like Buddhism and Daoism see it as a dynamic network of interactions that is intrinsically beautiful and good, even though it includes what is customarily regarded as bad and ugly. Just as with Nietzsche's 'Dionysian pantheism'.[24]

Believers in any form of pantheism, which understands the whole world as divine, will be inclined to revere and protect natural beings. Whereas a monotheist might regard a rock as sacred because created by God, a religion like Shinto in Japan considers any awe-inspiring natural phenomenon sacred because it's infused with a certain spirit (*kami*), or form of energy. So even though adherents of monotheism and non-theistic religions hold quite disparate beliefs, the resulting attitudes and behaviour may not be so different. There's a profound and passionate inquiry into the ground of such issues, from Shinto and Buddhist as well as Christian philosophical perspectives, in James Heisig's book, *Of Gods and Minds: In Search of a Theological Commons*.[25]

There's an important point here for interreligious or intercultural dialogue on climate: as long as we're agreed on how to move toward the kind of world we want to live in, the supporting belief systems don't matter so much. I came to understand this in the course of a dinner conversation some years ago with a colleague in Japan. Part way through a discussion of environmental issues, I realized that this distinguished Japanese scholar believed in the one God of Christianity. I wondered how the discussion would turn out, since my own approach was from a Daoist and Buddhist standpoint. (Odd that a Scotsman should be arguing the East Asian perspective with a Christian from Japan.)

So yes, my colleague's worldview – involving an omnipotent Creator, the Kingdom of Heaven, the immortal soul and so forth – was quite different from mine. But at the same time our ideas of what needed to be done about the natural world and climate change – by the individual, the government and the global community – were remarkably congruent. People concerned about the destruction of the biosphere often think (as I did too), that the problem is wrong ideas or beliefs: if others could only get behind *mine*, they would shape up just fine. But what do differences in belief matter as long as we can agree on what needs to be done?

At any rate, by contrast with the fundamentalists who insist on a literal (and highly selective) reading of Holy Scripture, most students of religion agree that most religious texts permit – and some even encourage – *multiple* interpretations, some of which will be more pertinent at one time, and others at other times. Ecologically-minded interpreters recommend broader readings of the Bible. Councils of various Churches and other official groups hold conferences and publish pamphlets on environmental issues. There is a movement and academic field known as Ecotheology, and a growing literature on the contributions of the world's major religions to the resolution of environmental problems, which often helpfully engages philosophical ideas concerning human relations to the Divine and to nature.[26]

Prominent religious leaders of the major traditions speak out ever more frequently in favour of action on slowing global warming. Archbishop Desmond Tutu and the Dalai Lama, and after them Pope Francis, have been some of the more outspoken. Although the Qur'an contains more passages than the Bible that praise the beauty of Creation and emphasize the sacred duty to protect it, and there's a great deal of scholarly discussion of Islam and the environment, Muslim leaders have been relatively less inclined to speak out on climate change. This is a pity, and so we do well to encourage more interfaith dialogue on these topics.

Compassionate Christianity

By contrast with the individualist ideology of the American Religion, most forms of Christianity value community and love of one's neighbour. (Buddhism is similar with its focus on the community of practitioners, the *sangha*.) It's remarkable how estranged today's right-wing evangelicals are from the roots of religion in America, in the ideas and example of the Puritans of New England, who display a consummate appreciation of the joys and duties of community. Instead of just thumping the Bible, the Puritans read it with care and strove to live in accord with its precepts.

A great exemplar here, who followed John Wycliffe in advocating a humane Christian society based on love and compassion, is John Winthrop. In his lay sermon 'A Model of Christian Charity' (which famously invokes 'a city on a hill'), Winthrop notes that God 'in His most holy and wise providence' made human beings 'ranked into two sorts': some rich and powerful and others poor and weak. He did this not so that 'the rich and mighty' might 'eat up the poor', but rather to give the former an opportunity to exercise 'love, mercy, and gentleness', and because he preferred to 'dispense his gifts by man to man' rather than by 'his own immediate hands'. He ordered these differences 'for the preservation and good of the whole' and 'the common good of the creature, man'. This in turn promotes a condition of healthy interdependence: 'that every man might have need of others, and from hence they might be all knit more nearly together in the bonds of brotherly affection.'[27]

In a wonderful essay on the question 'Which Way to the City on a Hill?', Marilynne Robinson debunks many false assumptions about the philosophy of the Puritans. She expresses Winthrop's main idea succinctly: '*inequality is the divinely created occasion for liberality*' – liberality in its earlier sense of 'a scripturally blessed and commanded open-handedness, a generosity based in faith and love.'[28] His idea of who we are – open to and caring for others in acknowledgment of our interdependence – is the absolute opposite of the mean individualism of the libertarians and Rand fans. And Winthrop's view is just what we need in the time of climate crisis: 'a community of perils', he says, 'calls for extraordinary liberality'. It's an opportunity to put our interdependence into practice: 'we must be knit together, in this work, as one man. . . . We must be willing to abridge ourselves of our superfluities, for the supply of others' necessities.' Beautifully put – and difficult to dispute.

This acknowledgment of our interdependence can be extended to things of nature, and the last fifty years have seen excellent studies by Christian thinkers in this area. Two pioneers are John B. Cobb, Jr. on the Protestant side, and Thomas Berry, CP on the Catholic – outstanding figures in part because of the breadth of their theological and philosophical knowledge, which includes Asian religions and thought. But let me focus on an emblematic contribution to the field by Pope Francis, which also has close affinities with Asian thinking.[29]

The pope has spoken eloquently of 'a special gift that allows us to grasp, through Creation, the greatness and love of God and His profound relationship with every creature'. Our appreciation of the goodness and beauty of the natural world means that 'we care for it and we use it for the benefit of all, always with great respect and gratitude.'[30] Since Creation is not anyone's property, 'let alone the property of a very few', it is simply wrong to exploit it. (As with the good Christian 'stewardship' discussed earlier.) We are not 'Masters of Creation' but rather 'Custodians', under obligation to respect and protect God's gift to the human race. As would-be dominators, we fail:

When we exploit Creation we destroy the sign of God's love for us, in destroying Creation we are saying to God: 'I don't like it! This is not good!'
– 'So what do you like?'
'I like myself!'
– Here, this is sin! Do you see?

This is *sin*! Narcissism rules. Do we see? No, it doesn't seem as if high-level consumers in the developed nations see this at all – or realize that such blindness may be fatal.

'Safeguard Creation,' Francis warns, 'because if we destroy Creation, Creation will destroy us! Never forget this!' Yes, a very good thing to keep in mind. The Righteous on the right have no compunction about destroying large parts of Creation if it will make them a profit, comfortable in their conviction that God will never send another Flood. But Francis surely has the more realistic understanding of God's Word.

That 'everything is interconnected' is a primary theme in Pope Francis's remarkable encyclical letter from 2015, 'Laudato Si', in which he shows himself to be a worthy bearer of the name of the Saint of Assisi. The letter is an impassioned and compassionate call for us to stop destroying the earth and exploiting the poor before it's too late, eloquently formulated and based on a firm understanding of the environmental and climate sciences.

The encyclical takes its name from, and begins by quoting, a canticle by St Francis that expresses gratitude for the gift of a familial relationship with the earth: 'Praise be to you, my Lord, through our Sister, Mother Earth, who sustains and governs us, and who produces various fruits with coloured flowers and herbs.' This emphasis on familial relationship, taking all creatures as kin, is unusual in the Western tradition, although it has always been central in Chinese philosophy. For St Francis, as the pope remind us, 'each and every creature was a sister united to him by bonds of affection: that is why he felt called to care for all that exists'.

But the fascinating thing about this document is the consonance of its underlying philosophy with ancient Chinese thought. Several times Pope Francis writes: 'It cannot be emphasised enough how *everything is interconnected.*' This is a central tenet of Buddhist, Confucian and Daoist philosophy in China.[31]

When the Neo-Confucian philosophers thought about the connection of the human body with the body of the world, they employed similar terms. Some two centuries before Francis of Assisi a Neo-Confucian thinker by the name of Zhang Zai, who was deeply influenced by Buddhism as well as Daoism, laid out the ground for compassion with all beings as follows:

> Heaven is my father and Earth is my mother, and even such a small creature as I am finds an intimate place in their midst.
>
> Therefore that which fills the universe I regard as my body and that which directs the universe I consider as my nature.
>
> All people are my brothers and sisters, and all things are my companions.[32]

The Chinese word for 'Heaven' has no connotations of a transcendent or other-worldly realm, but simply refers to what we experience when we're outside and look up (sky, sun, cloud, rain, lightning, etc.): more like our term 'the heavens'. It's often used as a shorthand for (the powers of) Heaven and Earth, as in the next quote, or 'Nature'.

Zhang's ideas resonated with many Chinese thinkers, such as the later Neo-Confucian Wang Yangming, who flourished some three centuries after Saint Francis.

The great man regards Heaven and Earth and the myriad things as one body. He regards the world as one family and the country as one person. As to those who make a cleavage between objects and distinguish between the self and others, they are small men.

Wang observes that 'the mind of the small man' is no different from that of the great man, except that the small man out of ignorance 'makes his mind small'.

The way to expand the mind is through extending familial love to everyone and the 'myriad' or 'ten thousand things' (meaning all processes and events in the world). 'Everything from ruler, minister, husband, wife, and friends to mountains, rivers, spiritual beings, birds, animals, and plants should be truly loved in order to realise my humanity, which forms one body with them.'[33] It's quite remarkable that Wang Yangming, who is for some scholars the greatest of the Neo-Confucian thinkers, should recommend 'regarding the world as one family' in the same spirit as St Francis.

At the end of a brilliant reading of relevant chapters and verses, the Pope concludes an exposition of the 'Wisdom of the Biblical Accounts' as follows:

These ancient stories, full of symbolism, bear witness to a conviction which we today share, that everything is interconnected, and that genuine care for our own lives and our relationships with nature is inseparable from fraternity, justice and faithfulness to others.

This too is powerful: the interconnections among all things mean that we have to deal with the problems of climate change and world poverty together, since they're in fact two sides of one and the same problem: a lack of global justice.[34]

A year after publishing the encyclical, Francis celebrated the World Day of Prayer for the Care of Creation with a message titled 'Show Mercy to Our Common Home'. Along with the plea for mercy he repeated his warning that in harming the earth, God's creation, we are sinning. 'God gave us the earth "to till and to keep" (*Gen* 2:15) in a balanced and respectful way. To till too much, to keep too little, is to sin.'[35] Francis again puts the climate crisis in the context of interconnectedness: 'The world's poor, though least responsible for climate change, are the most vulnerable and already suffering its impact. . . . Human beings are deeply connected with all of creation. When we mistreat nature, we also mistreat human beings.'

He also repeats some of the gentler passages from the previous year's encyclical, balancing the warnings with some glad tidings. When we undergo an 'ecological conversion', we develop 'a loving awareness that we are not disconnected from the rest of creatures, but joined in a splendid universal communion. As believers, we are . . . conscious of the bonds with which the Father has linked us to all beings.' This understanding of the place of the human being in Creation according involves a sense of interconnectedness that makes it the absolute opposite of the individualism that underlies the American Religion and libertarian ideology.

No surprise, then, that the pope has been criticized, especially by pious politicians in the US, for meddling in politics. But his sense of justice naturally drives him toward politics, insofar as avoidable global warming has harmful effects on the poorer nations, who are not responsible for the climate crisis. The reaction of James Inhofe to Francis's intervention was typical. In a keynote speech at an 'International Conference on Climate Change' sponsored by the Heartland Institute shortly before 'Laudato Si'' was published, Inhofe told reporters, yet again, that climate change is 'a hoax' and that the Pope could do little 'to change his [Inhofe's] mind' about that.[36] It's true; we haven't yet seen Francis perform any miracles.

The sense of interconnectedness we saw in Francis's Christianity is also to be found in several different philosophies that are non-theistic. If, for example, you substitute for the Father who links humans to all beings the ancient Chinese notion of Heaven, you have the same basic idea – with similar implications for how to behave toward the sentient creatures with whom we share the planet. Buddhist, Confucian and Daoist philosophies also regard everything as interacting, without positing a God who manages it all. (We'll be looking at these Chinese philosophies in Chapters 8 and 9, along with corresponding ideas in Stoic and Epicurean philosophy.)

The most remarkable affinity – remarked by President Xi Jinping in a Marxist context – is between Chinese yin-yang philosophy and the dialectical materialism of Marx's friend and collaborator, Friedrich Engels. When applied to the natural world, his dialectical perspective (deriving from Heraclitus and Hegel) sees interactivity everywhere. In *Dialectics of Nature* Engels writes, 'Everything affects something else and vice versa', and regrets that scientists mostly overlook 'this movement and interaction on all sides'. Yet the evidence is clear: he cites examples of different cultures acting upon the natural world in a domineering way – through deforestation, for example – and then being surprised when nature responds with drought or flooding.[37]

By 1883 Engels had developed a relational philosophy (along the lines of Alexander von Humboldt's) that accounted for adverse push-back from disrupting natural ecosystems. He warns against the hubris that accompanies human domination of the natural world:

> Let us not flatter ourselves too much for our human victory over nature. For every such victory she avenges herself on us. Each one does in the first instance have the consequences that we counted on, but in the second and third instances it has quite different and unforeseen effects that all too often annul those first consequences.[38]

A remarkable anticipation of the drawbacks of pushing ecosystems too hard – and of what the climate sciences are telling us about global heating. Beware the revenge of Gaia!

From the standpoint of this common ground between Christian thought and ancient Chinese and other non-theistic philosophies, the libertarian ideology of individualism appears as the historical and cultural aberration that it is.

A note on population growth

When religions tell stories about who we are, these sometimes involve estimates of how many of us there should be, and these numbers can on occasion clash with environmental conditions.

It wasn't so long ago that discussions of such topics always cited *overpopulation* as a factor in environmental degradation. Back in the 1960s, scientists like Paul Ehrlich drew attention to the dangers of burgeoning population, and especially for the natural environment. He formulated the influential IPAT equation ($I = P{\times}A{\times}T$), which says that the environmental impact of human activity is a function of population, affluence, and technology. Since then it has been pointed out that when it comes to climate change the formula should really be 'I=CAT', substituting 'consumers' for 'population'. Affluent consumers contribute to global heating at vastly greater rates than the world's poor, whose contributions are negligible in comparison.[39] Yet as we help people escape poverty, they will consume more; and if this isn't matched by a reduction on the part of the rich, pressure on the environment will increase.

Nonetheless, in recent decades the importance of restraining population growth has disappeared from most discussions of environmental issues and climate change. The topic has been fading from view, as if becoming taboo. A few decades ago disapproval from religious leaders, and especially from some of Francis's predecessors, was a major factor; but nowadays an obsession with political correctness may be contributing to this unhelpful shift. In any case a major factor is the growing political power of the Religious Right.

Promoters of piety as fecundity often point to holy Scripture, as E. Calvin Beisner does from his 'Biblical Perspective'.

> We affirm that human multiplication and filling of the Earth are intrinsically good (Genesis 1:28) and that, in principle, children, lots of them, are a blessing from God to their faithful parents and the rest of the Earth (Psalm 127; 128).
>
> We deny that the Earth is overpopulated ... and that godly dominion over the Earth requires population control or 'family planning' to limit fertility.[40]

How many more Beisners Beisner chooses to impose on the world is up to him, but it's telling that he has no interest in wondering how many people there would have to be before the Earth is finally 'filled'.

This equating of piety with fecundity is what one commentator has called *fecundism*, defined as 'the attribution of religious value and significance to reproductivity'. Not all religions promote fecundism: Buddhism, for example, while acknowledging the advantages of procreation, sees no particular virtue in propagating oneself to the maximum.[41] In a world of 7.7 billion people, projected to rise to 9 or 10 billion over the next thirty years, you might well regard fecundism with suspicion. Some people are choosing to have fewer children – or none at all – so as not to overburden the Earth. Some people in the developing world, women especially, would prefer to have fewer children and so would benefit from family planning; but conservative evangelicals work to deprive them of access to contraception. Such a use of politics to impose one's religious views on others is a strange way to practise the virtue of charity.[42]

When someone like Beisner encourages 'human multiplication and filling of the Earth', he's ignoring the *context* of the Biblical injunctions.

When God encouraged Adam and Eve to 'Be fruitful, and multiply, and replenish the earth', the world's population numbered only two, and so some replenishing was quite in order. And when He said to Noah and his sons, 'Be fruitful, and multiply, and replenish the earth', there were only three couples on the earth capable of procreating. And when He said to Jacob 'Be fruitful, and multiply', this was because the tribe of Israel was still small, and 'a nation and a company of nations' were yet to come from him.[43] But since the world is now home to almost 8 billion people and is already buckling under the strain of supporting them, the injunction to be fruitful and multiply is no longer appropriate. But again it's the 'conservative' rather than the 'evangelical' that's decisive, as this contrasting view demonstrates.

A major figure behind the 'Evangelical Call to Action on Climate Change' that so enraged Beisner and his conservative colleagues was the Reverend Richard Cizik, who continues to be outspoken on the duty of evangelicals to take the climate crisis seriously. On the population issue he is equally reasonable: 'Family planning is not only moral: it's what we should be doing. Be fruitful and multiply was superseded by a post-flood mandate to live peacefully with all of God's creatures.'[44] Compared to Beisner, Pope Francis is a moderate: he advocates 'responsible parenthood', reassuring Catholics that they don't have to breed 'like rabbits'.[45] That's also reassuring to the rest of us, since it's clear that population growth is preventing us from 'living peacefully with all of God's creatures'. The Protestant Church hasn't collapsed as a result of permitting contraception, yet Francis continues to uphold the Catholic ban, even though it would reduce our rate of species extermination.

In any case, when you look into the reasons behind enthusiasm for burgeoning populations they are rarely reassuring: aside from egocentric motives (surely more of *me* is better), it's usually a matter of people's wanting to have many more of 'us' so that there will be relatively fewer of 'them'.[46] And then – it gets sinister – perhaps even *none* of them. For anyone who doubts that the world would be a better place with not as many people in it, and that a smaller population will help mitigate the climate crisis, Alan Weisman's excellent book, *Countdown: Our Last, Best Hope for a Future on Earth*, is highly recommended.

But whatever you think about population growth, we can't resolve the climate crisis without Chinese cooperation – and that requires a more open attitude to, and better acquaintance with, their ideas about politics.

Political Philosophies, Greek and Chinese

In Part Two we saw the effects of the libertarian agenda and the harm it's doing to the public good; and if we're to fight back in the war of ideas, we need to examine their underlying assumptions about who we are as human beings and to come up with better ideas, and better forms of governance. We can neutralize the Three Obstructions by pushing back against the power of money and making our democratic systems work properly. But we then have to cooperate with the Chinese if we're to avoid the worst effects of global heating, with a powerful regime that doesn't do liberal democracy.

How to think about the climate crisis necessarily raises the question of how to think about China – and to judge by the deterioration of relations over the past decade, we haven't been thinking about China very well. Here's where intercultural philosophy can provide some guidance on successful dialogue across cultural and ideological divides. People who've been pondering the climate crisis are pretty much agreed that it demands a radical change in our thinking rather than just some improvements here and there. And what better way to gain a helpful perspective on our own ideas and presuppositions than to entertain ideas as different from ours as those of ancient Chinese philosophy?

Since Xi Jinping assumed power in 2012, the regime has promulgated its philosophy for the benefit of foreigners in two books of his speeches translated into several languages. Much of it is the Marxist socialism you would expect, but there's also a substantial core of ideas from ancient Chinese political thought.[1] The question of how far the regime lives up to the ideas it advocates is interesting, but beyond the scope of my project: the focus here is on how the ideas can help us think constructively about the climate crisis and facilitate fruitful dialogue with the Chinese. (Readers who are interested in exactly which ideas the regime advocates, and some reflections on the extent of the follow-through, can consult the appendixes to this chapter.)

But here's an objection: If their philosophical ideas didn't prevent the Chinese from despoiling the ancient (and modern) environment, how could they be helpful in thinking about the climate crisis – brought about by use of technology they could never have dreamed of?

Here's the response: it's true that China has a long history of controlling the aquatic forces of nature – especially as manifested in floods and droughts – by means of hydraulic technologies, though with only limited or intermittent success. Chinese civilization inflicted serious damage on its natural environment – especially through endless warring among the states – but not more serious than the Greek and Roman civilizations did, or the Egyptian, Mesopotamian, and Mayan for that matter.[2] Advanced cultures tend to be quite retarded when it comes to sustainability over the long term.

What distinguishes the Chinese tradition is more 'environmentally friendly' philosophies than were prevalent in the West, along with a greater awareness on the part of scholars and officials that technologies shouldn't be pushed too far. If these were sadly ineffectual in preventing environmental devastation, it's because if you want to win a war you destroy the enemy's natural resources whatever your philosophical position. As the author of a comprehensive environmental history of China concludes: practices shaped by good ideas are insignificant 'in comparison with the massive effects of the *pursuit of power and profit*'.[3] It's the same story everywhere.

But the story gets really grim again after the establishment of the People's Republic of China (PRC) in 1949, when the Communists and Mao Zedong took over a country ravaged by two decades of civil war, and ruthlessly promoted collectivization and industrialization for the purpose of 'making the country strong'. The reigning ideology was the complete antithesis of traditional Chinese wisdom: instead of aiming for a harmony between human beings and nature, Mao announced that 'Man must conquer nature' and 'overcome the natural' by deploying the power of the masses and industrial technology.[4] It didn't turn out well: in the Great Chinese Famine between 1958 and 1962, tens of millions perished.[5] By the end of the Mao era the country had indeed become stronger, but at the expense of severely weakening its basis in the natural world.

In sum: the Chinese thinkers had good ideas, but they were ineffectual against the lust for profit and power, especially lust backed up by large armies inclined toward slashing and burning. And Mao's war on nature was based on Western ideas (Communist Europe and Soviet Russia were just as hard on the environment) and an explicit rejection of traditional Chinese philosophies of nature. [7.1]

Toward fruitful intercultural dialogue

There are several reasons why negotiations between the West and China tend to disappoint, the first of which pertains to all intercultural dialogue. Depending on the language of the conversation, which often reflects power relations between the two parties, one of them will set the terms of the dialogue, the worldview and ideas that inform it, and the concepts in which the arguments are couched.

In the case of negotiating with the Chinese, we insist on framing the issues in Western terms that we presume to be universal. Thanks to the Scientific Revolution that took place in Europe several centuries ago, and the Age of Enlightenment that succeeded it, we have learned to employ human reason to discover universal concepts and values. Now all we need is to translate these ideas into Chinese, and we're ready to go.[6]

But Chinese philosophy is different: they have different ideas about how to think about things. There's no straightforward way to translate the idea of human rights, or liberal democracy, into Chinese: such notions don't figure in the Chinese tradition of political thought, which focuses rather on duties and responsibilities, and correspondences between family and state. It's not that their ideas are incommensurable with ours: a fruitful conversation on the topic of rights or democracy is feasible – but it requires acknowledgment of the difficulties and respect for the philosophy and culture of the other side.[7]

Lecturing from the moral high ground hasn't proved effective: it produces nothing but irritation from the Chinese side. And in view of the spectacular failures of liberal democracies toward the end of the century's second decade, the claim that democracy is the only decent form of government, along with the refusal to take the Chinese seriously until they adopt it, fails to convince.[8] The fact that someone as ignorant and corrupt as Trump could be elected president demonstrates for many people the utter inadequacy of democracy in its American form. [7.2]

From the Chinese perspective, the Western pretension to superiority and insistence on dialogue on Western terms smack of intellectual imperialism and conceptual colonialism – and remind the Chinese, understandably, of a dismal period in their recent history. We tend to ignore or forget what China remembers as 'the century of national humiliation', which began with defeat in the first Opium War (1839–42) and lasted until the Communists took power in 1949.[9] That memory continues to inform the attitudes and motivates the actions of the current regime, and we would do well to try to understand why.[10]

Other humiliating events were: a series of 'Unequal Treaties' that China was obliged to sign with European colonial powers and Japan; the Second Opium War, at the end of which British and French soldiers, in an act of utter barbarism, looted and destroyed the magnificent Old Summer Palace and several other historical sites in Beijing; the Sino-French War; and the First Sino-Japanese War – in all of which China suffered defeat. During this period, China was reduced from a world power to a weak country carved up by invading colonialists.

A major factor behind China's weakness during that period was civil strife *within* the empire, especially in the form of the Taiping Rebellion, one of the bloodiest civil wars ever, which raged from 1850–64. (The Second Opium War took place within this period.) The rebellion was sparked by Hong Xiuquan, a man who failed the Confucian public service examinations four times and then became a fanatical convert to Christianity. After a dream of meeting a celestial family and other heavenly visions, he came to believe that he was a Son of God and younger brother to Jesus Christ.[11]

Hong set out on a faith-driven mission to rid the country of Confucianism and its Manchu rulers, who were 'demon-devils' (foreigners, after all), and transform China into a Christian nation. He and his army of fellow 'God-worshippers' managed to conquer and occupy several provinces in the southern part of the country. More than twenty million people are said to have perished in the course of the fourteen-year conflict – according to some estimates millions more – before Hong finally died and his army was defeated. It's hardly surprising, in the light of the Rebellion's ravages, that Chinese rulers should now be wary of Christianity. This isn't to justify but rather to explain the current tendency to suppress the religion.

One last consideration should be mentioned, from China's ancient history, which has informed the development of Chinese political philosophy from its beginnings. China has been a unified country for the last two millennia, but its political philosophy developed during the centuries before the unification, a time known as the Warring States period (475–221 BCE). We Europeans think the Hundred Years' War went on for a horrendously long time, but the Warring States period lasted for 250 years. In reaction to those centuries of internecine strife, ancient Chinese philosophy and culture developed a distinctly *un*warlike ethos: all the major schools of Chinese thought (except Legalism) advocate avoiding war at all costs. *The Art of Warfare* would be more aptly titled 'the art of avoiding war'. That long period of conflict also gave rise to an obsession with maintaining order in the polity and keeping the empire *unified* – something that is also a priority for the current regime.

In any case, given the humiliations inflicted by Western powers on China in the nineteenth century and into the twentieth, and the urgency in the twenty-first of gaining Chinese cooperation to avoid climate breakdown, a less aggressive posture would be in order. This is not to deny that we also need to be firm in dealing with China, because the regime's behaviour since Xi Jinping assumed power has become steadily more assertive. There is a very even-handed report by a joint Task Force on U.S.–China Policy, 'Course Correction: Toward an Effective and Sustainable China Policy', which lays out the major issues from the Western perspective and recommends reasonable strategies for responding to Chinese belligerence.[12]

On the positive side, dialogue with the Chinese would be more likely to succeed if we expressed appreciation for their current shift from an industrial to an 'ecological civilization', a commitment that was incorporated into the Chinese constitution in 2012.[13] After all, China has a special interest in coping with global heating because of its vulnerability to the worst effects. The North China Plain, for example, with over 400 million people one of the most densely populated regions of the world, is becoming steadily hotter and also, after so much irrigation for agriculture, more humid. Climate models predict that it won't be long before it's simply too hot to live there. You can survive inside with air conditioning, but spend more than six hours outside, even without moving, and you die of hypothermia.[14] (And of course the more you use air conditioning, the more carbon emissions, and the hotter it gets outside.)

And then there are the low-lying cities on the country's east and south coasts, which will be devastated by sea-level rise. Among all the world's coastal cities, Shanghai may be 'the most vulnerable to coastal floods overall'.[15] Around 20 million people may have to leave the city as the waters rise. But where will they go? Certainly not to the North China Plain, because it'll be too hot there.

Although the Chinese lead the world in installed capacity of coal-powered plants, the urgent need to reduce air pollution (not only to save lives but also to forestall growing discontent on the part of the middle classes) is a powerful incentive to phase out coal and switch to renewable sources of energy.[16] Since China also leads the world in installed capacity and investment in solar and wind power, it's in a good position to effect considerable cuts in GHG emissions.[17] A comprehensive study by the prestigious Stockholm Environment Institute in collaboration with the Chinese Economists 50 Forum shows how China can make the transition to a low-carbon economy 'while still maintaining economic growth and aspirations for development' *and* 'within the finite global carbon budget for greenhouse gas emissions'.[18] If it's willing to incur some costs up front and to renounce short-term profits, China can manage a rapid phasing out of coal.

To the extent that China's domestic programme to reduce emissions will have a beneficial effect on global heating, this is good news for the rest of the world – as long as China doesn't just export its coal-burning plants elsewhere. Although the government insists that the gargantuan 'Belt and Road Initiative' (BRI) will be 'green', as of 2016 China was involved in 240 coal-fired power projects in twenty-five of the participating countries.[19] It does seem, unfortunately, as if China intends to 'export' its fossil fuel infrastructure – so that the BRI loses much of its lustre if it aggravates rather than alleviates the climate crisis.

This issue doesn't detract from the fact that the Chinese government, fortunately unencumbered by global warming deniers, has an intense interest in slowing global heating so as to mitigate disastrous effects on densely populated parts of the country. Another consideration that makes fruitful cooperation on the climate crisis more likely is that the ideas the regime subscribes to in the area of political philosophy are unusually apt in our current situation. What is more, these ideas from the Confucian tradition are consonant with key ideas in the foundational text for political philosophy in the West, the *Republic* of Plato.[20] This circumstance suggests that we share more common ground for a political conversation with the Chinese than we might think – and so an openness on our part toward those ideas would also contribute toward constructive conversations about what to do about the climate. [7.3]

Thinking about the climate crisis also means thinking about politics, and thinking *differently* about politics, insofar as our customary thinking hasn't helped us find any political solutions that work. One reason for our impotence in tackling global heating may be that we've become unmoored from some ancient and yet still valid political principles. Since our current political thinking has been hobbled by the ideology of the rich libertarians, it's time to entertain some ideas that are diametrically opposed to their individualism. Many more appropriate ideas are to be found in the works of Plato and the Confucian thinkers.

Political, familial, and personal order

Nothing could be farther from the individualist fantasy than the Confucian notion of the particular person as a node in a network of familial, social, and political *relationships*. While it may seem natural to take the individual as the basic unit of society, many cultures regard the *family* – a configuration of persons – as fundamental. One advantage of this way of understanding things is that you don't overlook interconnectedness, because you're in it from the beginning.

Chinese thought regards the network of relations within the family or clan as a macrocosm of the structure of the particular person, and as a microcosm of the society, or state. Just as the father is responsible for order in the family (it's a patriarchal philosophy, but can be adapted to our current situation), so the 'heart' optimally orders the forces within the person and the king, or emperor, is in charge of governing the people.

It's a hierarchical order, but dynamic rather than fixed: as children we are expected to obey, but if we grow up to be parents, the roles become reversed. And you have to play the role responsibly or else you lose the entitlement to deference: if I turn out to be a hopeless husband and deadbeat dad, my wife and daughter don't need to defer to me. Absolute obedience isn't required: if a father is failing, it's the son's duty to *remonstrate* with him (politely). And for our times we can change the hierarchical relation between husband and wife to the coequal Confucian relationship between friend and friend.

A great advantage of taking family relations as a model is that they work on the basis of *love*, which renders ethical responsibility and moral deliberation irrelevant. If a close family member is in trouble you help spontaneously, without calculating the costs in terms of time or money – simply because that's what parents do for children, and vice versa. (As long as the family isn't dysfunctional.) For Confucius and Mencius, the second great Confucian thinker, in order to become fully human and humane you have to extend the love you naturally feel for your parents, siblings and children to more distant relatives, and from there analogously to other members of society. (The Chinese word for 'nation' is *guojia*, 'country-family'.) By contrast with the Christian ideal of universal love, the love advocated by Confucius is 'gradated': my love for immediate family members is properly greater than for distant relatives, friends, or neighbours.[21] [7.4]

But before we follow the implications of expanding the dynamics of the family into larger social and political structures, let's turn to the microcosm and consider how these dynamics work within the particular person. For Plato as well as the Confucians, a political leader has to be both *competent* and *virtuous*: competent in being the best at governing, and virtuous in exercising self-restraint rather than being dominated by desires. Rulers with this virtue govern for the sake of the governed rather than for themselves.

Our current political systems appear to have little interest in such guidelines, which results in governments awash in corrupting money and filled with incompetents – a combination that precludes any meaningful response to the climate crisis. This is especially true in the US, though it wasn't always like that there: the Founding Fathers realized the importance of competence and virtue. As Robert Reich has reminded us, they wanted a system of governance 'that would produce the most virtuous people' (rulers as well as the ruled), and where 'virtue meant a concern for the common good'. He cites James Madison's insisting (in *Federalist No. 45*) that 'the public good, the real welfare of the great body of the people, is the supreme object to be pursued'. As far as the governors are concerned, Thomas Jefferson wrote in a letter to John Adams in 1813, the best government should take advantage of 'a natural aristocracy among men' (by contrast with 'an artificial aristocracy founded on wealth and birth') to appoint as leaders those with the most '*virtue and talents*'.[22]

On one level, politics is a system that tries to accommodate and coordinate people's desires, which usually go beyond the resources at a society's disposal. This requires a measure of restraint, or self-restraint. The ancient thinkers regarded those capable of self-restraint as the most fit to restrain others, while those incapable of restraining themselves, if their behaviour diminishes the well-being of their fellow citizens, have to be restrained. (An idea that libertarians vehemently reject.) Order within the polity derives from an order of rank based on people's ability to order themselves.

Many Western thinkers after Plato agree that you need a government to restrain people's desires when they threaten to disrupt the functioning of the polity as a whole, but no one has expressed the necessity as eloquently as the Irish statesman Edmund Burke.

> Men are qualified for civil liberty in exact proportion to their disposition to put moral chains upon their own appetites. . . . Society cannot exist unless a controlling power upon will and appetite be placed somewhere, and the less of it there is within, the more there must be without. It is ordained in the eternal constitution of things, that men of intemperate minds cannot be free. Their passions forge their fetters.[23]

And their passions thus preclude their freedom. Nietzsche takes this idea beyond politics, regarding it as a basic trait of the living. As his alter ego Zarathustra learns when he investigates in depth how life functions: 'Whoever cannot obey himself will be commanded. That is the way of the living.'[24] (Again not something that libertarians are interested in, because they want above all to be *free*.)

The Confucians have a similar idea: just as Socrates regards the human psyche as a microcosm of the *polis*, so Mencius and Xunzi (the third great Confucian philosopher) regard the particular person as a duality or multiplicity of power relations that corresponds to the structure of the family, which in turn reflects the political organization. On both sides you have a lower part, or character, of the person: the desiring or appetitive part, so closely linked to the body (and its desires for shelter, food, drink and sex) as to be powerful in its demands. And also a higher character that commands a broader and longer-term view, and which is capable of restraining and ordering the lower drives for physical pleasure (and love of money as a means to pleasures).

The basic Confucian distinction between the few 'gentlemen' and the far larger class of 'small' or 'petty men' is based on the ability to organize one's person so as to minimize selfishness. Mencius distinguishes parts of the person that are 'of greater importance' from parts 'of lesser importance', and warns against harming the former for the sake of the latter. For instance, people whose lives are dominated by the desire for food and drink are 'despicable' because the obsession leads them to neglect 'the parts of greater importance'.[25] It's not a matter of denying the flesh – it's quite appropriate to care about food and drink – but rather of getting one's priorities right. If desires for physical pleasure or personal gain predominate, this prevents one from acting appropriately in the wider world of society.

Socrates presents a similar picture of personal organization in the *Republic*, insofar as he distinguishes a 'thinking' and a 'desiring' part of the soul, equivalent to the parts of 'greater and lesser' importance. (He also posits between them a 'spirited' character that has no counterpart in the Confucian model: this part is angered by injustice and has the courage to fight for what is right.) Again the idea is not ascetic self-denial. but rather to prevent the desiring part, which easily becomes 'insatiable', from predominating. If it's allowed 'to enslave and rule' the other parts, it can end up 'subverting the person's entire life'.[26] Moderation may not be much fun, but if it's lacking you can end up as an addict.

For Socrates, the optimal intrapersonal organization is one where the thinking part of the soul is in charge. We flourish under such a regime because the thinking part 'is wise and has forethought about all of the soul', understanding what's beneficial for each part and the 'community of the three parts'. As in Mencius, it's not a matter of repressing or extirpating desires, but rather of satisfying the 'necessary' desires for food and drink while keeping the 'unnecessary' desires, for luxuries, in check. In cases where the thinking part fails to rule, the thinking must be 'set over one from outside': the immoderate person will have to be kept in check by someone in whom the thinking part *does* rule.[27] This kind of external restraint is just what the libertarians oppose because it restricts their freedom and takes the fun out of being enslaved to their desires.

The Chinese thinkers pointed to parents as paradigms for good rulers, because they restrain their own desires in order to do what's best for their children. Since Socrates in the *Republic* has proposed abolishing the family he can't use that analogy, but he finds an effective one in the profession of medicine. Inquiring into the nature of the good ruler, he remarks a parallel with the good doctor, who is in the medical profession for the benefit of the patient rather than himself. In caring for the sick he is not working 'for his own advantage', but is rather 'a ruler of bodies' for the benefit of the sick, who are temporarily incapable of ruling their own. True doctors, as practitioners of an 'other-benefitting' art, are quite different from 'businessmen' or 'money-makers' – which is also just what you want from true political leaders.[28]

In the case of the medical practitioner it clearly benefits society to disconnect professional activity from personal gain. If a doctor is also a businessman or money-maker, he's apt to be swayed in his professional decisions by the prospect of profit. Suppose I'm a surgeon, and it's my considered medical opinion that the chances of a certain procedure's benefitting the patient are 50:50, statistically even. If I stand to earn, say, $10,000 for performing the operation, of course I'll go ahead with it. But what if the chances are 60:40 against the procedure? Well, I may still be inclined to operate, just in case it helps. And what about 70:30 against? Shall we give it a try? You never know: it might work. Then 80:20, and 90:10? It's no coincidence, given the financial arrangements that prevail in the American medical system, that the nation leads the world in the number of unnecessary surgical (and other) procedures performed.[29]

If on the other hand a national health service pays me a fixed salary for being a surgeon, regardless of how many procedures I perform, it's easy to decide whether treatment is called for purely out of consideration for the patient. Whether I operate or not, prescribe medicine or provide any kind of treatment, it will have no effect on my earnings. Such an arrangement benefits everybody (except when a practitioner becomes lazy and takes advantage of his position, but you can guard against that). Correspondingly, the good ruler works for the benefit of the ruled and not at all for his own, and can make the best political decisions when insulated from financial considerations.[30]

The problem is that if you arrange the political system so that the rulers have no opportunity for personal gain, it's difficult to persuade anyone to take on the burden of governing. As Socrates aptly remarked: 'No one willingly chooses to rule and get mixed up in straightening out other people's troubles.' Indeed 'the best' potential rulers will regard 'love of honour and love of money' as reprehensible, and be reluctant to rule because they don't care about personal gain or fame. They'll have to be persuaded, and are likely to consent only if they're shown that all other candidates are inferior – because they'll be reluctant to be governed by people less competent than themselves.[31]

Political thought in China diverges from Platonic philosophy on this point: far from regarding government as a necessary evil, the Confucian tradition sees it as the culmination of the life of the gentleman, since the natural result of self-cultivation is an emanation of virtuosity that orders the state, and beyond, without coercion. (More on this shortly.) And while Socrates explicitly requires the best qualified women as well as men to be trained as political leaders (because the *polis* will benefit from having the very best leaders rather than the best *male* leaders), the Confucians always talk of the emperor, king and the consummately humane person as male. But the absence of a political role for women in Confucian philosophy reflects the tenor of the patriarchal times rather than being integral to the philosophy itself. Since the aim of the Confucian project is full humanity, political equality between men and women poses no problem.[32]

Once you have philosophical figures in positions of political power, you need to arrange things so that they *stay* uncorrupted, immune to the allure of fame and gain, and focused on the well-being of the people. Socrates ensures this by denying the rulers any private property except for the necessities, which will be provided as a 'salary' by other citizens, in moderate amounts that result in neither surplus nor lack. These arrangements prevent the prospect of personal gain from affecting decisions the rulers make concerning what's best for the entire community. After all, 'we are not looking to the exceptional happiness of any one group among us but, as far as possible, that of the city as a whole'.[33]

Although the Confucian thinkers rarely condemn the desire for profit as severely as Socrates does, they consistently warn that aiming for personal gain can divert one from doing the right thing.[34] But they also saw no need for precautions like Plato's against the ruler's acting out of self-interest, because they had greater faith in the persuasive and pervasive power of self-restraint. They trusted in the efficacy of self-cultivation on the part of candidates for rulership, a regimen designed to reduce selfishness and promote concern for others.

But what if the rulers, even after a long period of excellent education and assiduous self-cultivation, begin to act in ways that *don't* benefit the people? It would be a relatively simple matter to build the necessary checks and balances into a Platonic or Confucian meritocratic system to prevent or remedy that.[35] Indeed Confucian political philosophy insists with its notion of 'remonstrance' on the need for ministers not only to advise the ruler but also to *criticize*, diplomatically, when necessary.[36]

In any case, for both Plato and the Confucians the best way to ensure that the rulers will exercise self-restraint and govern for the sake of the people is to give competent candidates the right kind of education.

Ruling through radiant virtuosity

So what is the appropriate curriculum for better political leaders? The question is worth posing not only because Confucian and Platonic political philosophy give similar answers, but also because they are so different from our idea today of how rulers, or any of us, are to be educated. For those ancient thinkers say: teach *music* and *physical exercise* – rather than statecraft, which can come in later.[37] A measure of how far we've come since ancient times is the *absence* of these two disciplines from the curriculum in so many schools in the Western world.

Socrates stresses the importance of 'gymnastics' for the health of the body and the spirited part of the soul: a strong and fit body is the basis for a soul that's courageous – certainly something we want in our leaders. The foundation for the education of the Chinese gentleman is the 'Six Arts', five of which involve focused physical practice: archery, charioteering, calligraphy, ritual propriety and the playing of music.[38] The last two were the most important, insofar as their exercise hones and attunes one's interactions with both people and things.

The Confucian practice of ritual propriety is less strenuous than the Greeks' gymnastics, but more obviously something that would conduce to virtuous rulers. It's a matter of cultivating oneself, honing one's interactions with other people and things, in such a way as to 'overcome the self' (in the sense of egocentrism).[39] In the ancient rituals you had to integrate your actions with those of your fellow participants, while handling the ritual implements with the utmost care. You set self-will aside in order to practice 'the form' – what the Japanese call *kata*. I learn to do it *their* way, trusting in the wisdom of the ancients, and forget about 'my way'. (Sorry, Sinatra-san). The method is *reciprocal*, and involves putting yourself in the other person's shoes. The better you get at doing that, the greater the capacity for empathy, the easier it is to experience yourself as a network of relations, and the more you can let your energy and motivations come from the people and things around you as well as – and then *rather than* – from your limited self.

In ancient Greece and China 'music' included poetry and song, which in both cases portrayed heroes and rulers from ancient times, whose exemplary lives provide excellent models. Listening to the right kinds of music tempers the passions and lends harmony to the various drives within the person, while in playing music you conform your activity to the musical work as well as to the activity of your fellow players. You thereby perfect the practice of what Confucius calls 'taking one's place among others' in society.[40]

Music contributes to social and political order because it's attuned to a deeper and broader source of order, the natural world. The ancient *Book of Ritual* observes that music flows naturally from 'generation and change', from processes of growth and maturation. 'Music is an echo of the harmony between Heaven and Earth; ritual propriety reflects the orderly distinctions in the operations of Heaven and Earth.'[41] In playing music, you take your place among others – not only other people but in All-under-the-Heavens (*tianxia*). If you're looking to educate exceptional and above all humane human beings, not just polymaths or technocrats, you'll want to help the students attune their energies to those of other people and the world as a whole.

For Socrates, the ruler achieves inner harmony through a proper ordering of the inner regime. Thanks to the isomorphism between parts of the soul and classes in the *polis*, the ruler can extend this harmony into the world as if he were the musical director, or conductor, of the political symphony. In a later dialogue by Plato, the *Timaeus* (along with the *Republic* the most influential of his works), the context expands to the harmonizing of the rational part of the soul with the soul of the entire world.[42]

Just as, for Plato, it's the 'philosopher king' who is best able to bring about such harmony, so Xunzi writes: 'It is the lord of men who is the indispensable element wherewith to "arrange the musical scale" of the classes of men.'[43] Insofar as the ruler in the Chinese tradition gets his power to rule from the forces of Heaven and Earth, he can bring about harmony in the human world by resonating with the greater harmony of nature through appropriate music. The philosopher king in Plato and the Chinese sage-ruler both govern through resonance rather than coercion – an ideal perhaps, but one worth striving for. [7.5]

Upon completion of their education, the Chinese had an institution for gauging the success of the process: public service examinations. Confucian government officials developed a system of examinations open to everyone, the results of which would indicate fitness for a political career. Officially inaugurated in the second century BCE, it has prevailed – on and off, in some form or other – up to the present day. Of course the system has its shortcomings, but its longevity attests to a certain degree of success in appointing competent officials, which is most evident today in the competence of the Confucian-influenced government of Singapore.[44]

A century ago, in a speech in Tokyo, Dr Sun Yat-sen, who is known in China as 'Father of the Nation', deplored the state of American democracy and the ignorance of its politicians.

> With respect to elections, those endowed with eloquence ingratiated themselves with the public and won elections, while those endowed with learning and ideals but who lacked eloquence were ignored. Consequently, members of America's House of Representatives have often been foolish and ignorant people who have made its history quite ridiculous. ... The corruption and laxity of American politics are unparalleled among the nations of the world. This would seem to be entirely due to the inadequacy of its public service examinations.[45]

In fact, they've never had public service examinations: anyone can run, and be elected, even if they're totally lacking in qualifications and political experience. And so the situation today remains much the same.

The classic texts on the curriculum for the public service examinations share the premise that the successful candidate will understand that 'the people are the foundation of the state'. This maxim comes from one of the ancient histories, invoking the legendary emperor Yu the Great:

> Our inspired ancestor proclaimed
> That the people should be cherished
> And never abused!
> The people are the foundation of the state;
> If the foundation is secure, so is the state.[46]

The priority of the well-being of the people runs throughout the Chinese tradition of political philosophy (except for Legalism). Mencius especially emphasizes that 'the fully humane being loves others': 'Do things for the good of others', he wrote; 'Help the poor and assist those in difficulty.'[47]

For leaders to act in the interests of the people rather than their own, they will need to 'perfect' themselves through assiduous self-cultivation – thereby becoming less selfish. These exhortations, from Confucius and Mencius, show that self-cultivation in the Confucian tradition is the opposite of egocentrism, and rather a matter of overcoming one's selfishness by opening up to the network of personal, familial and social relationships that constitute one's life. It's a matter of *realizing* our interconnectedness – in the double sense of becoming aware of it and making it real.

The Confucian thinkers believed that self-cultivation on the part of the ruler results in a charismatic power, a virtuosity, that encourages and inspires his ministers and the people.[48] Confucius said: 'The rule of virtue can be compared to the Pole Star, which commands the homage of the multitude of stars without leaving its place.'[49] The power that emanates from the good ruler seems to operate magically, without coercion or overt force. An accumulation of virtuosity is effective because of the 'sympathetic resonance' that conditions the whole world as a field of *qi* energies. (More on this in the next chapter).

Because we lost the idea of sympathetic resonance in the Western tradition, we have to look to the notion of *charisma* which, as Max Weber showed, works powerfully in the realm of politics. 'Charisma is a certain quality of an individual personality by virtue of which he is set apart from ordinary men and treated as endowed with supernatural, superhuman, or at least exceptional powers or qualities.'[50] The power may manifest itself more physically, as with Theodore Roosevelt, Winston Churchill, or Charles de Gaulle, or it's a strong moral authority, as possessed by Mahatma Gandhi, Nelson Mandela, Martin Luther King or Václav Havel.

Or think of how virtuosity in the world of sports can be inspiring. When our daughter was playing basketball, I regretted not being able to take her to see Michael Jordan when he was playing for the Chicago Bulls. But if we had gone, there would have been no need to say 'Keep an eye on that player', because it would have been obvious who was the best, or 'You should follow his example', because the man's style and grace would naturally inspire any aspiring player to try harder. As long as we guard against letting the prospect of virtuosity provoke envy and resentment of others, it provides natural inspiration for us to do better ourselves.

This Confucian idea anticipates the modern notion of 'soft power' – characterized by Joseph Nye as 'the ability to get what one wants by attraction and persuasion rather than coercion or payment'. Having committed themselves to a 'peaceful rise', the Chinese are very concerned to build up their soft power. (Witness the amount of money spent on the 2008 Beijing Olympics, the 2010 Shanghai Expo, the Confucius Institutes.) For the Confucians, just as the best rulers lead by the example of their great virtuosity, a well-governed country can by its shining example bring order to international relations and set the world at peace. In the current regime's pursuit of soft power they do well with promoting traditional Chinese culture, but when it comes to the art of rulership and ways of governing, their example is less than shining. To govern non-coercively by the virtuosity of the leaders would compel the appreciation of the world; but to resort instead to coercive Legalist policies only brings opprobrium on the stage of world opinion.

One last point: self-cultivation on the part of the ruler brings order to the family and the state, and beyond those to the empire and All-under-the-Heavens.[51] The ancient Confucian classic *Great Learning* begins with an image of the ruler treating the people as his family. The text goes on to say that one's household will be well ordered only if the person in charge has cultivated himself successfully, the state will be well ordered only if the household has been, and that only if the state is well ordered can harmony be brought to All-under-the-Heavens. 'From the Son of Heaven to the common person, for all alike, cultivating the person is the root' – with effects that extend beyond the plurality of nation states to the whole world.[52]

In this sense Confucian political philosophy, by taking the whole world rather than the state as the ultimate political entity, displays cosmic ambitions as it imagines sympathetic resonance extending everywhere. Whereas the Chinese thinkers understand ordering as pervading ever larger configurations of relationships, Western political thought extends the individual to the next level up, so that the state is imagined to function as a super-individual.

The current world order of international relations is individualism writ large: under the Westphalian system that has prevailed for the past several centuries, nation states enjoy autonomy and above all *sovereignty*. The United Nations Charter acknowledges 'the sovereign equality of all its Members' and protects all 'matters which are essentially within the domestic jurisdiction of any state' (Article 2). How much fossil fuels a state burns within its borders, and the consequent emissions, are up to the leaders and citizens of that state. No wonder that twenty-five years of climate conferences among almost 200 sovereign states have yielded no results. We urgently need to rethink and reframe the process – and so why not along the lines of the Chinese idea of All-under-the-Heavens, the world as an interconnected whole: the natural world as well as the social, historical, cultural and political worlds? (More on this in the concluding chapter.)

As Nicolas Berggruen and Nathan Gardels suggest in their book *Intelligent Governance for the 21st Century*, which examines political philosophies and practices in China and the West, both sides can benefit by being open to learning from the other. They propose as a reasonable aim 'a balanced combination of meritocracy and democracy, of authority and freedom, of community and the individual'.[53] A new 'middle way' could indeed enable an effective collaboration between China and the West – and eventually the rest – on tackling the climate crisis. In any case, we do well to acknowledge that the ancient wisdom of both traditions is valid when it insists that the rulers be the most competent at ruling, and that they govern for the sake of the people.

If the United States as the country that has done the most (in terms of historical GHG emissions) to get us into the climate crisis persists in doing less than nothing to get us out of it, it would be in the best interests of other countries to persuade China, as the current top GHG emitter, to take the lead in slowing global heating. At least the regime appears to have the right idea about geopolitics. According to the 'America First!' approach, where the nation is regarded as an individual: 'The world is not a "global community" but an arena where nations, nongovernmental actors and businesses compete for advantage.' By contrast for China as the Middle Kingdom, where the country is like a large family group: 'This is a world where countries are linked with, and dependent on, one another at a level never seen before. Humankind is a community of common destiny in which everyone has in himself a little bit of others.'[54] I leave it up to the reader to decide which view is more apt in the globalized world of today.

China has to reduce its carbon emissions in order to prevent climate catastrophe domestically, and as a responsible member of the human community it wouldn't want to export coal-burning plants to other countries. The Chinese have been very concerned to increase their soft power: if as good Confucians they were to take the lead in tackling the climate crisis, it would be the greatest soft-power coup ever – one that would earn them the gratitude and admiration of all the world's nations. (I outline the benefits in an unsent letter to President Xi.) [7.6]

Part Four

Lower Consumption, Higher Fulfilment

The world is overfull with beautiful things, but nonetheless poor, very poor, in beautiful moments and revelations of these things.

FRIEDRICH NIETZSCHE[1]

Sage Advice from the Ancients

Supposing we succeed in getting rid of the Three Obstructions and cooperating with the Chinese on tackling the climate crisis, we're still going to have to adapt to some difficult conditions in a warming world, and people in richer countries will have to get used to less abundance and some scarcity. However, we can turn the necessity of changing our ways into an opportunity for living lives that are more fulfilled. To think productively about the climate crisis we need to rethink our relationships – to other people and things, and especially to the natural world because we depend on that for our survival.

Practically speaking, we're going to have to take a middle way between the high-consumption path of the developed countries and the low-income lives of people in the developing countries. There simply aren't sufficient resources on a finite planet to allow all 7.7 billion of us to live it up at the top level. Dividing the population into the richest, middle and poorest thirds, most of those in the middle are well enough off without being affluent by our standards. There's enough to eat, drinkable water on tap, a comfortable enough place to live and means of transportation such as bicycles. The poor third can be brought up to that level – but only if the rich third reduces its consumption, which any sense of fairness would require.[1] Or do we in the developed world presume we have the right to continue consuming the lion's share of the planet's resources while so many remain miserably poor? If we don't assume that, it's time change our ways.

When I suggest that saving the species means that we richer people have to reduce our consumption of energy and consumer goods, the response is often dismay: 'We'll be so *miserable* if we can't consume as much.' But how do we know? We might be pleasantly surprised. The reason people think they'll be miserable is that they've been brought up in, or have bought into, an ideology that says a good life is one of high consumption. To be human is to be a consumer; and to be a good human being is to consume a lot. But this shows what's lacking in discussions of the climate crisis: the question of *human flourishing*. Too often the baseline is set too low: it's true we can survive under a range of adverse conditions – but aren't we concerned with *thriving*, as societies as well as individuals, rather than merely surviving?

It's difficult to determine what human flourishing consists in because, as Plato observed long ago, people differ with respect to what makes their lives worth living. Certain needs obviously have to be satisfied: in order to be happy, let alone fulfilled, you need access to adequate food and shelter, potable water, education and basic health care. A certain satisfaction with *work* also appears to be necessary. Before the advent of capitalism, most people could participate in the production of something that others needed, whether food or other goods or services. But since the Industrial Revolution, opportunities for cultivating or crafting things by the skilful use of one's hands have diminished.

For many people religion is a major source of meaning in their lives, while the non-religious make do with social interaction, culture and the arts, history and traditions. But another key factor in human flourishing is contact with the natural world. The Chinese tradition has always taken this for granted, insofar as the worlds of Heaven, Human, and Earth are understood as one. In other words, human flourishing requires a context of healthy natural ecosystems, and declines when the environment is damaged and debilitated.

This is hardly surprising, since our bodies have evolved over millennia of involvement in the natural world: until recently, human existence was in close and constant interaction with the powers of nature. If we begin from *homo habilis* (the most ancient human genus, now extinct) the human being has been around for some two million years. And if we imagine that period reduced to a human lifespan of seventy, then the first village settlements wouldn't have appeared until eight months after the sixty-ninth birthday, and some indigenous groups in remote parts of the world would have remained hunter-gatherers until a day or two before the seventieth.

It's only in the last few generations – in effect, during the last thirty *hours* of our seventy-year lifespan as a species – that we've been able to insulate our lives from the vagaries of weather and climate by way of modern dwellings and workplaces, food production systems and modes of transportation. When citizens in the developed world are cut off from the natural environment so abruptly, it's no wonder that bodies register distress and souls feel impoverished.[2]

Insofar as we're suffering from the effects of a rupture, how can we best be healed? If we say 'by regaining our connection with the natural world', this raises the question of what *is* natural – of whether the human has pervaded the natural to the point where there's no nature left, and whether we can somehow get around the apparently inevitable 'social construction of nature'.

Natural philosophies

The climate crisis obliges us to revise our relations with nature because our predicament derives from our letting human-centred activities overwhelm natural processes. The ancient adage about 'living in accord with nature' could help us tackle the crisis *and* adapt to a post-crisis world of lower consumption; but if nature no longer exists, or is an empty concept, how are we going to manage that?

On the conceptual level, some progressive thinkers tell us that 'the categories of *Nature, the environment, natural*, and *unnatural* have long since been deconstructed'.[3] A common argument is this: because humans are natural beings, everything they do is natural. Just as it's natural for ants to live in colonies and beavers to dwell in lodges they've built, so all the trappings of civilization that human beings produce are natural. Yes, if everything is natural and there's nothing that's not natural, 'nature' does become an empty and meaningless category.

Another argument is that it makes no sense to recommend living in accord with nature because we have no direct experience of such a thing. All our experience of the natural world is 'socially constructed', conditioned by our upbringing and education, which precludes any experience of nature that's unmediated by culture. Anthropology shows through ethnographic studies from around the world that most cultures do not divide human culture from what goes on in nature.[4] Such a sharp separation is a recent and parochial phenomenon, peculiar to Europe after the sixteenth century.

What is true, and sad, is that toward the end of the last century we got to *The End of Nature* – as recounted by Bill McKibben in 1989, sounding a cogent early warning of the dangers of global warming. Since we're treating ourselves to 'a new atmosphere', with higher concentrations of GHGs, we're affecting *everything* under the Heavens, the whole Earth.

And in the course of heating up the planet, our industrial activity is also polluting it: 'Each cubic yard of air, each square foot of soil, is stamped indelibly with our crude imprint, our X.'[5] We have stained the entire earth with soot and other particulate matter, organic and synthetic chemical compounds – along with the occasional burst of radioactive particles. No pure nature any more: it's all marked by the human.

This is a loss, not least because scientists have always found it valuable to study the way *natural* ecosystems function, places untouched by humans. But now they are no more: we've transformed the world into a humanized place. Welcome to the Anthropocene. But there's still enough nature left – natural phenomena not being controlled by humans – to serve as a guide, if we want.

Whatever the merits of the objections mentioned earlier, and however we choose to draw the line between the activities of nature and of humans, it can mark a crucial distinction. The Big Question for many years in debates about the climate has been how far global heating is human-caused and how much is due to 'natural variation'. In this context there's an urgent need to distinguish between what is natural and what derives from human forcing. [8.1]

There are definite benefits from employing the category of the natural by contrast with the *artificial* or the synthetic. It's not that artifice is itself a bad thing: it's often called for, and can be enjoyable. But when our technology became able to develop *synthetic* products in the mid-twentieth century, we went beyond an inconspicuous but significant limit. Under the slogan 'Better Living through Chemistry', this phenomenon introduced a flood of synthetic chemical compounds into the biosphere – unnatural substances that can't be taken up into the natural cycles of ecosystems. (Remember E. F. Schumacher warning against this innovation.) Whereas natural products biodegrade and become food for something else, synthetic products became a new kind of *waste* that disrupts ecosystem functioning.[6] So it certainly helps to distinguish between what's natural and what's *artificial*, insofar as many of our problems stem from our letting the artificial overwhelm the natural.

That's all well and good, say the objectors, but the 'harmony of nature' is a myth. Nature is violent and disharmonious: forest fires, volcanic eruptions, asteroids crashing in, species extinction prior to human intervention. And on top of that, indigenous peoples are savage and brutal.[7] Yes, of course, nature includes all that – but why should we want to emulate it? As human beings we're capable of thinking about how to learn from nature, which activities to emulate. Some will let us flourish better than others: we just have to pay attention to how it's going.

One last objection before we get to the positive stuff: if we have changed the world so radically by our use of modern technology, why bother with what ancient thinkers, with no experience of the effects of such technologies, have to say about nature and human flourishing? Of course the conditions of contemporary life are quite different from theirs, but key features have remained the same: the human body and its physiology haven't changed significantly, nor has 'human nature' (whatever that is). It's true that we're now undergoing more rapid changes: with more prostheses being integrated into human bodies, and enthusiasts of artificial intelligence (AI) and ICT assuring us that we're facing an unprecedented acceleration of mental changes – into the 'post-human', or 'trans-human' condition.

But rather than dismissing the wisdom of the ancients as out-dated, we might let it help us question the *desirability* of these accelerating changes, and how much our modern ideas have contributed to our environmental predicament. And if the early philosophers in Greece and China would agree that the good human life involves living 'according to nature', it's surely worthwhile asking what they mean, in case it can help us thrive in difficult times.

By an interesting coincidence, the Stoic and Epicurean schools of philosophy were founded right around the time the two great Daoist classics, the *Laozi* and *Zhuangzi*, were taking final shape in response to the prevalence of the Confucian canon over the preceding century or two.[8] For all these thinkers it's a matter of understanding the good human life in *context*, since human flourishing depends on not just a healthy society but also a thriving natural environment. And if you're going to align your life to the prevailing circumstances, you'd better have an understanding of what they are and how they're changing.

The ancient thinkers share an idea of the natural world – which the Stoics and Epicureans call *physis* and the Chinese thinkers Heaven and Earth – as an ensemble of processes that produce birth and growth, and recycle the residues of decay and death. The Stoics imagine an all-pervasive 'breath' (*pneuma*) that informs all things with a simultaneously expanding and contracting force, keeping them together and in their proper places, an ordering principle they sometimes call divine reason (*logos*). The Epicureans also have the idea that all things are born from an original matrix (in this case, of atoms) and perish back into it – the difference being that they emphasize natural spontaneity rather than conformity to divine reason. In this sense they are closer to the Chinese philosophy of a world of *qi* energies constantly condensing and dissolving.

The Stoics share with the Chinese the idea that the whole of nature is pervaded by 'sympathetic resonance', whereby phenomena of similar kinds resonate with each other. The Daoists cite the example of two strings tuned to the same note on difference musical instruments: when one is plucked, the other vibrates in sympathy. They tell stories of emotional resonance between parents and children, charioteers and their horses, rulers and their people, as well as reciprocity between clouds and the forms of the land or sea beneath them.[9]

Following Plato in his dialogue *Timaeus*, the Stoics regarded the cosmos as a living being with all parts organically related to one another. In his dialogue *On the Nature of the Gods*, Cicero draws attention to 'the sympathetic agreement, interconnection and affinity of things'. While one character talks about things being 'held together by a single divine breath', another ascribes 'the system's coherence and persistence' to 'nature's forces' alone, and to the 'concord' (*sympatheia*) of its spontaneous growth.[10] Similarly, Marcus Aurelius, the last great Stoic thinker, makes it clear that interactivity informs the whole system.

> Think of the world as one living being ... and how all things work together to cause all that comes to pass, and how intertwined the thread and closely woven the web. ... And just as existing things are combined in a harmonious order, so also all that come into being display a wonderful kindred interrelationship.[11]

These last words mean that the interactions are inherent and above all *ecological*. By contrast with something fashioned or made, where the maker is external to the product, in the case of the cosmos, 'where things are held together by Nature, the power that made them is within and abides with them'.

Classical Chinese thought similarly credits the forces of Heaven and Earth with ordering the world, without the need for some external power to animate things and make them cohere harmoniously. The way (*dao*) of the world works through each particular thing or process as its own power, or virtuosity (*de*). They all respond constantly to the one breath of *qi* energy that flows through and animates them. The great Neo-Confucian thinker Zhu Xi explains that sympathetic resonance is possible because *mind* is all-pervasive (there's an influence here from Chinese Buddhism):

> Heaven and Earth reach all things with their mind. When the human being receives it, it then becomes the human mind. When things receive it, it becomes the mind of things in general. And when grass, trees, birds, animals receive it, it becomes the mind of grass, trees, birds, and animals in particular. All of these are simply the one mind of Heaven and Earth.[12]

Marcus Aurelius expresses the idea of pervasive intelligence through the analogy of the cosmic breath when he offers this practical advice:

> Be no longer content merely to breathe in unison with the all-surrounding air, but from now on also think in unison with the all-surrounding Mind. For the power of mind is diffused throughout and distributed for him who can absorb it, no less than the power of air for him who can breathe it.

Doesn't this lighten the burden of thinking somewhat – if we don't need to do it all ourselves, but can rather tap in to the spirit of the world around us? If we can all breathe the air, we can also allow the thinking of all that's around us to hold sway by letting it pass through us. (Nietzsche alludes to something comparable when he writes that in cases of profound thought one should say '*It* thinks' rather than 'I think'.[13])

Stoic and Epicurean physics (as the study of nature) are compatible not only with ancient Chinese philosophies of *qi* energy but also with modern Western physics – not Newtonian but quantum physics, and related fields such as chaos theory. Discussions of *qi* often involve something like the principle of conservation of energy under the first law of thermodynamics, and its transformability is compatible with Einstein's discovery of the equivalence between energy and mass (as in $E=mc^2$). A simpler analogy in Western science would be the electromagnetic field discovered by Michael Faraday in the nineteenth century, expanded to cosmic proportions. In general, analogies with notions like energy fields in contemporary physics, or systems in systems theory, won't be misleading.[14]

Great figures in physics – David Bohm, Niels Bohr, Albert Einstein, Fred Hoyle – talk about hidden interconnections and interactions, extending even to 'distant parts of the Universe'. Werner Heisenberg's uncertainty principle and Bohr's complementarity have resonances with Daoist ideas that both scientists actually acknowledged.[15] Inability to confront the climate crisis derives from the *lack* of a sense of inter-dependence with our fellows and environing natural phenomena. If both philosophers and physicists from different times and perspectives are asserting corresponding interconnections that we don't directly perceive, this gives us further reason to open up our customary worldview as broadly as we can.[16]

But for the ancient Greek thinkers, physics wasn't only a theoretical exercise but also an existential practice. Epicurus taught that we attain a serene and fulfilled life first by investigating and understanding the natural world, and then by 'living in conformity' with it. Natural science (*physiologia*) serves to dispel primitive dread of phenomena in the heavens above us and torment from the gruesome events recounted in ancient myths. Rather than following 'vain opinions' we do better to 'follow nature', and we can start by broadening our perspective and gaining some distance from our personal situation. If we assess our actions only on the basis of what's closest to us, our view of things is distorted: we need a sense of scale and space and time, which we get from keeping in touch with *physis* as we live out our days.

Living in accord with nature

The first Stoic thinker, Zeno of Citium, was apparently the author of a book with the title *Of Life in Accord with Nature* (like all his other works, lost). He is said to have said that happiness consists in 'a good flow of life' – just what the Daoists and traditional Chinese medical practitioners say about well-being and *qi* energies. Zeno's successors in the Stoic school understood living in accord with nature as two-fold: 'according to our human nature as well as the nature of the universe.' The idea is that 'our own natures are parts of the nature of the whole', and so the task – as with their Chinese counterparts – is to harmonize microcosm with macrocosm.[17]

At the beginning of his *Meditations* Marcus Aurelius thanks his teacher for advocating 'life in accord with nature', and encourages himself to keep on living that way. When he writes that 'all things come to pass in accord with the Nature of the Whole', he means that since we humans exist among all things, we do well to try to get a sense of the totality and where it's tending. We are able to accord with nature because our own nature is subject to the 'ruling' or 'guiding principle' within us, which is one with the rational, divine power that governs the cosmos.[18]

The reason we need to remind ourselves to live in accord with nature is that the human being, while remaining dependent on and to some extent in contact with the natural world from birth to death, is also alienated from it through socialization and civilization. Always a part of nature, we're also able to stand apart from it as we pursue the work of culture. Culture lets us surpass instinctual life and the condition of being driven by the needs of the body, in order to fashion for ourselves a 'second nature' as we come to embody the social practices of our milieu.

But are we sure we really understand the processes of nature, the powers of Heaven and Earth, and not merely our version of them – whether mythical, religious or scientific – our projections from the anthropocentric perspective? Because to live in accord with some merely subjective conception of the natural world won't help us much. If our experience of nature is always socially constructed, this would confound any attempt to live in accord with it, because that would mean merely in accord with ourselves.

It's true that we get socialized into the prevailing perspectives of the society we're in, including perspectives on the natural world. But once we realize that our experience of nature is conditioned by socio-cultural ideas and prejudices, it is possible to subtract some of them or withdraw the projections – especially if we take the trouble to appreciate alternative cultural constructions, and to consider our own set-up from the perspective of, say, the ancient Greek, or Roman or Chinese worldview.

Within any culture, there's a tendency to view natural phenomena from the perspective of *utility*, in terms of how we can use things of nature, or 'natural resources' as we call them. For survival purposes it's a valid set of perspectives, though it causes problems if it predominates – if, for example, 'the land and the creatures on it are looked upon as *nothing but* factors of production'. As E. F. Schumacher wrote: 'It is irrational for man to treat things that he has not made and cannot make and cannot recreate once he has spoilt them, in the same manner and spirit as he is entitled to treat things of his own making.'[19] Fixation on the perspective of utility also tends to promote narrowness and rigidity: the Daoists think we do better to broaden our worldview and keep it fluid.

Several stories in the *Zhuangzi* show the frequent irrelevance of the perspective of utility, and even 'the usefulness of being useless' where the perspective of utility is reversed. In one of them, a master carpenter arrives in a village where there's a gigantic oak tree that's regarded as sacred. He dismisses it with hardly a glance as 'worthless lumber'. But the tree later appears to him in a dream and points out that trees useful to humans suffer because of their utility: 'Thus do their abilities embitter their lives. That is why they die young, failing to fully live out their natural lifespans.' Does the carpenter suppose that the talking oak could have grown so huge if it had been useful?

The blight of our times is the predominance of the perspective of utility as enshrined in modern economics: 'to the extent that economic thinking is based on the market, it takes the sacredness out of life, because there can be nothing sacred in something that has a price'.[20] Conversely, the category of the sacred is crucial because it has nothing to do with utility or making a profit: when a tree or grove, a mountain or river, is declared sacred, people are more likely to treat it with respect and protect it.

If we entertain other perspectives on natural phenomena than the utilitarian – religious, aesthetic, scientific, mythic – we can enjoy a richer range of experience than if we remain stuck in the perspective of what we can get out of them. Zhuangzi shows how, by adopting a diversity of other and opposite points of view, we can find 'the axis of the Way' through the various directions that our value judgements present when they say 'this way' and 'not that way'. By letting all things 'bask in the broad daylight of Nature', the Daoist sage is able to 'remain at rest in the centre of the wheel' of the turning world, within the empty axis of the Way – and thereby to entertain and appreciate multiple perspectives as everything cycles around and through him. This is the advantage of our ability to stand apart from nature while staying a part of it: it allows us to entertain, with practice, a range of trans-utilitarian and more natural perspectives.

Another way of gaining a less anthropocentric view of nature is by a Daoist practice they call 'fasting the heart' or 'emptying the mind'. This involves waiting patiently until all assumptions, opinions and presuppositions about the world begin to drain or fade away. Free of mental clutter, the heart can then respond to the situation as it *is*, rather than as we would prefer it to be. (This corresponds to the Greeks' discipline of physics, which grants a 'distance perspective' on our situation.)

Zhuangzi acknowledges the difficulty of distinguishing between the natural and the human, because we are born from and nurtured by the powers of Heaven and Earth, which continue to work through the body as 'the life in us'. He concludes that what distinguishes us from the animals and other kinds among the myriad things is the ability *to deliberate*, to weigh up possible courses of action and choose among them. We tend to make our way by pondering alternatives in our hearts and minds, and then directing ourselves to act in one way, aim at one end, pursue this goal rather than one of those others. This kind of thinking is necessary, sometimes; but it tends to run counter to – because it ignores – the sympathetic resonances that attune our bodies to their surroundings and the rest of the natural world. (A matter of intuiting our 'gut feelings' about things.) Lacking such attunement, and because thinking often stimulates our desires, we let personal and short-term considerations obscure the bigger picture. In view of this tendency to let the human overwhelm the natural, the Daoists recommend that we compensate in order to attain a dynamic balance between the natural and the human.[21]

In one sense, then, living in accord with nature is tantamount to living in accord with reality, rather than with a humanized version of what is actually happening. Another method the Stoics and Epicureans practise – in perfect consonance with the Daoists – is to withhold the *value judgments* that distort our experience. Not that the latter are the only Chinese thinkers who recommend dropping the judgments except when we really need them, which is rarely: the idea is central to Chinese Buddhist thinking too.

This wonderful dictum of the Stoic thinker Epictetus could easily have come from the Buddha: 'What upsets people is not events themselves but their judgments about the events.'[22] While our power to affect events is limited, our judgments are a realm where we're free to change or refrain – if we choose to exercise that freedom. 'Some things are up to us and some are not up to us,' as Epictetus remarks. Foremost among what's up to us are 'our opinions, impulses, desires, aversions', and these we can change if we put our hearts and minds to it.[23]

Celebrating natural limits

Another aspect of living a truly human life in accordance with nature involves acknowledging natural *limits* – and even, as we'll see, celebrating them. At one point in his *Meditations*, Marcus gives voice to a part of himself that deprecates vigorous engagement with work and life in society, and recommends lingering in a warm bed instead. 'Nature assigns limits to rest', he replies to his inner idler, 'as well as to eating and drinking, and you nevertheless go beyond your limits, beyond what is sufficient'.[24] He was a Roman emperor, after all, as well as the last great Stoic thinker.

The Epicureans are in full agreement that life goes better when you acknowledge and respect natural limitations: one of their central teachings is that Mother Nature sets bounds when she produces things in their various kinds. In the words of the great thinker-poet Lucretius:

> a limit has been set
> For the growth of things and for their hold on life,
> Each after its kind, and it stands decreed
> What each by nature can and cannot do.

As he writes later in the poem, 'all things / Must stay within the law of their creation' – and if they don't, the penalty is severe (the severity stressed by three repetitions of these lines):

> For all things have their boundaries fixed and sure,
> Transgress them, and death follows instantly.[25]

Lucretius bemoans the failure of most people to understand that there are natural limits to the pleasures of material acquisition precisely because our desires in that realm are *un*limited:

> Therefore always in vain and uselessly
> Men labour, and waste their days in empty cares,
> Because they fail to see what bounds are set
> To getting, and what limits to true pleasure.[26]

This is crucial: acknowledgment of natural limits, far from making us miserable, can make for a more serene and joyous existence.

And yet for many people in the twenty-first century it's not so clear that the boundaries of the human are fixed and sure: couldn't it be that *we are* the one kind that isn't subject to the death penalty for transgressing the boundaries? The enthusiasts of cyborgs, artificial intelligence and immortality through cryonic suspension seem confident that we are indeed unique in this respect. They're so concerned with self-assertion that it never occurs to them that acceptance of limits may actually amplify serenity and joy.

Limits imposed by Heaven and Earth are also a central theme in Daoist thought, and understanding these limits is likewise a key condition for a fulfilling life. As the *Laozi* puts it:

> Violent winds do not last a whole morning,
> Torrential rains do not last an entire day.

There are rhythms to the ways of the natural world: when we act and move in accord with them, we do better than if we ignore or flout them.

> If even Heaven and Earth cannot go on forever,
> How much less the human being.

It's important to know when to stop, and how much is enough: 'To withdraw when the work is done is the Way of Heaven.'[27] There's no point in trying to obstruct that withdrawing, and every reason to discern the directions it's tending in – because pushing against natural limits is not in our best interests in the long run.

Certain limits are manifested in the cyclical reversions that condition natural processes, whereby the forces of light or heat or dryness increase to an extreme, and then revert and give way to the forces of dark or cold or wetness, which in turn increase to an extreme – and so the cycle continues.

| Yang | YANG | Yin | YIN |
| Spring | Summer | Autumn | Winter |

Working as the polarities of yang and yin, the interactions of Heaven and Earth produce the four seasons. If we imagine the white (yang) and black (yin) components cycling clockwise in the figure above, this represents the progressions of the forces of sun and shade, light and dark, heat and cold, dry and wet through the four seasons. The yang energies come into ascendance with the beginning of spring, reaching their maximum in midsummer; then the forces of yin take over, and prevail through autumn so as to predominate in mid-winter.

The changes also describe a simple sine wave: the yang beginning at the baseline in spring, ascending to a maximum in summer, reverting and descending – and so forth. The forces of yang never keep increasing indefinitely, nor do the forces of yin diminish forever: each side always reasserts itself, predominates, and recedes again, up and down, over and over.

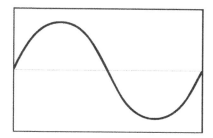

The climate sciences and paleoclimatology would agree that this is the way Heaven and Earth have been going so far: the geosphere has been in dynamic equilibrium since the beginning, with periods of 'hothouse earth' and 'snowball earth' alternating, and variable 'interglacial' periods in between. But now we humans have managed to upset the energy balance of the planet. Before we appeared, the most extreme swings could be destructive, causing mass extinctions, but it has never happened that one particular species is alone responsible for the damage. And why? Because we keep on overdoing it.

A well known line in the *Laozi* goes: 'Turning back is how the way moves.' Turning back, reversion, going around again in cycles. But human beings – unlike the rest of the myriad things – tend to lose the way; we go off on tangents and stride beyond the limits. By contrast, 'Knowing when to stop, one can be free from danger.'[28] Corresponding limits are germane to the *Zhuangzi*'s understanding of Heaven and its powers: 'Life and death are fated, and that they come with the regularity of day and night is from Heaven – that which humans can do nothing about, simply the way things are.'[29]

Heaven assigns years to every kind of thing, which may last out the allotment, or be cut short, eaten by some other creature – or else, as in the case of a tree that's good for lumber, cut down by humans and put to use. Our all-too-human assertiveness finds it hard to accept 'that which humans can do nothing about', because we can always think of some way to change it. This cleverness leads in turn to further problems, as another passage from *Zhuangzi* helpfully explains.

> The flow of my life is bound by its limits; the mind bent on knowledge, however, never is. If forced to follow something limited by no bounds, the bounded current of life is put in danger. And to meet this danger by enhancing knowledge even further – that merely exacerbates the danger.[30]

This passage could just as well be warning of the risks of too much Promethean spirit. As natural beings, our lives are limited by the bodies we receive and sustain from the powers of Heaven and Earth; but if we use our minds to pursue knowledge, we come to feel as if we're beyond limitations because we can envisage possibilities that transcend our physical capabilities. We can get so caught up in our thinking that we neglect what the body is telling us, and end up exhausting its energies. If we damage the life in us, it can be hard to heal – and it's the only one we get.

It's not just ancient Chinese science and Stoic physics that acknowledge limits: our contemporary natural sciences do so too. James Lovelock, for example, begins his answer to the question 'How does Gaia work?' by saying this: 'The key to understanding Gaia is to remember that it operates within a set of bounds or constraints.'[31] That's how the whole Earth System works. And while it may seem as if modern technology lets us push beyond natural limits, William Ophuls reminds us, in his fine book *Plato's Revenge*, of the price we're going to pay when our high rate of extinguishing other species jeopardizes our own existence.[32] Although scientists warn us of the consequences of the Sixth Mass Extinction of species other than the human, we go on destroying heedlessly, under the illusion of separateness, or separability, from natural phenomena.

There's a limit to the amount of human-generated carbon dioxide the atmosphere can absorb before the climate turns catastrophic. And there's a limit to what we can take from the bounty of the earth through industrialized agriculture, and especially factory farming. That's simply the way things go, and it's Promethean hubris to fight it. Limits to the continuous growth that capitalism requires are evident, as Ophuls shows, in the losses from converting the energy contained in fossil fuels into electricity: 'The challenge to exponential growth is exacerbated by the laws of thermodynamics, which operate as internal or systemic checks on continued economic growth and technological progress.'[33] But we may have already thrown off the Earth System's energy balance so much that such checks will be irrelevant. The ancient thinkers wouldn't have considered the human species capable of such a feat – but that doesn't mean that they were wrong about the consequences of transgressing the boundaries.

When Promethean technophiles insist that we can always develop cleverer technologies that will allow us to transcend natural limits, they are ignoring the lessons from Earth System Science. Johan Rockström, Will Steffen and their colleagues have identified nine 'planetary boundaries' that ensure a 'safe operating space for humanity'. Human activity is pushing the two 'core' ones, climate change and biosphere integrity (formerly 'biodiversity loss'), along with biochemical flows (of phosphorous and nitrogen) and land system change, toward tipping points beyond which the Earth System as a whole is destabilized. Push climate change or biosphere integrity too far – and either one can drop us into a new and distinctly inhospitable climatic regime.[34]

On top of that, they all interact: so if we push too hard on one, it's likely to tip over another and lead to a 'planetary cascade' of unpleasant consequences. The silver lining to this cloud is that when we take care of climate change and biosphere integrity at the same time, the benefits are mutually reinforcing, and with the other seven areas as well. To avoid catastrophe, we have to think along the lines of ESS and adopt a kind of 'planetary' thinking that will in turn let us thrive better under more constraining circumstances.

We ignore or disrespect natural limits, the boundaries of the Earth System, at our peril: they may teach us a painful lesson in humility. So why not learn the lesson beforehand? Just as our ancient philosophers found natural limitations to be something to celebrate, so William Ophuls salutes in the same spirit this teaching from natural science: 'Once we abandon our anthropocentric point of view, we can see limitation as a creative force that fosters *quality* instead of quantity. The life process responds to limited matter and energy by using them more efficiently.'[35] Living in accord with nature thus involves accommodating ourselves to natural limits, *and* finding joy in this as long as we're fitting in creatively.

And when you have respect for natural limits, you have a better sense of how much is enough.

A sense of sufficiency

Among the ancient Greek thinkers, the closest to the spirit of Laozi and Zhuangzi is Heraclitus 'the Obscure', who wrote these fine lines:

> It is not better for human beings to get all they want.
> It is disease that makes health sweet and good,
> hunger satiety, and weariness rest.[36]

It isn't better for human beings to get all they want? Why is it so hard for us to get this?

It has to do with the contrast effect: we tend to think that conditions like disease, hunger and weariness are bad, and need to be made better by replacing them with their opposites. But Heraclitus is pointing out (in the spirit of yin–yang thinking) that we find conditions such as health, satiety and rest pleasant only by *contrast* with their opposites. After a hard day's work there's nothing better, some would say, than kicking back with a cold beer. But if you spend most of your waking hours laying back with a series of cold beers, the pleasant effect soon diminishes. Or so I'm told.

On the same topic, Plato suggests there's something inherently self-defeating about dedicating your life to pursuing pleasure and avoiding pain. In the opening scene of the dialogue *Phaedo*, Socrates is released from his fetters. He rubs his ankles with relief and comments on the strange connection between pain and pleasure: 'If anybody pursues one of them and catches it, he's always pretty well bound to catch the other as well, as if the two of them were attached to a single head.'[37] It's the sine wave again. Suffering the pain of the fetters around his ankles, Socrates was down in the trough of the wave, and this lowered the baseline in such a way that when the cause of the pain was removed, he experienced the mere absence of pain as pleasure. After all, he didn't have anything else to be pleased about, for he would soon have to drink the hemlock.

When you're recovering from a bad case of influenza, and the symptoms finally subside, simply *not* to be aching in every part of the body feels wonderful. In the case of something like heroin addiction, the huge high raises the baseline, so that when you come down, the 'normal' condition is experienced as painful. If you dedicate your life to pursuing heightened highs, you'd better be prepared for some depressed lows as well. The Stoics and Epicureans, like the Daoists in China, suggest ways of escaping from the pleasure-pain cycle and attaining a joy, a contentment with life, that's on a different level.

The Epicureans regard knowing how much is enough as 'the greatest freedom', since you're then not enslaved by cravings for more. Here is Epicurus, eloquently explaining in a letter to a friend how this works:

> We regard self-sufficiency as a great good, not so that we may enjoy only a few things, but so that, if we do not have many, we may be satisfied with the few, being firmly persuaded that they take the greatest pleasure in luxury who regard it as least needed, and that everything that is natural is easily provided, while vain pleasures are hard to obtain.

It's by no means a matter of austerity, or asceticism, for its own sake, but of adjusting one's desires to broader circumstances and to the longer term of a whole life.

> To be accustomed to simple and plain living is conducive to health and makes a man ready for the necessary tasks of life. It also makes us more ready for the enjoyment of luxury if at intervals we chance to meet with it, and it renders us fearless of fortune.[38]

I have to admit that my very few brushes with luxury have been most enjoyable – and to become 'fearless of fortune' sounds better still.

Again, it's a matter of living in accord with nature: 'We obey nature if we satisfy the necessary desires and also those natural, physical desires that do not harm us, while sternly rejecting those that are harmful.' The necessary desires relieve pain – the desire for drink when you're thirsty, or for food when hungry. And because the desires that might harm us arise 'from idle imagination', Epicurus thinks they are 'easily dispelled'.[39]

Like the Buddha, who recommended a Middle Way between indulgence and asceticism, Epicurus warns against taking austerity too far: 'Frugality too has a limit, and the man who disregards it is in like case with him who errs through excess.'[40] Now here's a nice twist to the teaching of moderation. I'm sure my father never read a word of Epicurus, but his maxim was more than Epicurean: 'Moderation in all things,' he used to say, '– and *especially* in moderation.' It wouldn't do at all to be excessively moderate.

Turning to Confucian culture again, we find that the central practice of ritual propriety (discussed in the previous chapter) can involve considerable expense. However, Confucius himself said that expense should be spared when appropriate, and in general the Confucians recommend a dignified frugality, and regard riches and extravagance with suspicion.[41]

The Daoists are more vocal in their opposition to greed and in their promotion of moderation. The *Laozi* lays it out clearly:

Of crimes, none is greater than indulging desires;
Of disasters, none is greater than overlooking satisfaction;
Of calamities, none is greater than desiring to acquire.
Thus, for satisfaction, knowing how much is enough suffices.[42]

Because capitalism depends on constant growth, consumerism ignores the issue of sufficiency and encourages continuous consumption and indulging of desires. It's no surprise that those free libertarians who run the capitalist system, as well as the governments they've bought, do the opposite of what happens in the realm of Heaven and Earth.

It is the Way of Heaven to take from what has in excess in order to make good what is deficient. The Way of the Human is otherwise. It takes from those who are in want in order to offer it to those who already have more than enough.

The human is often perverse like this – think of all those 'advanced' societies where economic inequality is accelerating.

What the super-free humans overlook is the tendency toward reversion or turning back at the end of a cycle. The *Laozi* again:

Excessive meanness is sure to lead to great expense;
Too much storing is sure to end in immense loss.
Know contentment and you will suffer no disgrace;
Know when to stop, and you will meet with no danger.

The *Laozi* is remarkable for the way it seems to anticipate the drawbacks of consumerism, as in this sage advice offered to the ruler:

Not to value goods that are hard to come by
will keep the people from theft;
Not to display what is desirable
will keep them from being unsettled of mind.[43]

High crime rates in capitalist societies derive from people's valuing goods that are hard to come by for those without enough money. Consumerism depends for its success on advertising that displays as desirable goods that are in fact unnecessary – which renders people so unsettled of mind that they buy them anyway. And even once they've bought them they remain unsettled of mind, and so throw themselves into further getting and spending (which Wordsworth warned would 'lay waste our powers').[44]

The dangers in wanting to be rich are often highlighted in the New Testament, and especially by Paul the Apostle. He warns against associating with 'men of corrupt minds' who suppose that 'gain is godliness' – whereas in truth 'godliness with contentment is great gain'.

For we brought nothing into this world, and it is certain we can carry nothing out. And having food and raiment let us be therewith content. But they that will be rich fall into temptation and a snare, and into many foolish and hurtful lusts, which drown men in destruction and perdition. . . . For the love of money is the root of all evil.[45]

What's the point anyway, if 'we can carry nothing out' with us?

So if you live in the developed world, and you're confronted with the latest, irresistible product of super-capitalism, you can always consider at least

Nine Reasons Not to Buy It.

1   You save money, in the amount of the purchase price.
2   You don't have to maintain it, or repair it if it breaks.
3   No need to protect against theft, insure it or in any way secure it.
4   You never have to bother with storing it or moving it.
5   If you don't own it, you can't lose it, or waste time looking for it.
6   There's no need to dispose of it, or take the trouble to recycle it.
    And when the Grim Reaper comes to tell you it's time to go

7   You can't take it with you – so there's no need to pack it.

And since you can't possibly bequeath it if you don't own it

8   Your heirs can never squabble over it.

Finally:

9   If you don't buy it, and enough other people are persuaded they don't need it either, they'll eventually have to stop making it!

This will save natural resources and reduce pollution, and as long as we help the people who were making it find a better line of work, everyone will benefit – especially once we all get used to not having or needing as much. Then we won't need to bring down global capitalism: it will gradually implode and collapse.

Sources of fulfilment

When it comes to saving natural resources, more frugality doesn't have to mean less enjoyment. There are many energy-squandering indulgences – solo car-driving, for example – that we can moderate without incurring misery. But let me take excess illumination as just one example where cutting down leads to unforeseen benefits. If you look at maps of light pollution worldwide (easily accessible on the Internet), you see it's the global North that's lit up – like a forest of garish Christmas trees. Toning down those extravagant lighting practices would save energy and money, and open up new realms of experience for city dwellers. Yes, the night lights of Manhattan, or Shinjuku in Tokyo, or Lujiazui in Shanghai are impressive – but they come with a cost: they obstruct a sight that promotes sanity by showing us our place in the world, a source of wonder that our modern technology conceals.

We get so used to light pollution in cities that we don't realize how much it blunts our sense of where we live – on Earth under Heaven. When the earth blocks the sun's light, we have a dark backdrop against which we often see nothing but opaque haze. But if we get out of the artificial brightness, we can finally behold the firmament in all its glory, the Milky Way and innumerable other stars in our galaxy. Only a few generations ago, our ancestors lived in frequent contact with the glories of the night sky.

Who knows how early humans perceived that phenomenon, and what images from myth and folklore conditioned their perceptions? A common idea was that the night sky is an opaque dome blocking the brightness of the heavens, but with innumerable tiny holes in it, (stars) through which the brightness can shine. And in the constellations they saw various figures: rams, bulls, archers, water carriers and so forth.

For us moderns, a clear view of the night sky occasions a different experience – thanks to what we *know* about what we're seeing. The most distant entity visible to the naked eye is the nearest major galaxy to ours (which includes the Milky Way), the Andromeda Galaxy. It's not that near, at a distance of some 2.4 million light years (one light year is 9.46 trillion kilometres).[46] So when we see Andromeda in the night sky, we know that the light entering our eyes, although it's travelling faster than we can imagine, has taken almost two-and-a-half million years to reach them. What is more, or less: some of the stars we see have probably exploded already, and so no longer exist.

Contemplation of the night sky gives us a sane sense of proportion and perspective on our existence – a sane sense because so many of our problems stem from our obsession with bigness and the gigantic. Yes, it's impressive that we can know that we're seeing a galaxy that's very, very far away – but that sight can also impress upon us the smallness of human existence. Pascal found 'the eternal silence of those infinite spaces' frightening, but it doesn't have to be if we drop our individualism and regain a sense of our interactivity.[47]

Coming down to earth, there are further benefits to limiting our energy indulgence in over-illumination. I happened to be teaching a seminar in Tokyo not long after the Fukushima Daiichi nuclear disaster in 2011. On our first evening there, my wife and I found her home city transformed: because other nuclear power plants had been shut down, the authorities had mandated an austere energy-saving regime. Much of the city's neon lighting in commercial districts was off or muted, while buses and taxis turned off their engines when waiting at traffic lights or in stalled jams. But the most striking change was the dimmer light in the acres of subway stations linked to underground shopping precincts by broad tunnels and walkways.

Before, the neon lighting used to blaze at headache intensity everywhere, but now the underground places were mysterious in their restrained luminosity. The dimmer conditions seemed to incline people to pay more attention to where they were going, and to walk more slowly.

Altogether a mellower experience – enhanced by the knowledge that the lower lighting was taking a lesser toll on the atmosphere. And above ground as well, where the Spectacle plays out in huge neon displays announcing the latest products of consumer capitalism, it didn't seem as if people really missed all that. (Does anyone living in a place that banned billboards actually miss them?) In any case, the aesthetic improvement came along with savings in energy expenditure – demonstrating that reduction of GHG emissions from the lighting sector can be achieved quickly when necessary.

When capitalism goes global, it becomes incompatible with the basis on which it depends for its growth: a planet that's finite. And when viewed from a broad perspective that includes the other species and natural phenomena with whom we share the geosphere, the capitalist enterprise has been disastrously destructive. We can't afford it any longer – we've run up against the limits – but in any case we don't need it. The wisdom of the ancients that we've considered – and indeed many great thinkers from Plato to Nietzsche – would regard the whole system as inimical to human flourishing and based on a false understanding of what makes for a fulfilled human life.

Once our basic needs are satisfied, it isn't hard to lead fulfilling lives even in the absence of sources of meaning beyond this world – as long as we pay attention to our social and cultural interactions as well as the world of nature. The problem in the developed world is that urbanization and industrialization restrict our access to natural phenomena, and so many people screen themselves from contact with what's actual by staying focused on their smartphones and surrounding themselves with consumer goods (sold to them mostly by the advertising on their phones).

What high consumers are missing isn't just the beauty of the natural world, but also its beneficial effects on human health. Japanese researchers have determined that getting out into the woods (they call it 'forest bathing') vitalizes the human body, and especially the immune system, because trees and surrounding plants emit organic compounds called 'phytoncides' which boost the body's 'natural killer cells', which in turn fight infections and tumours.[48] This is no surprise, since the human body evolved from and in the world of nature.

The great biologist E. O. Wilson has written of the human urge 'to affiliate with other forms of life', calling it 'biophilia', love of what is alive. He comes close to the insights of the Daoists when he writes: 'We are human in good part because of the particular way we affiliate with other organisms. They are the matrix in which the human mind originated and is permanently rooted.'[49] The Daoists would broaden the field of consideration beyond the living to include the inorganic realm, the world of rocks and waters, and the Buddhists, too, would find mind there as well.

Accessible joys of nature range from appreciating a leaf or flower in a city park to contemplating the wonders revealed to us by the natural sciences, from geology to oceanography, from botany to zoology. Many cities have parks and libraries, botanical gardens and college campuses, which afford their citizens access to accounts and experience of the wondrous processes that sustain our existence – and mostly free of charge. Let me give an example, from an autumn morning when I was living in Ireland.

I was returning to my office on campus from having given a lecture to a large class of first-year students. The topic had been the experience of enlightenment in Zen Buddhism, which is 'nothing special' but simply an awakening to the reality of the present moment, an awareness of what is going on right here and right now, as well as in the broader context of time and place.[50] I was climbing a flight of stone steps flanked by a variety of deciduous trees. It had been raining, but now the sun was shining. I stopped to look at a step a few higher than the one my front foot was on – and all of a sudden: one of those experiences when, in Emerson's words, 'the world reaches its perfection'.[51] The step in question was covered with leaves of many kinds and autumn colours, all glistening in the sunlight. The beauty was riveting, and rooted me to the spot. The more I looked, the more perfect the scene before my feet appeared.

It wasn't just that the shape of each leaf was just right in its difference from the others, but that each particular leaf – whether overlapping, overlapped or adjacent – was in the perfect place in relation to the leaves around it. And the harmony of the different colours, all enhanced by the rain residue that coated every leaf surface, provided an intenser joy. The various forms of wonder intermingled delightfully.

How long I stood there gazing at the leaves and basking in such a sensuous scene, I don't know. (Should I mention I had ingested nothing stronger than coffee that morning?) But at some point I began thinking, and wishing I'd had my camera with me because the composition – or self-composition – of that rectangle of leaves was so artistic that I wanted to capture an image to show to others. (Never having used Instagram,

I was envisaging a photographic print.) After all, many of the thinkers we've been considering in this book – Plato, Zhuangzi, Nietzsche et al. – consider nature, or heaven and earth, to be the original, greatest artist, on whom all human artistry depends.

But then I thought, No, better not to let technology intrude, so that I can pay undivided attention to what's actually going on here, and if appropriate tell my friends (which I've done) and perhaps write about it (which I'm now doing). Eventually I raised my gaze to the next leaf-covered step and noticed that, though the arrangement of the leaves was of course different, the scene looked as perfect as the one I had just spent so long contemplating. But my office hours were about to start, and so I had to climb the remaining steps without stopping to look any further. I suspect that many of those steps would have been worth contemplating as frames for images produced by the Earth's central life.

The weather in the days that followed stayed more or less the same, mainly sunny but with occasional showers to dampen the still falling leaves. I made a point of looking out for areas of leaf-covered ground – and saw many perfect leaf tableaux. The autopoiesis of the Earth System; spontaneous creation at its most aesthetic. This kind of thing is happening all around us, in all seasons; we just have to pay attention, or else we miss it – because these moments, like all moments, are ephemeral. As Nietzsche once remarked: 'The world is overfull with beautiful things, but nonetheless poor, very poor, in beautiful moments and revelations of these things.'[52]

As natural beings, bodies that evolved over millennia of interaction between Heaven and Earth, we fail to flourish if we artificially insulate ourselves from such interaction. And if we cultivate sympathetic resonance with things, we can then engage and contribute to the ongoing processes. Then it won't matter that the opportunity to indulge in consumerism has passed away, because a proper sense of sufficiency can generate genuine *joy* in living.

A Good Life with Congenial Things

A large part of the problem, in the developed countries, is our dysfunctional relationship with *things*. Our relations with our fellow humans, and with the animals and plants that we eat or whose habitats we destroy, are fraught enough, but our attitude toward what we call inanimate or non-living things, things we buy and own and use, is even worse. Since the Scientific Revolution of the seventeenth century, when the Cartesian thinkers separated matter and mind, and acknowledged soul in humans alone, we've lived in a soulless world, amidst things made of inanimate matter, in a dead space containing lifeless atoms. If we think about how we produce and consume things in the context of the climate crisis, it becomes clear that we need to change our ways. If we can befriend things, and so treat them better, we'll discover saner ways of living that don't imperil our existence.

The central life of Earth

We live our lives symbiotically, not only with other living beings, from animals and plants down to bacteria and other microbes, but also, through the interactions of the various Earth Systems, with the life of Earth itself – with what Henry David Thoreau called the 'great central life' of Earth. As well as being one of our more poetical thinkers, Thoreau was a keen observer of the natural world and made some contributions to botanical science. But at the same time he subscribed to the ancient idea of the world as 'a living being', as shown in this passage from his masterpiece *Walden* (1854).

> The earth is not a mere fragment of dead history, stratum upon stratum like the leaves of a book, to be studied by geologists and antiquaries chiefly, but living poetry like the leaves of a tree, which precede flowers

and fruit – not a fossil earth, but a living earth; compared with whose great central life all animal and vegetable life is merely parasitic.[1]

Together with his mentor Emerson, Thoreau offered a philosophical and poetical account of the ways of nature which set the stage for the ecosystem science that eventually followed. This in turn tries to understand the life of the earth by tracking flows of energy through 'food webs' and other systems from the perspectives of biology, organic chemistry and related sciences.

A later pioneer in this field was the American ecologist Aldo Leopold, who was an expert in forestry and a scientist of wildlife, an eloquent essayist and also something of a philosopher. His account of natural ecosystems presents nature in terms that a Chinese philosopher of *qi* energies would understand. 'Land is not merely soil', he wrote: 'it is *a fountain of energy flowing through a circuit of soils, plants, and animals.* Food chains are the living channels which conduct energy upward; death and decay return it to the soil.' The eventual sink for the energy fountain is the ocean, and the gradual 'net loss by downhill wash' is counteracted over the long term by volcanic and tectonic activity that raises the earth up again to the beginning of a new down-cycle.[2]

On the basis of all this interactivity, Leopold recommends that we think of ourselves as 'members of a community of interdependent parts', and that we 'enlarge the boundaries of the community to include soils, waters, plants, and animals, or collectively: the land.' Ethics traditionally deals with interactions among people, as suggested by the need to say 'animal ethics' if you want a broader understanding. But Leopold proposes a 'land ethic' that obliges human beings as citizens of the land community to have 'respect for fellow-members, and also respect for the community as such'.[3] For a natural scientist in the mid-twentieth century to encourage extending our respect for life to the earth itself is rather unusual.

It's natural, Leopold writes, for the Earth's energy systems to change over time, but 'man's invention of tools has enabled him to make changes of unprecedented violence, rapidity, and scope'. The biosphere is 'like a slowly augmented revolving fund of life', but intensive agriculture 'makes overdrafts on the soil', and in the longer term these 'derange the channels of flow or deplete storage'. The violence of human activity threatens 'the integrity, stability, and beauty of the biotic community', because the denser the human population the more violence it inflicts, and the greater the eventual 'penalties' in the form of a 'reduced carrying capacity' of the land we live on and from. The restoration of fertile soil is a slow process that takes centuries, and the lesson of ecology is that there are limits to the Earth's carrying capacity: 'Ecology knows of no density relationship that holds for indefinitely wide limits. All gains from density are subject to a law of diminishing returns.'4 We've heard this message before: it's high time to begin heeding it.

Overall, Leopold recommended 'thinking like a mountain', which is the title of one of his briefest essays. Thinking like a mountain means not only thinking over long time frames so that we avoid making short-sighted decisions, but also thinking holistically in a way that's sensitive to the relevant interconnections. Hunters kill wolves so that there will be more deer to hunt, but with too many deer the mountain loses its cover of vegetation – and this can take decades to regenerate.5 And that's nothing, as we saw, compared to the time the atmosphere and oceans will take to recover. [9.1]

Robust though Earth's central life may be, as humans developed ever more powerful technologies it began to suffer damage from human violence. In response, the land ethic would affirm – on the part of soil, water, plants and animals – 'their right to continued existence, and, at least in spots, their continued existence in a natural state'. As members of the biotic community, we have to let other members thrive in the ways they're accustomed to. It's all very Daoist, and in fact Daoism provides helpful guidance on keeping the technology in check, offering suggestions that Leopold would have applauded.

Guidelines for technology

If we consider from the perspective of Chinese thought the damage our unwise use of fossil fuel and other technologies is doing to the central life of Earth, we discover some ways to mitigate the harm. In a world of qi energies, the question is whether a particular human activity harmonizes with the sympathetic resonances that prevail naturally or else disrupts them; whether it's aligned with the ebbs and flows of energy or else blocks them. This isn't a universal rule that dictates which technologies should or shouldn't be deployed, nor a criterion for distinguishing 'good' technologies from 'bad': it simply suggests some guidelines or rules of thumb.

Imagine arranging various kinds of technology along a continuum from non-disruptive at one end to deeply invasive at the other. The former work by following, or integrating themselves into, natural processes, while the latter instrumentally impose human will onto natural processes in order to push them beyond their limits. At the non-disruptive end would be things like windmills, sailboats, watermills, wind turbines: constructions that make use of the natural forces of wind, water and gravity without abusing or using them up. When a sailor, for example, positions her boat so that the wind fills its sails, this in no way reduces the amount of wind available for other boats nearby. Toward the invasive end of the continuum we'd have set-ups like the nuclear power plant and equipment for producing genetically modified organisms, which penetrate to the core of matter and life, and monkey around with the innermost physical and biological processes.

Although uranium occurs and degrades naturally, the reaction that powers nuclear plants can only be achieved through highly complex technical procedures, and the radioactive waste they produce is difficult to deal with, expensive to store, and remains dangerous for a very long time. The aftermath is unnaturally protracted. The problem with genetically modifying organisms lies in the possibility of their escaping into the wild, such that our modifications wreak havoc on natural ecosystems – with potentially worse consequences than we've managed to bring about already with invasive species. A Daoist rule of thumb would suggest that the closer to the *non*-disruptive pole the technology, the more likely it is to enhance human existence and the flourishing of the geosphere in the long run – and the farther away, the riskier things become.

The ancient Chinese thinkers thought about the central life of Earth on the analogy of the living human body, and the practical art and science of feng shui is based on the premise that the *qi* energies of the earth are concentrated in 'veins', or channels, which correspond to the body's vascular system. According to traditional Chinese medicine (TCM), illness results from a blockage in the body's energy flow, or from an imbalance between the forces of yin and yang. As it goes in the microcosm, so it goes in the macrocosm and its various systems: gross *imbalances* and obstructive *blockages* in the central life of Earth have unpleasant consequences.

This book is a response to the problems that result when our emissions of heat-trapping gases from burning fossil fuels block the solar radiation that bounces off the surface of the earth and prevent the heat from dissipating into space – a clear case of blocking the energy flow. The consequent imbalance in the Earth System, as James Lovelock keeps telling us, is making the Earth sick. 'Humans on the Earth behave in some ways like a pathogenic microorganism. We have grown in numbers and in disturbance to Gaia, to the point where our presence is perceptibly disabling, like a disease.' Don't we see in rising temperatures the signs of terrestrial fever? Don't we worry that Earth's body might destroy 'the invading disease organisms'?[6]

When it's pointed out that we need to stop burning oil if we're to avoid frying the planet, some people respond that there are other useful things we can get from petrochemicals: *plastics*, for example. Whereas GHGs do their blocking high up in the atmosphere, invisibly, petrochemicals as plastics work their magic on the ground, and in the oceans. They are proving almost as deadly to the life of the earth as fossil fuel burning, thanks to their ability to block the 'fountain of energy flowing through soils, plants, and animals'. They are symptoms of global illness, human distractedness and our deeply dysfunctional relationship with things.

The first synthetic plastic was invented in England in 1856. It was called 'Parkesine', after its inventor, Alexander Parkes (who I fear may be a distant relative). Of course, plastics have brought us many benefits – the demand for ivory went down after high-quality plastic became available – but along with many problems stemming from our careless use and disposal of them.

Recent research has discovered this depressing circumstance: 'the dramatic rise of produced plastics, from the less than 2 million tonnes manufactured in 1950 to the 300 million tonnes made annually today. The cumulative amount produced as of 2015 is of the order of 5 billion tons, which is enough to wrap the Earth in a layer of cling film, or plastic wrap.' By the year 2050, on current trends, the researchers project 40 billion tons annually – enough to plastic-wrap the globe many times over.[7] The image is apt: by smothering the planet in plastic, we're stifling the diversity of its life.

It's marvellous that twentieth-century technology can produce synthetic materials that never existed in nature, but their potential for disruption can be lethal. When something non-biodegradable like plastic is introduced in large quantities, it can't be food for anything else and so stays in the system, blocking the flow, for an unusually long time. To make matters worse, as plastics degrade, they release toxic substances – over a period of several centuries (!) in the case of plastic bottles.[8]

Plastic waste is lethal for many of the animal species with which we share the planet – especially sea creatures, because there's so much plastic in the oceans. Yet plastic production increases relentlessly, and the deadly debris continues to accumulate. There are micro-particles of plastic everywhere, including in the stomachs of whales, fish and sea-birds – and of many people who eat seafood. Projections of plastic production predict a steady increase, which will wreak further havoc on ecosystems around the globe. We know very little about the long-term effects of so much plastic in the environment on our own health, but they probably aren't that good.

If we step back to consider the *ideas* behind this dismal state of affairs, we find a view of the physical world as mostly lifeless. This worldview regards animals as lacking soul or personality, vegetation such as grass, flowers and trees as lacking awareness, and 'inanimate' things such as rocks or tools as lacking any kind of life. Such things are to be used and manipulated for our own purposes, and cared for only insofar as they're useful to us. However, evident as this may seem to us moderns, regarded historically it's a recent and rather unusual way of viewing things.

The presumption of animism

We saw earlier that Platonic cosmology understands the whole world as 'a truly living thing, endowed with soul and intelligence', and as animated throughout by what the Neoplatonic tradition would later call the 'world soul', or *anima mundi*.[9] Indeed a couple of centuries before Plato the first philosopher of the Western tradition, Thales of Miletus, is believed to have said 'the whole world is ensouled', and to have ascribed soul to what we would call 'inanimate' things – in part because 'the Magnesian stone and amber' are able to move iron.[10]

Around the same time another, quite different, idea of the human soul emerged in Greek culture, deriving from shamanism and what has been called the 'Orphic-Pythagorean' tradition. On this view the human soul exists prior to the body (is even 'eternal' and thus infinitely more 'real'), and the body is its 'tomb', a prison from which it is finally released at death.[11] Christian philosophy would later develop a corresponding version of this dualism, which regarded the body as fallen and a site of sin, and the soul as a candidate for salvation.

Western philosophy took an extraordinary turn when the Cartesian thinkers 'de-souled' the physical world (*res extensa*, 'extended stuff'), denying soul even to animals, in spite of their name (*anima* = *psychē* = soul). They affirmed that only human beings, as thinking things (*res cogitans*), are ensouled. The physical world became inanimate, dead matter in motion, machine-like, an enormous mechanism. Dualism taken to the extreme.

This way of thinking had become mainstream by the nineteenth century, when Western anthropologists studying so-called 'primitive' cultures started wondering how their subjects experienced the world. So when the pioneer of cultural anthropology E. B. Tylor introduced the term 'animism' in his monumental classic *Primitive Culture* (1871), he applied it in a special sense to 'savages and barbarians', who are strongly inclined to 'personify' things and regard 'inanimate objects' as having souls. From Tylor's post-Cartesian perspective, which understands material objects as lifeless, if 'primitives' experience the world as alive with 'personal souls' and 'spiritual beings' inhabiting natural phenomena, they must be unconsciously projecting features of their own psychic lives onto the inanimate world around them.[12]

But this sense of 'animism' – soul projected onto material things by primitive minds – refers to a remarkably recent notion (just a few hundred years old). Indeed it's only when you get the parochial (northern Europe) and peculiar idea (never occurred to the Chinese) of Cartesian 'mind-matter' dualism that you even *need* a word like 'animism'. For most people during most of human history, the world has naturally presented itself as animated, or ensouled, from the start. Animism is a modern – and typically condescending – presumption.[13]

Bruno Latour questions this presumption from a different perspective, but with similar effect, with his idea that insofar as 'mute' and 'inanimate' things are embedded in the same relational networks as we humans are, they have a voice and are also actors in the sense of 'actants, acting agents, interveners'.[14] There's no space, sadly, for discussion of this idea here – except to say that in spite of Latour's different understanding of the nature of nature, his relational thinking has deep affinities with the East Asian philosophical perspective on the presumption of animism.

Now that the environmentally devastating consequences of the modern scientific worldview are becoming obvious, we are retreating from the extreme view that only humans are ensouled. Nevertheless, while Western advocates of biophilia and deep ecology extend their concern to all living things, they tend to get stuck at the stage of 'biocentrism', failing to go all the way and include the mineral realm of rocks and mountains – and from there also things of use and other artefacts. As James Lovelock wrote: 'To ameliorate the fix we are now in over global change requires us to know the true nature of the Earth and imagine it as the largest living thing in the solar system, not something inanimate like that disreputable contraption "spaceship Earth"'.[15]

Are we in any case so sure that 'inanimate' things are lifeless? Or is there some basis for the feeling that a high-tech gadget like a laptop computer can seem to pick up on our moods? (Especially surprising to me since they're now all electronic rather than mechanical: no moving parts.) When we shout at a tool that breaks at the worst possible moment, usually due to our own carelessness, even though we may seem to be regressing to a primitive belief system, aren't we actually responding to some kind of 'will' or 'intention' that we experience in the thing? After all, if we revert to the sophisticated philosophical tradition that developed in China, we find that the distinction between animate and inanimate is relatively irrelevant in a tradition that understands the world as a field of vital energies.

Careful attention to interactions with *things* was central to the Confucian way of life that prevailed in China for well over two thousand years. When the Confucians promoted ritual propriety as a way of enhancing social harmony, this required a careful cultivation of one's interactions with things as well as persons. Not only must one's garments be appropriate to the occasion, but also how one wears them: you have to pay close attention to the angle of the hat, the sweep of the sleeve. And special care is required when handling ritual implements – and, by extension, all other things that we use.

The Daoist thinkers recommended moving beyond anthropocentrism by extending Confucian practices of reciprocity – putting oneself in the other person's position – to animals and plants *and* the rest of the myriad things as well. The aim for the Daoists is to attune their energies to the whole field of *qi*, and the *Zhuangzi* presents as exemplary practices an expert craftsman's interaction with tools and materials, which at its acme results in an an almost supernatural or 'spirit-like' outcome.[16]

A well known story in the *Zhuangzi* ascribes the consummate skill of a butcher to his contact with the realm of spirit – in the sense of the 'daemonic', as the realm between humans and gods. After many years of cutting up oxen, he no longer perceives the carcass with his senses but rather handles it through spirit, at a level beneath conscious experience where he can intuit the natural 'energetic' structure of the matter at hand. In short, he's carving on the basis of 'sympathetic resonance' with the ox carcasses – such that after nineteen years of use, his cleaver is still 'as sharp as if it had just come off the whetstone'.

If we can 'get the *qi*' of things, as the Daoists say, and understand ourselves as being 'one body' with natural and human-made things, this will transform our experience – and thereby our interactions with the world. If by contrast we regard things as absolutely 'other' than ourselves, we tend to produce too many of them, lose respect for them, and let the excess as rubbish destroy natural ecosystems. But what if we were to *drop* the presumption of animism, and 'bracket' our assumption that the things around us are merely inanimate? That could enhance not only our experience but also the condition of the world around us.

To get a better idea of the *qi* of things let's begin not with artefacts, which we might expect to absorb something of human vitality in the process of being made, but with things at the opposite end of the traditional 'animateness' scale from us – namely, rocks. Rock and stone figure prominently in the art of *fengshui* (understood as practical environmental science, rather than as an expensive way of learning how to arrange the furniture in your Hollywood mansion). Basically feng shui – literally, 'winds and waters' – is a science that maps patterns of *qi* energy in various landscapes, and the associated art of integrating human constructions and activities with those energy patterns. Feng shui thus played a key role in the development of *garden* making in China, and later in Japan: an activity that constructs a landscape in microcosm for the purpose of vitalizing the activities of people inhabiting the place.

Regarded as a field of energies within the earth, rocks are revered as concentrated 'kernels' of *qi* energy, and so they generally constitute the framework and focal points of East Asian gardens. By contrast with the French formal garden, where a preconceived plan in the mind of the landscape architect is imposed upon the site (think of the gardens of Versailles), the Chinese garden is built *in response to* the natural setting. Insofar as the Chinese tradition reveres nature as 'the greatest of all artists', the human artist will follow 'the natural processes of making and transforming', taking these creative processes 'as his master and teacher'.[17] Then it's more a matter of letting a garden take shape than of deliberately constructing it, and of responding to and working with the rocks rather than dictating where they belong.

In suggesting a different approach to things, let me go beyond China to a development of Chinese Buddhism in Japan – namely Zen – since it provides more accessible examples of closer relations.

The Zen of befriending things

As with gardens in China, the Japanese garden derives from the maker's response to the place and to the rocks that have been brought there – with the additional consideration that the maker keep in mind the country's most renowned landscapes as well as the work of past masters of garden making.

The world's first manual on this topic, *Notes on Making Gardens* (*Sakuteiki*) by a Japanese nobleman from the eleventh century, contains this instruction, to be followed after collecting the rocks that will establish the garden. 'Choose an especially splendid rock and set it as the principal rock. Then, following the request of this first rock, set others accordingly.... Then set the back rock, following the request of the first group of rocks.'[18] By paying attention to the presence of the principal rock and the feeling of the surrounding ground (what in the West is called the *genius loci*, the spirit of the place), the garden maker can learn where the other rocks need to be situated.

Some commentators dismiss the idea of following the request of the rock as a remnant of primitive animism, perhaps deriving from the indigenous Japanese religion of Shinto. But behind this practice is a history of highly sophisticated philosophy in Japan, which understands natural phenomena as spontaneously expressing themselves in sound and signs. Influenced by Indian as well as Chinese Buddhism, the ninth-century thinker Kūkai wrote that all things are constantly 'expounding the Buddhist teachings'.

> Being painted by brushes of mountains, by ink of oceans,
> Heaven and Earth are the bindings of a sutra revealing the Truth.

Not only do things expound the teachings orally and audibly, but they also express themselves through inscriptions, and even in scripture (sutra, in Buddhism).

We find a similar idea in the thirteenth-century Zen master Dōgen, whose influences include Zhuangzi as well Chan Buddhist thinkers. Dōgen talked of the power of 'voices of the river valleys' to enlighten poets, and gave a presentation to his students with the title 'Mountains and Waters as a Sutra', which encouraged them to see landscape as a kind of scripture, manifesting the Buddhist teachings.[19] (The equivalent to 'landscape' in Chinese and Japanese is 'mountains waters'.)

We should not expect, both thinkers say, that what we regard as non-sentient things will express themselves by speaking or writing anything like a human language. Think rather of the sounds of the wind or waves, or the way striations on rocks or tree bark patterns can appear meaningful. In order to appreciate the meaning of such natural expressions, Dōgen says, we have to 'slip out of our old skin, and not be constrained by past views', because 'conditioned views' are like 'looking through a bamboo pipe at a corner of the sky'.[20] We need, and can attain, a new and broader perspective if we're to appreciate the fullness of existence and find the things around us truly familiar.

As far as *things of use* are concerned, Dōgen encouraged the monks who worked in temple kitchens to use the polite forms of the Japanese language when referring to the materials of their craft: 'Use honorific forms of verbs for describing how to handle rice, vegetables, salt, and soy sauce; do not use plain language for this.'[21] He also stressed the importance of treating the kitchen utensils as well as the ingredients with careful attention, which involves knowing where in the kitchen they belong, getting acquainted with their 'home ground'.

Dōgen tells the monks who work there: 'Put what is suited to a high place in a high place, and what belongs in a low place in a low place. Those things in a high place will be settled there; those suited to a low place will be settled there.'[22] This is the key point: in a well-ordered kitchen the order doesn't derive from a plan in the head of the cook, but rather from our paying attention to suitabilities suggested by the things themselves. This allows us to situate the utensils so they're 'settled' there, and thus less likely to fall down or get damaged.

When it comes to cooking, Dōgen calls the creative handling of utensils and ingredients 'turning things while being turned by things'.[23] We need a sense both for how things are turning so that we can align ourselves aright, *and* for how our turning is in turn affecting what is going on. Optimally, through it all, there's an unforced interplay among hands, implements and ingredients. All in all, a rather sane approach to working in the kitchen – one that's to be generalized to all things and activities. In zazen meditation practice you bow to your cushion before and after the sitting, as an expression of respect. Also as a sign of gratitude for the support the cushion gives you, literally, in your practice.

After the cooking, there's always the cleaning-up. If we wanted to make this kind of activity into a chore, we could – simply by framing it in terms of means-to-ends: I need to keep the kitchen tidy *in order to* cook and eat efficiently, *so as to* make time for the really important stuff (whatever that may be). The way we so often structure our experience and activities, distinguishing the fulfilling ends we aim for from the burdensome chores we have to discharge in order to achieve our goals, condemns us to a great deal of drudgery. Of course we need *some* means–ends thinking in order to survive: but beyond that, if we free things from enslavement to our purposes, we find our engagement with them is much enhanced.

The *Tassajara Cooking* book, which I mentioned in the Introduction, begins with a section called 'The Knife', in which the author discusses how to care for kitchen knives, how to sharpen them and how to use them. Preparing food is easier and more pleasurable if your knives are sharp, and a sharp knife is an implement you definitely want to stay on good terms with. The book ends with a section called 'Good Friends', which discusses the benefits that flow from befriending everything in the kitchen, including the ingredients you bring into it and the other people who may work there.

Here's an example concerning a room other than the kitchen. Some years ago my wife and I were living in Japan, which meant that every morning after getting up we had to remove the bedding from the tatami-matted floor and store it for the day on shelves behind sliding doors along one side of the room. We realized after a while that if we didn't want this first shared task of the day to be a chore, we could make it into something more like a dance. (It had been clear early in our marriage that we would never be the next Astaire and Rogers, but the field of putting away bedding is far less competitive.) That way we could refresh activities that would otherwise seem repetitive.

When folding the sheets, once you synchronize your actions with those of your fellow folder, the interplay becomes a joy to participate in. Attention to efficient body movements lets you avoid unnecessary exertion and postures that produce strain: then the motions flow easily and smoothly, and on a cold morning the exercise has a pleasantly warming and tonic effect. The enjoyment becomes richer as you learn to harmonize your movements not only with your partner's but also with the size and weight and texture of whatever you're folding, responding to the item of bedding as a third participant in the early morning dance.

What's interesting here is not just that the better ways to put away the bedding take less effort and use less energy: they also *feel* better as you perform the movements. (They probably look better, too, if anyone happens to be watching.) The optimal way would be distinguished not only the pleasure it affords the actors but also by the attendant style and grace.

In our dealings with larger things such as mattresses, there's sometimes a tendency, especially for men, to manhandle them: intent on our own goals, we misjudge the weights or pliabilities of things, and end up making one obstruct another, or even hurting ourselves with them. Violent language may then ensue, or even violent actions against things perceived as 'recalcitrant'. It's easy to forget that *they* are always innocent.

But with the futons, after a bit of attentive practice the process became more spontaneous: you lose the sense of performing the movements, and gain a feeling for the activity's unfolding from a centre that's somewhere *among* all the participants. You know where the futons, once folded, belong; and things go better if, instead of your having to heave them into place, you simply help them get to where they need to be – again as suggested by the things themselves.

It was easier to pay better attention to things during that stay in Japan because we lived with so few of them: the contents of a few suitcases and basic furnishings of a rented apartment. Life was simpler than usual. I thought of Thoreau, thinking he would appreciate the simplicity. After all, he went to live in the woods for a while because he 'wished to live deliberately, to front only the essential facts of life', and he realized that would be easier if he could make a temporary escape from the busy-ness of life in Concord, Massachusetts. He wanted to make sure that when he came to die, he wouldn't make that most irremediable of discoveries – that he *had not lived* properly.[24] And to that end he resolved to rid himself of anything that might obscure 'the essential facts' – which is the point, at one level, of Zen meditation.

Thoreau found he didn't need much to live properly. 'As I find by my own experience, a few implements, a knife, an axe, a spade, a wheelbarrow, &c., and for the studious, lamplight, stationery, and access to a few books, rank next to necessaries, and can all be obtained at a trifling cost.' There were few things, then, in the cabin he built for himself: minimal furniture – on the principle that in general 'our houses are cluttered and defiled with it'. At one point he put three pieces of limestone on his desk, but found to his dismay that 'they required to be dusted daily, when the furniture of my mind was all undusted still'. And so he threw the stones outside – simplifying, simplifying. He could always enjoy looking at them outside after all, 'for no dust gathers on the grass'.[25]

Nietzsche is another Western thinker with a Zen-like attitude toward (what he calls) 'the closest things'. He ascribes much of our modern malaise to the fact that our attention is so often 'misdirected and artificially diverted away from the smallest and closest things'. (This in 1880, long before the advent of ICT.) Words and concepts, he writes, mislead us into thinking of things 'as being simpler than they are, separate from each other, indivisible, each existing in and for itself'. The reality is that they're all interconnected. What we need is less isolation, more intimacy: 'We must again become *good neighbours* to the *closest things*.'[26]

Nietzsche's alter ego Zarathustra sounds very much like a Zen master or Daoist sage when it comes to his practice of 'redeeming things from their bondage under Purpose'. Having attained mystical union with the openness of a cloudless sky before sunrise, when all things bask in even illumination, Zarathustra finds himself able to affirm the world impartially, to say Yes to every thing by blessing it:

> But this is my blessing: to stand over each and every thing as its own Heaven, as its round roof, its azure bell and eternal security: and blessed is he who blesses thus! For all things are baptized at the fount of eternity and beyond good and evil ...

Let's free things, he's saying, from the oppressive and constricted positions we subject them to as 'objects' – free them from being beholden to their Creator, or weighed down by divine Providence, or willed by some eternal will, or simply from being bound up in our instrumental view of them as things made or adapted for human purposes. Then we find all things bounding with joy, coming and going in 'the innocence of becoming', 'dancing on the feet of chance', on 'a dance-floor of godlike accidents'. With all this appealing activity going on, how much easier it is to befriend them.

But now I need to distinguish these philosophical ideas and practices from some others that are superficially similar.

The KonMari Method

When I first began to give talks on the Zen of befriending things, which is basically what Dōgen was advocating, people would ask if I knew of Marie Kondo, and whether Zen practices are different from what she recommends. I didn't know of her, but I soon discovered she's a master of 'the Japanese art of decluttering and organizing' and star of the popular Netflix reality series *Tidying Up with Marie Kondo* (2019).

Her best-selling book, *The Life-Changing Magic of Tidying Up*, is the breathless New-Agey self-help manual that the title leads you to expect – and yet her attitude toward things often resonates with what Dōgen and other Zen masters have advocated.[27] If the Kondo phenomenon persuades people to get rid of lots of stuff that's cluttering up their lives, it's doing some good. Even better would be if she could dissuade people from buying so much stuff in the first place – but bringing down global capitalism doesn't appear to be high on her agenda. (A year after I wrote that sentence, any doubt was dispelled: Kondo-san opened the 'Shop at KonMari' online, where she sells 'meaningful objects' for us to welcome into our lives.)

Of course, you're only going to need the Japanese art of decluttering if you're affluent enough to buy too much stuff in the first place. Or if you missed the earlier wave of 'Simplify Your Life' books in the 1990s (some of the titles ran, surprisingly, to several hundred pages). Or, going back further, if you failed to heed Thoreau's simple exhortation in *Walden*: 'Simplify, simplify.' It's more than a century-and-a-half since he taught the Yankee art of not even letting the clutter accumulate.

Kondo-san's attitude toward things was apparently influenced by her spending five years 'working as a Shinto shrine maiden'. Shinto regards the world (the natural world especially) as being full of spirits, or *kami*. Any awe-inspiring natural phenomenon – an enormous tree, a powerful rock, a majestic waterfall – is thought to be vitalized by a special concentration of *kami*.[28] This understanding is compatible with Zen, so that Kondo's attitude has a lot in common with what Dōgen recommended to his students.

Here are some representative passages from her book, concerning clothes.

> Clothes, like people, can relax more freely when in the company of others who are very similar in type, and therefore organizing them by category helps them feel more comfortable and secure. . . .
>
> Treat your socks and stockings with respect. . . . The time they spend in your drawer is their only chance to rest.

A little sentimental perhaps, but when Kondo recommends frequent handling of one's possessions as a good way of keeping in touch with them, you can't argue with that. For some reason, however, the respect she advocates for clothing doesn't extend to the category of books.

With books she recommends the ominously named 'bulk reduction method'. She can't imagine wanting to reread a book, although she acknowledges that a book could contain some 'words and phrases' that she might want to read again, so she tried copying those into a notebook. Since that took too long she turned to photocopying, cutting and pasting, but that took even longer. In the end she 'decided to rip the relevant page out of the book'.[29] Ouch! What happened to the respect? Doesn't that ripping hurt the book? It certainly renders it useless for any subsequent reader if all the best parts have been torn out.

Otherwise, Kondo encourages her clients to express gratitude to their possessions, to thank them for the benefits they've provided in the course of the day. This infuriates her critics, or at least the post-Cartesians among them, who mock her for treating possessions as if they were alive. But this doesn't detract from her advice to pay attention to, and take good care of, our possessions, which is well taken – and all the better if we can resist the allure of the Shop at KonMari and keep their numbers down.

So what *is* the difference between what Kondo is advocating on the basis of Shinto and a cheerful disposition, and what I'm recommending on the basis of Chinese and Zen thought? The answer has to do with the role of the 'I', the issue of control, and the philosophies' emphasis on interdependence.

Whereas Zen recommends paying attention to things so that we can be 'turned by' them, with Kondo-san there's a need to stay in charge of the turning. Whereas the Zen idea is for me to 'get out of the way' so that I can learn where and how the things around me will be at their best, for Kondo it's she, or her client/reader, who is the Decider. 'The essence of effective storage is this: designate a spot for every last thing you own. . . . So decide where your things belong and when you finish using them, put them there.'[30] It's a matter of organizing according to human-imposed categories. But why not take respect for things further by taking *their* inclinations into account as we interact with them?

Now suppose that we come to feel that some of our possessions are no longer 'sparking joy' in us: then we need to get rid of them. But in good Shinto style – 'Make your parting a ceremony to launch them on a new journey. Celebrate this occasion with them. I truly believe that our possessions are even happier and more vibrant when we let them go than when we first get them.' Even more happy and vibrant because they're being liberated from the prison of the storage box? And on a journey into what kind of new world that delights them so?

This is where the sweetness and light method again takes on a darker aspect. In her introduction Kondo writes: 'I have assisted individual clients who have thrown out two hundred 45-liter garbage bags in one go.' This is what makes the KonMari method easy to practise: once you decide to part with your excess belongings, you just throw them away and transfer responsibility for coping with them to other people (ultimately some poor person in South Asia, in many cases). And what kind of ceremony could possibly make those thousands of poor things thrill at the prospect of ending up in a landfill or garbage dump?[31]

However, these shortcomings don't detract from the sane core of Kondo's project: if people can learn to take better care of things, treat them with respect, converse with them more, and consume fewer of them, this will afford joy and help make the world a better place. But because of its shadow side, the KonMari method doesn't provide the whole answer to sparking our joy and mitigating the destruction of the biosphere. (If it did, there would be no point in my writing this chapter.)

In the next section I propose another view of things, this time from depth psychology – one that takes us deeper than KonMari and closer to the Zen way of interacting with things.

Respecting the soul of the world

James Hillman, who is regarded as the founder of post-Jungian 'archetypal psychology', was in my view the greatest psychologist of the late twentieth century. After thirty years as a successful writer and psychotherapist, he began to realize that the problems he was helping his clients deal with in the consulting room were not being resolved there. As the title of one of his later books puts it: *We've Had a Hundred Years of Psychotherapy – and the World's Getting Worse*. The reason was that the problems were coming up not just in his clients' psyches and bodies but also, and primarily, in the society and world around them.[32] A focus on the person and human relationships no longer works because our environment – domestic, urban and natural – is so polluted. Not just the patient but 'the whole world is sick'.[33]

What's missing is a consideration of the vitality of animals and plants, rocks and rivers, tools and cities – of all the soul that is *anima mundi*, world soul, which Hillman began writing about in the early 1980s. His primary concern was less with the world's 'unifying panpsychic life-principle' than with 'the *anima mundi* as that particular soul-spark, that seminal image, which offers itself in each thing ... God-given things of nature and man-made things of the street'.[34] I don't know whether Hillman knew this passage from Martin Buber, citing an old Hasid master, but it fits perfectly:

> When you walk across the fields with your mind pure and holy, then from all the stones, and all growing things, and all animals, the sparks of their soul come out and cling to you, and then they are purified and become a holy fire in you.[35]

It's a matter of the world soul as manifested in particular things, and Hillman believes that 'care for the soul' in this broader sense can help heal the deeper and more pervasive sickness.

Whereas for Marie Kondo the joy sparked is in *us*, for Hillman the soul-spark is first and foremost in the thing. Unlike Kondo, who comes across as the boss who organizes, Hillman likes to reverse the relationship and begin from the thing.

> Doesn't the tool in your hand teach you to use it? Take a needle: my eye, my fingers have to adjust to that needle's eye and pass the thread through it. The needle teaches me a strict discipline, a refinement of eye-hand coordination. If I do it wrong, the needle pricks me or gets out of my grip. Things are our 'masters' in that sense. And when you kick the TV set or curse the car because it doesn't work, it's because we are being bad students.[36]

Ouch. To think of the all innocent tools and gadgets I cursed when younger and more impetuous, I'm ashamed at how lousy a student I was. (When I practised motorcycle maintenance it was not, sadly, as a Zen art.) Sadly, because the 'wisdom', *sophia*, that philosophy is love of (*philo-sophia*), originally meant 'skill, in handicraft and art, as in carpentry' – an intelligence in dealing with and handling things.

Hillman's emphasis on what things reveal to our sense-perception (*aesthesis*), together with his phenomenological inclination to *let them show themselves* rather than imposing our views of what and how they can or should be, introduced a strong aesthetic component into his therapeutic recommendations. The aesthetic turn sensitized him to what was behind 'the acknowledged superiority of Japanese quality' that put Japan ahead of the US in the 1990s: 'The Japanese mind is set in a culture that pays devout attention to sensate details. Their refined arts ... bespeak a "precision consciousness" of sensate aesthetic qualities.'[37] He's talking about what the Japanese call *dō* (Chinese, *dao*): *ways* of living, artistically; practices that derive from, and in turn encourage, a long-standing culture of attention to aesthetic detail.

Hillman came to see the *arts* as key factors in the healing of a sick society, and to advocate creativity on the psychological level, regardless of whether something new is actually produced. He recommends

Individuating each act we do and thing we live with, actualizing its potential ... so that the innate dignity, beauty, and integrity of any act or thing from doorknob to desk chair to bed sheet may become fully present in its uniqueness.[38]

This could well be a description of the Zen way of living, though Hillman didn't show much interest in Zen ideas. His practice – thanks to its basis in careful attention to things as participants in the world soul – came to correspond remarkably with what the Buddhists regard as awakened activity.

If we can develop the knack of '*fitting ecological response*', Hillman suggests: 'tasks now imagined mainly as duties, or penalties – cleaning up, detoxification, repair, scrubbing, recycling – become models for a therapeutic and aesthetic idea of service to the world.'[39] (The Greek root *therapeia* means 'service' or 'attendance', and the sentiment is pure Dōgen.) Yes, we can keep on regarding those tasks as chores, and get bored and stop paying attention; or else we can attend carefully, and find ourselves participating in the central life of Earth and serving a function in the play of the world.

Insofar as we find the myriad things beautiful, we're likely to love them – and for Hillman, like Plato and Freud, the motivating factor is primarily *erōs*, or love. Ancient Greek thinking about love imagined a 'cosmogonic Eros', a force that generates the whole world and keeps it going, usually by bringing opposites together in productive union. But psychotherapy, in thrall to the recent Western notion of *romantic love* as the paradigm form of erotic relations, tends to focus unhelpfully on the individual and its relations with others, restricting the erotic realm to the human. If you misguidedly regard the non-human world as inanimate, Hillman observes, 'there's nowhere for love to go but to another person'.[40] And that's too bad: too cramped and narrow.

He thinks that both we and things would be better off if we opened up a bit. After all, some of us love our dogs, or our cars, if we have them; and I imagine some gun-owners even love their guns. But Hillman, ever the provocateur, wants to go further and take sexual fetishism into account. If we ask what a 'perversion' is saying with its attachment to nylon shower curtains or pieces of rubber, the answer is: '"Look, you can make love to material things, dead things" – dead, that is, according to Descartes.' Here's another indictment of Cartesian thinking: it 'makes our love for the world into a perversion'. In that light, one can see 'consumerism and advertising' as perverse ways of encouraging something that's actually salutary: 'rekindling our desire for the world'.[41] But preferably a desire for natural phenomena and a sufficiency of things that are well made.

Another great thinker from Hillman's generation, the French philosopher Michel Serres, also calls for loving the world. In his brilliant little book *The Natural Contract*, Serres exposes the problems that result from our entering into 'social contracts' that ignore nature. 'Through exclusively social contracts', he writes,

> we have abandoned the bond that connects us to the world, . . . the bond that allows our language to communicate with mute, passive, obscure things – things that, because of our excesses, are recovering voice, presence, activity, light. We can no longer neglect this bond.[42]

And when it comes to love, Serres holds that there are 'two double laws'. The first (common to Confucius and Jesus) is 'love one another', both neighbours *and* humanity. If you separate these two you let hatred in, because loving only one's neighbours leads to tribalism: 'the team, the sect, gangsterism and racism'. However, 'this first law remains silent about mountains and lakes, for it speaks to men as if there were no world'.

To compensate for that lack, the second law 'asks us to love the world'. For a long time there has been a local love, of the home land, *Heimat*, which on its own has led to 'inexpiable wars caused by the passions of belonging'. The climate crisis, in Serres' prescient formulation, exposes the need for 'a new, global law . . . which requires of us universal love of the physical Earth'. This doesn't require that we neglect the local, but simply expand our concern: 'Never forget the place from which you depart, but leave it behind and join the universal. Love the bond that unites your plot of earth with the Earth, the bond that makes kin and stranger resemble each other.'[43]

But instead we neglect the Earth, and fail to love it.

Those who share power today have forgotten nature, which could be said to be taking its revenge but which, more to the point, is reminding us of its existence . . . . We have lost the world. We've transformed things into fetishes or commodities, the stakes of our stratagems . . . . At the very moment when we are acting physically for the first time on the global Earth, and when it in turn is clearly reacting on global humanity, we are tragically neglecting it.[44]

Twenty-five years later, there is no doubt whatsoever about the force of the reacting, yet our neglect tragically persists. (Bruno Latour elaborates this theme in his recent works.)

If we step back and regard our treatment of the world mythologically, we might expect our neglect of things to provoke an angry reaction from the Gods or spirits. Regarding things as sparks of *anima mundi*, we shouldn't be surprised if they turn against us because they feel neglected and disrespected. This is just what's happening with environmental pollution and the things around us that can make us sicken and die. Because we fail to 'recognize how alive everything is and how desirable', Hillman suggests (who wasn't a reader of Serres, as far as I know), 'the world is taking revenge.'[45] He and Serres are saying this several years before Lovelock published *The Revenge of Gaia*, which presents it in terms of basic physics: we act up, and the natural world reacts.

If psychotherapy's exclusive concern with the human poses 'an ecology problem', which it obviously does, it also gives us 'a political problem' through its concern with 'bringing people into line so that they can function within the system and cope'. For Hillman this is unhelpful because if we're going to heal the psychosomatic sickness of our world, we to *change* our political systems rather than adapt ourselves to them.[46] Yes! – and a paramount symptom of that sickness is the climate crisis.

It turns out, then, that love is not *all* you need. But a more expansive kind of love that embraces the soul of the world – that will take us quite some way in a better direction. If we can celebrate turning things while being turned by them, we'll appreciate them better – not as a substitute for, but as an enriching complement to, our social and interpersonal interactions. And that in turn will reduce our levels of consumption, and so inflict less damage on other people, fellow animals and the geosphere. And with fewer needlessly manufactured things around, and more that we've taken the trouble to make beautiful, our natural and built environments are likely to treat us less harshly and reciprocate our new-found affection.

Inconclusions (What and How?)

Since the 0.1 per cent have been winning their war of ideas so far, what are we to do now? The first half of this book outlined their strategies and what's at stake, and I trust the second half has provided a context for understanding how to take the power back from the rich libertarians so that we can tackle the climate crisis. Even though there are signs that the tide of public opinion is turning in favour of taking appropriate action, the opposition remains powerful and deeply entrenched. Let's be inspired by the passion of Rage against the Machine: 'Ignorance has taken over / We gotta take the power back!'[1]

So what do we do now?

In 2019 Philip Alston, a professor of law at New York University, issued a report in his capacity as the UN Special Rapporteur on extreme poverty and human rights. Called 'Climate Change and Poverty', it shows how the climate crisis constitutes a human rights issue of unprecedented proportions, and proposes various ways of addressing it. In discussing the neoliberal drive to let 'the private sector' deal with climate change, Alston warns of the risks of privatization: 'An over-reliance on the private sector could lead to a climate apartheid scenario in which the wealthy pay to escape overheating, hunger, and conflict, while the rest of the world is left to suffer.'[2] His concluding paragraph berates UN human rights bodies and (most of) the human rights community for ignoring the challenge of global heating: 'Climate change is, among other things, *an unconscionable assault on the poor*.'[3]

The answer to the question of what do we do now depends on understanding what *they* are doing now: the super-rich are planning for 'a climate apartheid scenario' in which they avoid, and the rest of us suffer, the effects of their destruction of the climate. Some of them are going to take up 'seasteading', establishing communities of libertarians on the high seas, 'sovereign nations in international waters, free from the laws of any country'. Floating out there, conveniently offshore, they'll be free from government regulation and taxation.

But when the rocket technology is sufficiently advanced, they'll be off to 'the vast reaches of outer space', which for someone like Peter Thiel, one of the more intellectual billionaires, constitute 'a limitless possibility for escape from world politics'. Prototype rockets are already under construction, for planned bases on the moon and – even better because farther away from the devastated earth – on Mars.[4] I used to think that such fantasies were the converse of (Berkeley) Luke's imaginings about aliens from outer space, except with darker motivations – until I discovered that the Ames Research Center at NASA hosted a website for over twenty years that was concerned with the challenges and delights of space settlements. The site is now run by the National Space Society, and dedicated to 'spreading life throughout the solar system'. Having arranged for the devastation of one planet, some people are ready to move on.

Here we have the apotheosis of the post-Cartesian mindset: a type of person so disconnected from the conditions of their embodiment that they can envisage a joyful life on the moon, or Mars, or in a huge space station floating farther out. But then who needs a body when you can cheat death by uploading the contents of your brain to some supercomputer or the Cloud? Yet, if futurists like Ray Kurzweil and Peter Thiel plan to escape the consequences of global heating by using 'brain-computer interfaces' to achieve 'digital immortality', they'd better take the hardware off-planet so that none of the poor souls left behind can pull the plug on them.[5]

While they're waiting for the great escape technology to be perfected, the climate wreckers are buying large amounts of property in places like New Zealand to retreat to, while providing financial backing for another kind of haven: climate crisis-proof 'gated' cities.[6] Now that real estate is the most valuable form of property in the world, the 0.1 per cent are investing their billions in safe places that will be easier to get to than the moon when the climate gets really rough.[7] Projects like NEOM in Saudi Arabia and Eko Atlantic in Nigeria, places 'with their own laws, taxes and regulations', promise to provide the perfect refuge for rich libertarians seeking to avoid the sight of poverty and the ravages of climate change.[8]

This sad phenomenon reminds me of the realization I had long ago that people were making huge profits by destroying the natural environment in the name of 'development'. Now, when I think about how today's billionaires are making fortunes from wrecking the climate and then using their money to insulate themselves and ultimately escape from the ensuing chaos, the words of the Berkeley graduate student Mario Savio come to mind. At a crucial point in the Free Speech Movement of the mid-1960s, Savio made a memorable appeal to a huge crowd assembled on the UC Berkeley campus, which has since influenced civil resistance movements the world over.

> There's a time when the operation of the machine becomes so odious, makes you so sick at heart, that you can't take part. . . . And you've got to put your bodies upon the gears and upon the wheels, upon the levers, upon all the apparatus, and you've got to make it stop.[9]

The students staged a 'sit-in', non-violent civil disobedience; Joan Baez sang 'We Shall Overcome', and students were jailed – but eventually they prevailed. However, the Machine shows no signs of stopping, so we have to *make* it stop before it grinds us all down.

As I was revising this last chapter in September 2019, a much anticipated United Nations Climate Action Summit took place in New York City, the results of which I hoped would let me sound an optimistic note toward the end here. Several million young people all over the world had taken to the streets a few days before to protest the unconscionable impotence of the world's leaders in the face of the climate crisis. But their performance at the Climate Action Summit confirmed the worst fears of the climate-striking students: nothing more than the usual 'Yes, we really must do something' routine. China failed to inspire by strengthening its commitments, and the US – the world leader in historical carbon emissions – didn't even participate.[10] Time for Rage against the Machine!

What do we do now, geophysically?

If we are to avoid dangerous disruption to the Earth System, we have to drastically reduce our burning of fossil fuels – in coal-fired power plants and factories, diesel engines and jet fuel-guzzling planes – while making deep cuts in concrete production. Concrete because 'if the cement industry were a country, it would be the third largest carbon dioxide emitter in the world with up to 2.8bn tonnes, surpassed only by China and the US'.[11] Fortunately there's a perfect alternative, a reliable material that has been used for millennia: stone. However, the IPCC has shown that global heating can't be slowed sufficiently by reducing emissions from those familiar sources without also making radical changes in *land use.*[12]

Deforestation for the sake of providing pasture for cattle and growing soybeans for cattle feed, or for the production of palm oil or whatever, is on the rise – and has to be reversed if we're to reduce global heating. (Many of its initial supporters now see the US-initiated palm oil boom as a disaster for the planet.[13]) We need more trees, because we have to extract as much as possible of the CO_2 that we've emitted since the Industrial Revolution, which can be done by restoring ecosystems and engaging in extensive reforestation. The climate crisis and the ongoing mass extermination are interrelated, so restoring ecosystems will help us mitigate climate change. George Monbiot has founded an initiative called 'Natural Climate Solutions' to promote this idea. It's not a substitute for reducing GHG emissions but a necessary complement to it. When it comes to extracting CO_2 from the air:

The greatest potential identified so far is in protecting and restoring natural forests and allowing native trees to repopulate deforested land. The greatest drawdown potential per hectare ... is the restoration of coastal habitats such as mangroves, salt marsh and sea grass beds. They stash carbon 40 times faster than tropical forests can. Peaty soils are also vital carbon stores.[14]

We've known for a long time that planting trees is a way of taking carbon dioxide out of the atmosphere, but scientists recently discovered that the amount of carbon that could be sequestrated by this method may be greater than previously thought.[15] In view of the steady stream of stories about the dire effects of climate change, this is a welcome piece of news. Tree planting is a measure that can be initiated in countries all over the world, but for it to have the desired effect we would need to be moving toward a zero-carbon economy at the same time.

The good news about land use change is that the first thing we can do is easy, because it consists in *not* doing things we're currently doing: *stop* deforestation, stop draining peatlands and stop destroying wetlands. This would naturally lead to a reduction in destruction of wildlife and the many other species we're driving to extinction. We can do this, starting tomorrow.[16]

One 'negative emissions technology' that we could employ more widely, and that received favourable mention in the IPCC *Global Warming of 1.5°C* report, is *biochar*, defined as 'solid material obtained from the thermochemical conversion of biomass in an oxygen-limited environment'. It's a form of charcoal that you get from burning organic matter such as leaves and other vegetation in a special stove that keeps the oxygen out, and it helps sequester carbon in the earth and at the same time improves the quality of the soil. It appears to be especially beneficial for newly planted trees, and by some estimates could offset almost 2 billion metric tons of carbon emissions annually.[17]

The IPCC *Climate Change and Land Use* report makes it clear that the way we use – and abuse – the land simply isn't sustainable. Global warming is threatening the viability of the world food system, and soils are being seriously depleted all over the world. Industrial farming promotes too much monoculture, and sustaining the livestock industry through corn and soy further impoverishes the soil. Re-diversifying agriculture will let us re-diversify our diet, which would be good for our health *and* the health of the planet.[18]

As for low GHG-emission energy systems, the price of clean and renewable energy is coming down, and the efficiency of the lithium-ion storage batteries required for storage is going up – with the result that fossil fuel sources of energy are becoming economically uncompetitive. A 2019 study of coal-fired plants in the US found that electricity costs from three-quarters of them were higher than what wind or solar facilities within 35 miles would have to charge.[19] People would pay less for electricity, and public and environmental health would benefit greatly from a shift to clean renewables. But the Trump administration 'digs coal', and so everyone except the fossil fuel industries, and the politicians they're paying, has to suffer.

The good news is that in India solar and wind power are replacing coal-fired plants more rapidly than expected. As Bill McKibben reports, 'Over the first nine months of 2018, India installed forty times more capacity for renewable than for coal-fired power'.[20] The bad news is that the Indian equivalent to Koch Industries, the Adani Group, is doing all it can to keep the country hooked on coal. They've persuaded politicians in Australia to let them extract coal from a huge mine in Queensland and ship it past the Great Barrier Reef and a further 5,000 miles to a new

$2 billion power plant in India (carbon emissions from this trip?), which will then send the electricity to Bangladesh.

The billionaire in charge, Gautam Adani, said that it's unfair to criticize coal because 'India doesn't have a choice'. Well, there is the solar and wind power just mentioned. He also says that 'nation building' is part of his business philosophy: he should tell that to the poor people living in the villages around the Godda Thermal Power Project, who will suffer from its pollution for decades. Adani claims it's a matter of 'how to make India energy secure', but it's hard to see how importing coal from a foreign country 5,000 miles away, along the Axis of Shame, will bring energy security.[21]

I call it the Axis of Shame because Australia will make a lot of money on this deal at the expense of its neighbours to the east of Queensland – and the Australian government added insult to injury by refusing to make any concessions on a climate change communiqué at the Pacific Islands Forum in 2019. Prime minister Scott Morrison vetoed any mention of 'coal' or limiting warming to 1.5°C. Australia's neighbours are already suffering from sea-level rise caused by global warming – salinization of the water supplies – and some islands will soon become uninhabitable. It's no wonder the Pacific Island nations are coming to prefer dealing with China than Australia.

China is increasing solar power and reducing coal, which is good; but they're now financing coal-fired plants abroad instead, which isn't. We need to persuade the Chinese to cut their losses on coal equipment and refrain from selling countries power plants that pollute – and make a greener profit (if somewhat smaller at first) by selling clean energy systems instead.

The geopolitical benefits of the shift to renewable energy are enormous, as outlined in a report by the International Renewable Energy Agency titled 'A New World: The Geopolitics of the Energy Transformation'.[22] Many developing countries, in Africa and South Asia especially, can afford to set up decentralized solar and wind installations without the need for a national power grid. And the world will be a more peaceful place when the fossil fuel-rich nations aren't calling the shots: for one thing, the US will presumably start fewer wars in the Middle East. And the profits that currently flow to the Gulf States and Russia will be earned locally, supporting domestic employment and the economy.

This 'new world' sounds like a far better world; yet when a group of investors representing $34 trillion in assets 'called upon world leaders to bring in carbon pricing and phase out coal power to limit global heating to 1.5C' – this was just before the G20 Summit in Osaka in 2019 – the response was typically lame: Well, yes, the G20 leaders will be working on it, sometime soon.[23] We know what needs to be done geophysically to mitigate the climate crisis, and if our leaders keep refusing to act we need to replace them.

What do we do now, socially?

A painless first step is to stop squandering electricity: our energy use in the developed world is shamefully wasteful, and we can easily conserve *and* save money by changing our habits and doing with less – and enjoying life just as much if we adopt the right attitude (as discussed in Part Four). We have to curb our consumption of goods and services as well as energy, eat less meat and not fly around so much. Our activity is simply unfair to other people, animals, things and future generations; and we can enjoy life perfectly well without such excess.

The most extensive study to date (2018) of the environmental impacts of the global food supply chain estimates that a shift 'from current diets to a diet that excludes animal products' would reduce GHG emissions from world food production by a stunning 49 per cent (not to mention equally substantial reductions in land use, water consumption and pollution of fresh water and soil).[24] People don't like to be told, understandably, they can't eat something they like eating; but if they become acquainted with the horrendous conditions and environmental pollution under which most meat is produced, and with the carbon emissions and health hazards of a high-meat diet, many of them will cut down voluntarily. The more meat we eat, the more other people will starve as global heating devastates the world food system.

We can make the change by incorporating the full social, environmental and health costs of meat production into the price, leaving people free to spend their money on meat that is justly more expensive, or else to move to a more healthy and reasonably priced diet that's largely plant based and thus more sustainable. The possibility of generating protein from hydrogen-oxidizing bacteria, electricity, water and air – no agriculture or aquaculture involved – gives some further grounds for optimism in this area.[25]

The same goes for air travel, which is a luxury enjoyed by a small proportion of the world's population and a growing contributor to carbon emissions.[26] Again, if you were to incorporate the full costs into the price of an airline ticket, the increase would deter most people from flying so much. But it wouldn't have a substantial effect on the super-rich, so a fairer way would emulate carbon-trading schemes: you set an individual cap on how many miles per year a person can fly on commercial airlines, and set up a market for buying and selling the allowances, so that if you don't fly you gain income, and flying more will cost more.[27] Yes, it's a restriction of my freedom; but surely I have no *right* to travel in such a way as to cause harm to less fortunate people and the planet?

In 2019 global tourism was estimated to account for some 8 per cent of the world's carbon emissions.[28] Since a growing number of the world's most tourist-filled cities (Amsterdam, Barcelona, Dubrovnik, Venice, etc.) are suffering from a surfeit of visitors that's straining their social fabric and civic infrastructure, the reduction in air travel that's needed for resolving the climate crisis would improve the quality of life in many places. Instead of flying all over the world to meetings, business people can use more videoconferencing, and academics will have to make do with smaller conferences closer to home.*[29]

If we want political action that tackles the climate crisis and aims for a more just society, there are many organizations dedicated to translating good ideas into social activism. We need activism that can influence politicians currently in office and help to get better ones elected – better in the sense of concerned with the well-being of their constituents rather than their own enrichment. Some groups deserving of support are Fridays for Future, Extinction Rebellion (XR – heavier duty!), Power Shift Network, Zero Hour, and YouthStrike4Climate.[30] Climate Outreach has been working in Europe since 2004 to promote more robust public engagement with climate change. One of the most effective advocates for change has been 350.org, co-founded by Bill McKibben and colleagues in 2008 (a time when a reduction of atmospheric CO_2 to 350 ppm still seemed feasible).[31]

Similar organizations – such the Mobilisation Lab, the Sunrise Movement, the Climate Advocacy Lab, Climate Mobilization and PowerLabs – are concerned with translating ideas into action by mediating between people with good ideas and policymakers. Their websites offer helpful information on what's going on and how people can get organized politically to make changes for the better.[32] There is also a movement with a more specific goal – but one that, if reached, would have vastly beneficial effects: putting an end to the travesty of the *Citizen's United* decision.[33]

Another way to reduce the political influence of the fossil fuel industry is by shareholder engagement that encourages sustainable practices and decarbonization. Further pressure on the industry to change its ways comes from the growing fossil fuel divestment movement, which encourages pension funds, insurance companies and sovereign wealth funds to shift their investments away from fossil fuels. Students played a major role in getting this movement going, and between 2014 and 2018 divestment rose from $52 billion in assets to over $6 trillion, with almost 1,000 institutional investors committed to divesting.[34] According to a notification from 350.org in the autumn of 2019, the figure had reached $11 trillion. If this encouraging trend continues, many companies will have far less money to spend on prospecting for more fuel to burn, and thus less opportunity for inflicting harm on other human beings and natural ecosystems.

But perhaps what we need most of all – and this is something that the young can bring about more effectively than the older generation – is a number of shifts in what's regarded as socially acceptable. (Think of the immense change in attitudes in the US toward smoking: from super-cool in the days of Bogart and Bacall, to almost totally unacceptable in 2019.) Older people often have an unjustified antipathy to non-preachy vegans, and so it's a good sign that among the young a vegan diet is becoming acceptable. The latest research has shown that 'fruit, vegetables, beans and wholegrains were best for both avoiding disease *and* protecting the climate and water resources', and that 'eating more red and processed meat causes the most ill health and pollution'.[35] But it's crucial to avoid preaching and rather to lead by quiet example – otherwise you lend credence to the former Trump aid Sebastian Gorka, who warned a thrilled audience at the American Conservative Union that supporters of the 'communist' Green New Deal 'want to take away your hamburgers!'[36]

I can imagine a time when it will be considered uncool to fly all over the world for the sake of Instagramming. And could we arrange something similar for the strangely named Sport Utility Vehicles? When Keith Bradsher's great book *High and Mighty: The Dangerous Rise of the SUV* came out in 2002, I naively thought it would help deflate the ballooning enthusiasm in the US for those hazardous hybrids.[37] He shows how the SUV-makers managed to get around safety and environmental regulations to produce vehicles that are lethal to pedestrians, cyclists and occupants of cars – and, surprisingly, to drivers and occupants of SUVs too, because of their alarming tendency to roll over. Not to mention their appetite – obscene in the context of climate change – for guzzling fossil fuels. Bradsher's meticulous and eloquent exposé of the auto industry's cynical lies and cover-ups received widespread critical acclaim (except in Michigan) – but failed to put even a modest dent in the market.

In fact, almost twenty years later, the market is booming as never before. When Bradsher did his research, SUVs accounted for 17 per cent of new passenger vehicle sales in the US. According to a 2019 report by experts at the International Energy Agency, that figure is now almost 50 per cent, and SUVs now account for around 40 per cent of annual car sales worldwide – a market share that continues to grow. As a consequence of this boom, 'SUVs were the second-largest contributor to the increase in global CO_2 emissions since 2010 after the power sector, but ahead of heavy industry (including iron & steel, cement, aluminium), as well as trucks and aviation'![38]

Don't people know that by driving an SUV they are recklessly endangering the lives of other people on and beside the road? Or don't they care? Don't the 50 per cent of US new car buyers who go for SUVs know that they are unduly contributing to the global heating that's devastating communities in many states by hurricanes, flooding, wildfire and drought? (Not to mention destroying the livelihoods of people in the developing world.) Or don't they care? If you're striking for the climate, it's up to you to make sure that people know that driving an SUV is nowadays far from cool – and rather a badge of shame.

What do we do now, politically?

A fundamental problem in current politics is the prevalence of 'fake news', thanks to which increasing numbers of people have no idea what's happening. Interference with elections, especially by foreign powers, together with the popularity of conspiracy theories, makes nonsense of democracy. Politicians can change that, if they want: Finland leads European countries in encouraging media literacy so that its citizens can avoid being misled by fake news – and other places around the world are learning from the Finns' example. In the US, the Democratic National Committee has created a website 'Combating Online Disinformation' to help make the 2020 elections more fair.[39] Of course, many politicians have no interest in combating fake news because they themselves lie and rely so much on generating falsehoods.

People who get their news mostly through social media will need to switch to more reliable sources if the various climate movements are to gain momentum. School strikes and demonstrations put the politicians on notice that there's massive support for change. But there's a danger of getting stalled, if people think all they need to do is take to the streets every now and then. Unless accompanied by direct and well-informed political engagement, demonstrations will be ineffectual.

Policymakers need to be told that unless they take swift and effective action to slow global heating they'll be voted out of office. Young people will have to vote in greater numbers than they traditionally do, so they can help get more responsible candidates elected. We need political leaders who will mandate conservation of energy and natural resources, end subsidies for the fossil fuel industry, and divert funding into clean and renewable sources of energy.

The regime change that's most urgently needed is of course in the United States, which as of 2019 suffers under the most inept and corrupt administration in living memory. The country is also, according to a YouGov poll from the same year, a 'hotbed of climate change denial', with only Saudi Arabia and Indonesia boasting a larger percentage of deniers. (No mere coincidence that the US and Saudi Arabia are the world's top oil producers.) In the US 'a total of 17% of those polled agreed that "the idea of manmade global warming is a hoax that was invented to deceive people". Unsurprisingly, 'a total of 52% of Americans who described themselves as "very rightwing" to YouGov insisted global warming was a hoax.'[40] Well of course: the president said so. Conspiracy theories abound – otherwise the 'hoax' lie wouldn't still be viable.

If you're in the US, you have to oppose the Republicans' war on young voters and citizens of colour through voter suppression, gerrymandering of electoral districts and other shady practices. Compared to other liberal democracies, the US ranks second to last in 'electoral integrity'. According to the Brennan Center at New York University,

> Over the last 20 years, states have put barriers in front of the ballot box – imposing strict voter ID laws, cutting voting times, restricting registration, and purging voter rolls. These efforts . . . have kept significant numbers of eligible voters from the polls, placing special burdens on racial minorities, poor people, and young and old voters.[41]

The Republicans put a lot of effort into keeping people who would vote against them from voting at all; but informed citizens who are determined to vote can prevail.

When practised properly, however, the law can be one of the most powerful weapons in the fight against the climate-wreckers, as shown in the inspiring book by Martin Goodman and the environmental activist lawyer James Thornton, *Client Earth: Building an Ecological Civilisation*. One strategy is to ensure that the environmental laws that are already on the books are actually enforced: many of them aren't because the corporations are paying off the politicians. And another is to create new and better laws to prevent climate catastrophe. And if industry continues to violate those laws, you have to use the law to make it so expensive for them to continue that they'll stop.

As far as the Three Obstructions are concerned, we can use the democratic system to neutralize them. We can get money out of politics as much as possible, and hold the politicians responsible for working for our benefit rather than their profit. If there are rules that require members of governmental committees to be competent and knowledgeable in their fields, this will disqualify the religious zealots. And we have to wean ourselves off our gadgets enough to find out which candidates are the most competent and responsible, and vote for them – candidates who will tax and regulate the Tech Titans, reining them in and obliging them to promote responsible use of their products.

When it comes to getting fossil fuel money out of politics, there are movements like the No Fossil Fuel Money pledge, which encourages politicians to stop taking contributions from coal, gas and oil companies. Under the circumstances, any politician who refuses the no fossil fuel money pledge needs to be voted out of office immediately. In fact, there ought to be a law against accepting contributions from fossil fuel concerns. An organization called Represent US is dedicated to solving the corruption of the American political system by the 0.05 per cent of the people rich enough to keep the right politicians in business. The actor Jennifer Lawrence is the presenter of an excellent short film on how to go about fixing things: *Unbreaking America: A New Short Film about the Corruption Crisis*.[42]

The equally important question is whether our political leaders, or candidates for leadership, are committed to tackling the 'supply side' of the climate crisis at its roots by discouraging further extraction of fossil fuels. You have to look carefully, past the bright green facade presented to the public to the more shadowy aspects. Barack Obama was proud of what he did for the environment, but he encouraged the country's enthusiasm for fracking, so that the US is now the world's largest producer of crude oil. As governor of California, Jerry Brown did wonderful things for the environment, but he never restricted oil drilling in the state. And the greenest-washed leader of all, Canada's Justin Trudeau, declared a 'climate emergency' in June of 2019 – and the very next day approved an expensive extension to a pipeline running from the world's dirtiest oil in Alberta to the west coast for shipment to Asia.[43] This kind of duplicity is common, and practitioners need to be named and shamed.

Back in 2002 the Bipartisan Campaign Reform Act made headway in keeping private and corporate millions out of politics, but that progress was annulled eight years later by *Citizens United* and the subsequent legal decisions that gave the libertarian billionaires and fossil fuel industries the freedom to buy the politicians, policies, and laws they want – and to get rid of the regulations they don't want. However, as the example of the Scandinavian countries shows, where election campaigns are mostly funded by the government, it *is* possible to keep private money out of politics and still have a strong enough economy. If you want a functioning democratic system, you need to strictly limit financial contributions to political campaigns and impose reasonable spending limits.

Further improvements would come with moving away from hugeness altogether, by devolving power from government at the top to smaller entities 'on the ground' such as counties, cities, and other communities. George Monbiot gives examples of successful projects in this kind of participatory politics, and argues plausibly that such local initiatives flourish as naturally diverse ecosystems do when humans refrain from trying to govern them. And in his book *Out of the Wreckage: A New Politics for an Age of Crisis* he offers not only intelligent proposals for political reforms but also examples of practical ways of bringing them about.[44] The ancient Chinese thinkers would approve of a system that encourages spontaneous self-organization of this kind.

In any case, we need to aim for deeper reforms in our democratic systems, making them more responsive to the well-being of the people. This would involve a move toward socialism (democratic socialism, social democracy) – again we can look to the model of the Scandinavian countries. And since we have to cooperate with the Chinese, why not incline toward socialism with ancient Chinese and American pragmatist characteristics? That would surely help us gain the cooperation of the Chinese government on confronting the climate crisis.

In *geopolitics* we need to shift from the current system, based on the Westphalian model of sovereign nation states competing for their rational self-interest, to a more cooperative model like the Chinese notion of All-under-the-Heavens. After a quarter-century of trying, the member states of the United Nations have failed to achieve any meaningful agreements on slowing global heating. There isn't time to found a new organization more appropriate for the internetworked and globalised world we now inhabit, but the UN could create a Climate Crisis Council (like the Security Council except larger) with representatives from all 193 countries.

There has to be an agreement that absolute national sovereignty is an out-dated and dangerous notion, that the parties are engaging a dialogue on the understanding that the fates of their respective homelands are inextricably intertwined.

What do we do now, economically?

For a start, we need to acknowledge that the discipline of economics has not been serving us well and is in need of reform. (By 'us' I mean here the world's population, of whom some 700 million live in extreme poverty while the 0.1 per cent get richer than ever.) In her revolutionary and revelatory book *Doughnut Economics*, Kate Raworth has proposed ways to revision and reform the discipline so that our economic systems will serve the needs of more of the world's people as well as future generations. She dismisses as pernicious the obsession with increasing GDP, and asks instead the basic question (one that should inform all discussions of climate change, but rarely does): 'What enables human beings to thrive?'

Influenced by Earth System Science, Raworth emphasizes the need to respect limits to growth, and respectful of social equity and global justice, she proposes twelve 'basics of life on which no one should be left falling short'. In the place of increasing GDP as the goal of economics, she proposes an aim symbolized by the 'doughnut', which, envisaged simply, is a pair of concentric rings.

Below the inner ring – the social foundation – lie critical human deprivations such as hunger and illiteracy. Beyond the outer ring – the ecological ceiling – lie critical planetary degradation such as climate change and biodiversity loss. Between those two rings is the Doughnut itself, the space in which we can meet the needs of all within the means of the planet.[45]

To attain such a goal will take time, and since it doesn't look as if the Revolution will rid us of capitalism by the end of the working day tomorrow, we need to start from where we are now. We live mostly under conditions of capitalism that permit deformities in the free market that are destroying the environment. We can get rid of these by internalizing the negative externalities. In the longer run, capitalism isn't viable because it's predicated upon unlimited growth within a limited earth system. We have to reform our economic system into a 'steady state' economy, and also dismantle it into smaller, local economies.[46]

We can fix the negative externalities by making the prices of goods and services reflect the social and environmental costs of their production and consumption. Massive investments in low- and zero-carbon infrastructure are needed, but in the meantime a tax on carbon and other GHG emissions – imposed mainly on the 1 per cent and with exemptions for people with low incomes – would immediately make the price of high-emission goods and activities reflect their true costs and discourage people from indulging.

It's a matter of applying the 'polluter pays' principle consistently, and preventing people from passing on the costs of their economic activity to others, including future generations. Farms in the US, for example, are exempted from the polluter pays principle under the Clean Water Act (for some reason no doubt having to do with money). Factory farms pollute the soil and water and air around them, inflicting gratuitous costs on their neighbours. Fertilizer and manure run-off cause toxic algae blooms that jeopardize the livelihoods of people on the coasts, and sicken innocent bystanders on the way.[47] And when it comes to factory farming of animals for meat, the costs (leaving aside the suffering of millions of animals) fall on everyone on earth who suffers from an overheating climate.

In view of the complex nature of the climate crisis, and the multitude of interacting factors that need to be addressed, the scale of the transformations we need to undertake is daunting. But we have managed vast transformations before, and not just in times of war: the most relevant model is Roosevelt's New Deal in the 1930s. As mentioned earlier, we can't tackle the climate crisis effectively without 'global financial system change' – which is just what Roosevelt achieved when he took the power back from Wall Street and put it in the hands of the government and the central bank (Federal Reserve).[48] But the super-rich hijacked the system again during the 1970s – so now it's time to take it back again.

Talk of a Green New Deal (GND) began around 2007 and action followed not long after, in the UK and Europe as well as in the US. The original New Deal employed millions of victims of the Great Depression, especially the impoverished and unemployed, to do meaningful work building all kinds of infrastructure, planting trees and making state parks, and pursuing public projects in literature, history and the arts. The GNDs aim to tackle the climate crisis by transforming our infrastructure in the direction of zero carbon, while at the same time reforming our socio-economic and political systems in the direction of zero exploitation and fulfilling employment.

Naomi Klein provides a helpful discussion of the shortcomings of the original New Deal in her book *On Fire: The Burning Case for a Green New Deal*. (Women, African- and Mexican-Americans, farm and domestic workers didn't fare as well as white males.) The GNDs are to be localized rather than centralized, and to be enacted through democratic discussion at the grass roots level rather than edicts from the top down.[49] The 2019 resolution sponsored by Representative Alexandria Ocasio-Cortez, with the support of Senator Ed Markey, acknowledges these issues. Their GND proposal is designed to achieve 'net-zero greenhouse gas emissions' *and* promote social justice through 'a national mobilization effort' that will transform the US economy.[50]

However, as Naomi Klein remarks, it's important to ensure that the wages from the new 'green' jobs that are created don't fuel high-consumer lifestyles that increase GHG emissions, and that shorter work weeks give people more time for more meaningful activities than shopping. She makes a convincing case for the feasibility of a vast, government-funded overhaul of almost everything, a reconstruction that offers the benefits of fuller employment and a fairer economic system, and enjoys broad public support – especially from young people.[51]

Ann Pettifor's short book *The Case for the Green New Deal* makes the case convincingly, and shows that it won't work unless we first take the power back. The super-rich have hijacked the financial system and now control it for their own profit. But they don't own it: it is rather 'a great public asset, financed, guaranteed and sustained by millions of ordinary taxpayers in all the economies of the world. In other words, a great public good has been captured by the 1 per cent. It needs to be restored to collective ownership.'[52]

If we're going to deal with the climate crisis other changes are needed: ending the hegemony of the dollar (which will also restrain the US from acting like a rogue state) and replacing it with an international currency, putting a stop to the profligate production of credit, and bringing all that offshore capital back onshore. We also need to transform the capitalist system into a 'steady state' economy, as advocated by the ecological economist Herman Daly, who was one of the first to expose the absurdity of pursuing economics, and economic activity, while disregarding the natural environment. Designed to function in the context of a finite planet, a steady state economy doesn't grow in size but rather develops in quality, affording citizens a richness of experience that isn't captured by Gross Domestic Product.[53] Think of Bhutan's Gross National Happiness.

Another task is to undo the damage wrought by imperialism, colonialism and 'globalization-minus' by returning to local-scale economies, especially in food production. Pettifor cites John Maynard Keynes, who in 1933 warned of the drawbacks of 'economic entanglements' among nations:

> Ideas, knowledge, science, hospitality, travel – these are the things which should of their nature be *international*. But *let goods be homespun* whenever it is reasonably and conveniently possible, and, above all, let finance be primarily national.

Economic entanglements among the US, China and Russia may be making war less likely, but destruction of livelihoods and the Earth is a high price to pay for over-globalization.

Pettifor demonstrates that the transition away from a fossil fuel-based economy is at any rate *affordable*: there's enough credit and savings, private as well as public, to pay for it. And she shows how it can be done.[54] Expert economists may disagree about some of the details, but as Brian Eno said at the launch of the Democracy in Europe Movement 2025 (DiEM25): 'Start cooking; the recipe will follow.'[55] The movement soon produced a draft at least, in the form of a 'Green New Deal for Europe'. One of the movement's original initiators, Yanis Varoufakis (former finance minister of Greece), advocates an *International Green New Deal* to coordinate the efforts of the various GNDs. Following the model of the Marshall Plan and its funding of the Organisation for

European Economic Cooperation after the Second World War, he proposes establishing a new version of the OEEC, the Organisation for Emergency Environmental Cooperation, whose reach this time would be global.

Making the cooperation international has benefits for the *production* of renewable energy (more sun from southern countries and wind from the northern), for *innovation* through 'pooling the brainpower of the global scientific community' to combat the crisis, and for *reparation* to those countries that were victims of European and American imperialism. These nations are have been 'doubly dispossessed': first we stole all their natural resources, and now we're giving them global heating in return.

Whereas the chronically unsuccessful UN climate conferences emphasize contraction, the International Green New Deal reframes the problem in a positive way: 'Rather than pleading for restraint, it sets out a positive-sum vision of international investment, in which the gains from joining in outweigh going it alone.'[56] I think we're going to need some restraint as well, but the reframing is great. Another brief text by Varoufakis inspires by introducing *The Communist Manifesto* as an inspirational text that is perfectly relevant for our current situation. With the aim of encouraging young people especially to take political action toward the goal of 'authentic human happiness and the genuine *freedom* that must accompany it', this Introduction shows the way toward saner ways of living.

And what do we do about climate justice?

Those developed countries that have contributed most to causing the hotter conditions that are destroying lives and livelihoods in developing countries are responsible, if not solely or directly, for the suffering their actions are helping bring about. Common-sense notions of fairness and considerations of global justice require the developed countries to finance the costs of adaptation in the developing countries, which they reluctantly agree they should do – though so far they've been dragging their feet rather than paying up.

Responsibilities for the crisis vary, and assigning them is a contentious business. Whereas the United States has been the major contributor to global warming, but will lose a relatively small proportion of its land to sea-level rise, the low-lying Pacific Island nations who comprise the Alliance of Small Island States have contributed negligibly to the warming that is gradually putting them underwater.[57] Their fate is more cruel than that of Bangladesh, which is almost as unresponsible, and where floods come and recede: the Islanders face a permanent inundation of their homeland by the waters of the ocean. And yet the Australian government doesn't care about the part its energy policies play in consigning its neighbours to drowning.

The situation is complicated because while the US is the greatest contributor historically to rising GHG emissions, the Americans can justly say 'They knew not what they did', since the global-warming effects of carbon emissions weren't known in the early years of industrialization. But since James Hansen's testimony to Congress in 1988, the American government has known perfectly well what's going on; but now they simply censor the science and deny the facts.

When the member states of the United Nations made the commitment in 1992 to 'stabilize greenhouse gas concentrations in the atmosphere at a level that would prevent dangerous anthropogenic interference with the climate system', they began by acknowledging that 'change in the Earth's climate and its adverse effects are a common concern of humankind'. They agreed that the developed countries are responsible for the bulk of the world's GHG emissions, and that for the developing countries to develop sufficiently they will have to increase theirs.

The global nature of climate change calls for the widest possible cooperation by all countries and their participation in an effective and appropriate international response, in accordance with their *common but differentiated responsibilities and respective capabilities* and their social and economic conditions.[58]

Responsibilities differentiated by a country's historical contribution to GHG emissions and its current wealth – generally derived from a long period of carbon-emitting industrialization. Because the developed nations have emitted vastly more GHGs than the developing nations (with only 20 per cent of the world's population they're responsible for 75 per cent of carbon emissions since 1860), 'the developed country Parties should take the lead in combating climate change and the adverse effects thereof'. And because the current prosperity of the developed countries derives from their vast fossil fuel burning, they have greater financial 'capabilities' for fixing the problem, and should be helping the developing countries, who have hardly contributed to global warming at all.

In any case we must now face the fact that there is only so much, or little, in the way of further GHG emissions that we can afford before we risk major climate collapse through going over one or more tipping points. (It's the idea of the world's carbon budget from Chapter 2.) It's a hard sell politically to get the developed nations to take responsibility for their cumulative historical emissions, and since the urgent priority is to lower GHG emissions as much and as fast as possible, it makes sense to try and arrange fair compensation for damage inflicted, and then focus on a fair allocation of the emissions budget from now on.

It's a complicated business, but the main issues are clearly laid out in a study from 2017 under the title 'Fairly sharing 1.5: national fair shares of a 1.5°C-compliant global mitigation effort'.[59] As the title suggests, in the context of efforts to keep the temperature rise below 1.5°C, the authors discuss the complexities of ascertaining fair allocations to the world's countries 'in accordance with their common but differentiated responsibilities and respective capabilities'. If we agree that 'this global budget of cumulative CO_2 emissions needs to be equitably distributed among all countries', the fairest method is 'to equally allocate emissions on a per-capita basis, so that national emissions budgets can be calculated according to the size of the population'.

We would also want to agree on tying the allocation to the country's population in a given year, because this would discourage population growth (if your population goes up, your per capita allocation goes down) which would further lessen the burden on the environment. Based on the data available, the allowance per person would be 2.7 tons per year.[60] Presumably the allowance in 2019 is significantly less – certainly many times less than the per capita emissions of the US, at a little over 16 tons.[61]

It would be hard for the Americans to argue that, because they're so exceptional, they should be allowed to emit more per capita than, say, citizens of Burkina Faso, who currently emit far less than the allowance. Because you can't transform transportation and power-generating facilities overnight, or remake cities and suburbs so that they're sustainable, you can't expect Americans to reduce their emissions immediately. But you can set up an emissions trading system tomorrow whereby the US can purchase emissions rights from developing countries who emit less than their fair share. Then the rewards for lower emissions nations are partial compensation that can be used for adaptation. A bit of climate justice restored.

But what if the United States simply refuses to participate because the global warming deniers are still in power? And fossil fuel rich countries like Russia who will suffer economically from the shift to a zero-carbon economy? The US may be more tractable: if they lost over $300 billion to extreme weather events in 2017, there are surely much larger bills on the way – and eventually the economics will overwhelm even the Republican deniers. In the case of Russia and other non-players, there are instruments like carbon tariffs that may persuade.

If, as is likely, a majority of the world's nations commit to coping with global warming, the spoilers who continue to pollute ('pollution havens') will gain a temporary economic advantage from exploiting the atmospheric 'commons' when most countries have agreed to refrain. The low-carbon countries can then impose carbon tariffs collectively on imports from the non-players, in order to re-level the field and persuade the non-players to join the game.[62] If properly coordinated, such tactics would bring the outliers into the fold of a protected global commons.

If the young people who are going to suffer the worst from the effects of global warming become politically engaged in getting our democratic systems to work properly, they can make the needed difference.[63] But it's crucial to realise that it can no longer be a matter of left or right, progressive or conservative. Robert Reich, a professor of public policy at UC Berkeley, published a brilliant piece in *The Guardian* showing how those traditional categories no longer apply in the US – though his argument also applies more broadly. Since it all comes down to 'Trump and the oligarchs against the rest', Reich urges us to look behind that 'puppet master' of a president to 'where the real danger lies'.[64] Yes, it's those libertarian oligarchs who have bought, and now control, the political system.

Although they have the power, while we at 99.9 per cent have the numbers, we are split into factions. Populists are good at promoting divisiveness, pitting various groups against each other, and misdirection, convincing people that it's those 'elites' that are the problem. To deal with the climate crisis effectively, we have to disempower the oligarchs; and to do this, Reich advises, we need to set aside the factions and come together into 'a multi-racial, multi-ethnic coalition' of people of all classes from all over the world. Wise advice: we can do it.

We began with a *Wake up!* call from Rage in the Machine. Now that we realize how much 'ignorance has taken over', we may want to follow their further urgings and *Take the power back*. Some rage is appropriate to our current situation, even outrage (as long as it doesn't get too moral). Plato regarded this particular affect as a proper response to injustice, a key political emotion that can energize the fight for what is fair.[65] A measure of clear rage may also prevent despair from becoming overwhelming.

The climate crisis inspires such strong emotion that I tried to craft a conclusion infused with feeling, something more poetical and emotionally satisfying. But when I recalled Michel Serres' elegy for Mother Earth at the end of *The Natural Contract*, I deleted my own attempts, because thirty years ago he put it better than I ever could.

> Indescribable emotion: mother, my faithful mother, our mother who has been a monastic for as long as the world has existed, the heaviest, the most fecund, the holiest of maternal dwellings, chaste because always alone, and always pregnant, virgin and mother of all living things, better than alive, irreproducible universal womb of all possible life, mirror of ice floes, seat of snows, vessel of the seas, rose of the winds, tower of ivory, house of gold, Ark of the Covenant, gate of heaven, health, refuge, queen surrounded by clouds – who will be able to move her, who will be able to take her in their arms, who will protect her, if she risks dying and when she begins her mortal agony?[66]

If not we, then who? And if not now, then when?

When I think of the younger generation and the climate challenge we're burdening them with, there's a deep sadness. I worry for our daughter's sake. I'm sorry, sorry for what my generation is doing, and ashamed. Sometimes I weep; not so often, but I do. But thank Heavens, and Earth, there are still some grounds for joy.

Notes

Preface

1 Damian Carrington, 'Humanity has wiped out 60% of animal populations since 1970, report finds', *Guardian,* 29 Oct 2018; M. Grooten and R.E.A. Almond, eds, *Living Planet Report – 2018* (Gland, Switzerland: The Zoological Society of London and World Wildlife Fund, 2018). *IPBES Global Assessment Report 2019*, https://lp.panda.org/ipbes; Jonathan Watts, 'Human society under urgent threat from loss of Earth's natural life', *Guardian*, 6 May 2019.

2 Timothy M. Lenton et al., 'Climate tipping points – too risky to bet against', *Nature*, vol. 575 (2019): 592–95. Also Will Steffen et al., 'Trajectories of the Earth System in the Anthropocene', *Proceedings of the National Academy of Sciences*, 6 Aug 2018.

3 See recent works (in the bibliography) by authors such as Clive Hamilton, Dale Jamieson, Naomi Klein, Bruno Latour, Bill McKibben, George Monbiot, Roy Scranton and David Wallace-Wells. Most recently, Bill McKibben, 'A Very Hot Year', *New York Review of Books*, 12 Mar 2020.

4 See Damian Carrington, 'Halt destruction of nature or suffer even worse pandemics, say world's top scientists', *Guardian*, 27 Apr 2020; Jonathan Watts, '"Promiscuous treatment of nature" will lead to more pandemics', *Guardian*, 7 May 2020.

5 Bruno Latour, 'What protective measures can you think of so we don't go back to the pre-crisis production model?' (translation modified), http://www.bruno-latour.fr/sites/default/files/downloads/P-202-AOC-ENGLISH_1.pdf.

6 Dominic Rush and Mona Chalabi, '"Heads we win, tails you lose": how America's rich have turned pandemic into profit', *Guardian*, 26 Apr 2020.

7 David Wallace-Wells, *The Uninhabitable Earth: Life after Warming* (New York: Tim Duggan Books, 2019).

8 International Energy Agency, 'Global Energy Review 2020', April 2020, https://www.iea.org/reports/global-energy-review-2020; UNEP, 'Cut global emissions by 7.6 percent', 26 Nov 2019, https://www.unenvironment.org/news-and-stories/press-release/cut-global-emissions-76-percent-every-year-next-decade-meet-15degc.

Acknowledgements

1 See Damian Carrington, 'Why the Guardian is changing the language it uses about the environment', *Guardian*, 17 May 2019.

Introductions (Background and Book)

1 See Dom Phillips et al., 'Revealed: rampant deforestation of Amazon driven by global greed for meat', and Jonathan Watts, 'We must not barter the Amazon rainforest for burgers and steaks', *Guardian*, 2 Jul 2019; Matt The, '"Sandy Amazon is Completely Lawless": The Rainforest after Bolsonaro's First Year', *New York Times*, 5 Dec 2019; Alexandra Heal et al., 'Revealed: fires three times more common in Amazon beef farming zones', *Guardian*, 10 Dec 2019

2 For an excellent discussion of 'food chains' in relation to the environment, see Michael Pollan, *The Omnivore's Dilemma: A Natural History of Four Meals* (New York: Penguin Press, 2006). Another treatment of food as the traditional locus of our basic engagement with the natural world is Pollan's *In Defense of Food: An Eater's Manifesto* (New York: Penguin, 2008).

3 Adam Gabbatt, '"It's hyped up": climate change sceptics in the path of Hurricane Florence', *Guardian*, 20 Sep 2018.

4 Glenn Thrush, '$2.5 billion in Storm Losses, but Don't Ask Georgia Farmers about Climate Change', *New York Times*, 19 Oct 2018. The $306 billion figure comes from the Office for Coastal Management in the National Oceanic and Atmospheric Administration (NOAA), https://coast.noaa.gov/states/fast-facts/hurricane-costs.html. Adam B. Smith, '2018's Billion Dollar Disasters in Context', NOAA, Climate.gov, 7 Feb 2019, https://www.climate.gov/news-features/blogs/beyond-data/2018s-billion-dollar-disasters-context.

5 On attribution science, see the American Association for the Advancement of Science, SciLine (2019), 'Attribution Science: Climate Change and Extreme Weather', https://www.sciline.org/evidence-blog/climate-attribution. For particular events, see Michael E. Mann, et al., 'Influence of Anthropogenic Climate Change on Planetary Wave Resonance and Extreme Weather Events', *Scientific Reports*, vol. 7, no. 45242 (2017); also the discussions by Damian Carrington in 'Climate change: "human fingerprint" found on global extreme weather', *Guardian*, 27 Mar 2017, and 'Extreme global weather is "the face of climate change" says leading scientist', *Guardian*, 27 Jul 2018. Finally, Michael Mann, 'Hurricane Florence is a climate change triple threat', *Guardian*, 14 Sep 2018.

6 Niina Heikinnen, 'What Do Farmers Think about Climate Change?', Climate Wire, *Scientific American*, 28 Jan 2015. For a broader survey of the issues, see George Marshall, *Don't Even Think about It: Why Our Brains Are Wired to Ignore Climate Change* (New York & London: Bloomsbury, 2014).

7 D. R. Reidmiller et al., eds, *Impacts, Risks, and Adaptation in the United States: Fourth National Climate Assessment*, Vol. II (Washington, DC: U.S. Global Change Research Program, 2018); available at https://nca2018.globalchange.gov.

8 Oliver Milman, 'Climate change group scrapped by Trump reassembles to issue warning', *Guardian*, 4 Apr 2019 (with links to earlier reports on the Assessment). 'Donald Trump Believes Climate Change is a Hoax', MSNBC, 2 Jun 2017, https://www.youtube.com/watch?v=yqgMECkW3Ak.

9 With *Sgt. Pepper*, to get the full effect you had to stop the record and then rotate the turntable backward by hand evenly and at the right speed.

10 See, for example, Jesse Walker, *The United States of Paranoia: A Conspiracy Theory* (New York: HarperCollins, 2013) for a good history, and for an account of more recent developments, Anna Merlan, *Republic of Lies: American Conspiracy Theorists and their Surprising Rise to Power* (New York: Henry Holt, 2019).

11 Francis Bacon, *New Organon*, XLVI.

12 See Eli Pariser, *The Filter Bubble: What the Internet Is Hiding from You* (New York: Penguin, 2011).

13 Two excellent sources are Jane Mayer, *Dark Money: The Hidden History of the Billionaires behind the Rise of the Radical Right* (New York: Doubleday, 2016), and Nancy MacLean, *Democracy in Chains: The Deep History of the Radical Right's Stealth Plan for America* (Melbourne & London: Scribe Publications, 2017).

14 For a powerful and beautiful account of the joys *and* horrors of the natural world, which moves smoothly between ecstatic-lyrical and unsentimental-empirical, see Annie Dillard's wonderful, Pulitzer Prize-winning book, *Pilgrim at Tinker Creek* (New York: Harper's Magazine Press, 1974).

15 Garrett Hardin, 'The Tragedy of the Commons', *Science* (1968), vol. 162: 1243–8.

16 Adam Smith, *An Inquiry into the Nature and Causes of the Wealth of Nations*, Glasgow Edition (Oxford: Oxford University Press, 1976), Vol. 1, Book IV.ii, 456.

17 Hardin, 'The Tragedy of the Commons', 1244–5.

18 Elinor Ostrom, *Governing the Commons: The Evolution of Institutions for Collective Action* (New York: Cambridge University Press, 1990). George Monbiot argues persuasively for an extension of the commons as the basis for thriving communities in *Out of the Wreckage: A New Politics for an Age of Crisis* (London & New York: Verso, 2017), ch. 6.

19 Lynn White, Jr., 'The Historical Roots of Our Ecologic Crisis', *Science*, vol. 155, no. 3767 (1967), 1204, 1203.

20 Genesis 1:26-28.

21 White, 'The Historical Roots', 1205–07.

22 Zentatsu Baker-Roshi, 'Introduction', in Edward Espe Brown, *Tassajara Cooking* (Berkeley: Shambhala, 1973).

23 Frances Moore Lappé, *Diet for a Small Planet* (New York: Ballantine Books, 1971).

24 Peter Singer, *Animal Liberation* (New York: HarperCollins, 1975). The novelist J. M. Coetzee offers deep imaginative insights in two chapters of *The Lives of Animals* (Princeton: Princeton University Press, 1999), which he later integrated into his brilliant philosophical novel *Elizabeth Costello* (London: Secker & Warburg, 2003). Coetzee's *Diary of a Bad Year* (New York: Viking Penguin, 2008), another humorously philosophical gem of a novel, contains some 'strong opinions' that are relevant to the political philosophy discussed below.

25 E. F. Schumacher, *Small is Beautiful: A Study of Economics as if People Mattered* (London: Vintage, 1973), 31, 52–3, 29–32 (emphasis in the original).

26 Schumacher, *Small is Beautiful*, 3–7.

27 *Small is Beautiful*, 16–17 (emphasis added).

28 *Small is Beautiful*, 30–6.

29 *Small is Beautiful*, 39–44.

30 *Small is Beautiful*, 126, 131.

31 Leopold Kohr, *The Breakdown of Nations* (New York: E. P. Dutton, 1978), xviii.

32 George Santayana, *The Life of Reason* (Cambridge, Mass.: MIT Press, 2011), 1:172.

33 Brandon Miller and Jay Croft, CNN, 8 Oct 2018, https://edition.cnn.com/2018/10/07/world/climate-change-new-ipcc-report-wxc/index.html.

34 Brian Eno, 'Foreword', Martin Goodman and James Thornton, *Client Earth: Building an ecological civilisation* (Melbourne & London: Scribe, 2017), xi.

Part One

1 Friedrich Nietzsche, *Jenseits von Gut und Böse* (*Beyond Good and Evil*), aphorism 156.

Chapter 1

1 Heraclitus (flourished around 500 BCE), Fragment I in Charles H. Kahn, *The Art and Thought of Heraclitus* (Cambridge: Cambridge University Press, 1979), 29; fragments IV, II.

2   Brian Kennedy, 'U.S. concern about climate change is rising, but mainly among Democrats', Pew Research Center, 'Fact Tank', 28 Aug 2019.

3   Marshall, *Don't Even Think about It*, 2.

4   See, for example, John Cook, 'Heat stress: setting an upper limit on what we can adapt to', *Skeptical Science*, 11 May 2010,

5   For a comprehensive discussion of this issue, see David Michaels, 'Manufactured Uncertainty: Contested Science and the Protection of the Public's Health and Environment', in Robert N. Proctor and Londa Schiebinger, eds, *Agnotology: The Making and Unmaking of Ignorance* (Stanford: Stanford University Press, 2008).

6   See Robert N. Proctor, 'Agnotology: A Missing Term to Describe the Cultural Production of Ignorance (and Its Study)', in Proctor, *Agnotology*.

7   See Michael Polanyi, 'The Republic of Science: Its Political and Economic Theory', *Minerva* 1 (1962): 54–73, reprinted in vol. 38 (2000): 1–32.

8   John Cook et al., 'Consensus on Consensus: A synthesis of consensus estimates on human-caused global warming', *Environmental Research Letters* (2016), vol. 11/4, https://iopscience.iop.org/article/10.1088/1748-9326/11/4/048002. Abel Gustafson and Matthew Goldberg, 'Even Americans highly concerned about climate change dramatically underestimate the scientific consensus', Climate Note, 18 Oct 2018, https://climatecommunication.yale.edu/publications/even-americans-highly-concerned-about-climate-change-dramatically-underestimate-the-scientific-consensus/. Dana Nucitelli, 'Is the climate consensus 97%, 99%, or is plate tectonics a hoax?', *Guardian*, 3 May 2017.

9   An excellent history is Spencer R. Weart, *The Discovery of Global Warming* (Cambridge, Mass. and London: Harvard University Press, 2008).

10 See 'Science Is Not About Certainty' by Carlo Rovelli, an eminent theoretical physicist, *New Republic*, 11 Jul 2014.

11 Zeke Hausfather et al., 'Evaluating the performance of past climate projections', *Geophysical Research Letters*, 47/1 (2019), https://agupubs.onlinelibrary.wiley.com/doi/abs/10.1029/2019GL085378.

12 United Nations Framework Convention on Climate Change (New York: United Nations, 1992), article 3, sec. 3 reads: 'The Parties should take precautionary measures to anticipate, prevent or minimize the causes of climate change and mitigate its adverse effects. *Where there are threats of serious or irreversible damage, lack of full scientific certainty should not be used as a reason for postponing such measures* ... taking into account that policies and measures to deal with climate change should be cost-effective so as to ensure global benefits at the lowest possible cost.' (Emphasis added)

13 'The SYR was made possible thanks to the voluntary work, dedication and commitment of thousands of experts and scientists from around the globe, representing a range of views and disciplines.' IPCC, 2014, *Climate Change 2014: Synthesis Report* (Geneva: IPCC, 2015), v.

14 Michael Oppenheimer, Naomi Oreskes, Dale Jamieson, eds, *Discerning Experts: The Practices of Scientific Assessment for Environmental Policy* (Chicago: University of Chicago Press, 2019).

15 See, for example, Judah Cohen et al., 'Warm Arctic episodes linked with increased frequency of extreme winter weather in the United States', *Nature Communications*, vol. 9, article 869 (2018).

16 See, for example, Linda Qiu, 'The Baseless Claim that Climate Scientists are "Driven" by Money', *New York Times*, 27 Nov 2018.

17 Michael Marshall, 'The History of Ice on Earth', *New Scientist*, 24 May 2010 (see also the website snowballearth.org); Michon Scott and Rebecca Lindsay, 'What's the hottest Earth's ever been?', The National Oceanic and Atmospheric Administration's Climate.gov website (2014), https://www.climate.gov/news-features/climate-qa/whats-hottest-earths-ever-been.

18 James Lovelock, *The Revenge of Gaia: Why the Earth is Fighting Back – and How We Can Still Save Humanity* (London & New York: Penguin Books, 2007), 59.

19 James Lovelock, *Gaia: A New Look at Life on Earth*, with a new preface by the author (Oxford: Oxford University Press, 2000), ix; *The Revenge of Gaia*, 211. See also Lovelock, *The Vanishing Face of Gaia: A Final Warning* (New York: Basic Books, 2009).

20 Bruno Latour, *Facing Gaia: Eight Lectures on the New Climatic Regime*, trans. Catherine Porter (Cambridge, UK and Medford, Mass.: Polity Press, 2017), especially 92–101.

21 See David P. Turner, *The Green Marble: Earth System Science and Global Sustainability* (New York: Columbia University Press, 2018), ch. 1. This book provides an accessible introduction to ESS.

22 UNFCCC Declaration 1992, article 2. For the 'differentiated responsibilities', see 'What Do We Do about Climate Justice?' in the Inconclusions, below.

23 '2001 Amsterdam Declaration on Earth System Science', available at http://www.igbp.net/about/history/2001amsterdamdeclarationonearthsystemscience.4.1b8ae20512db692f2a680001312.html.

24 'Amsterdam Declaration'; Proverbs, 16:18.

25 Lovelock, *The Revenge of Gaia*, 4, 60. See also Clive Hamilton, *Defiant Earth: The Fate of Humans in the Anthropocene* (Cambridge, UK and Medford, Mass.: Polity Press, 2017), chs 1 and 2.

26 See Eugene Linden, 'How Climate Scientists Got Climate Change so Wrong', *New York Times*, 8 Nov 2019. Bruno Latour, *Down to Earth: Politics in the New Climatic Regime* (Cambridge: Polity Press, 2018).

27 For 'threat multipliers', see the United States Department of Defense, *Quadrennial Defense Review 2014* (Washington DC, 2014), 8. Some scientists see species and ecosystem destruction as a greater danger than global heating, but much of that destruction is actually a result of increasing temperatures.

28 Global Report on Internal Displacement 2019, http://www.internal-displacement.org/global-report/grid2019/; Oxfam International, 'Forced from home: climate-fuelled displacement' (Dec 2019).

29 ReliefWeb, UN Office for the Coordination of Humanitarian Affairs (Dec 2019), https://m.reliefweb.int/report/3422113. Colin P. Kelley et al., 'Climate Change in the Fertile Crescent and implications of the recent Syrian drought', *Proceedings of the National Academy of Sciences*, vol. 112, no. 11 (2015): 3241–6.; Aryn Baker, 'How Climate Change is behind the Surge of Migrants to Europe', *TIME Magazine*, 12 Sep 2015. See also Marshall Burke, et al., 'Climate Change and Conflict', *Annual Review of Economics*, vol. 7 (2015): 577–617.

30 Rupert Cornwall, 'Bush: God told me to invade Iraq', *The Independent*, 7 Oct 2005.

31 See Roberto Saviano, 'The Migrant Caravan: Made in USA', *New York Review of Books*, 7 Mar 2019. Michael D. Shear and Julie Hirschfeld Davis, 'Shoot Migrants' Legs, Build Alligator Moat: Behind Trump's Ideas for Border', *New York Times*, 1 Oct 2019.

32 Jeff Goodell, *The Water Will Come: Rising Seas, Sinking Cities, and the Remaking of the Civilized World* (New York: Little, Brown and Co., 2018).

33 Dale Jamieson, *Reason in a Dark Time: Why the Struggle Against Climate Change Failed – and What It Means for Our Future* (New York: Oxford University Press, 2014), 61; see the index for further discussions.

34 See IPCC, 'Summary for Policymakers', in V. Masson-Delmotte et al, eds, *Global Warming of 1.5°C. An IPCC Special Report on the impacts of global warming of 1.5°C above pre-industrial levels and related global greenhouse gas emission pathways, in the context of strengthening the global response to the threat of climate change, sustainable development, and efforts to eradicate poverty* (Geneva: World Meteorological Organization, 2018), sec. C2. (Full report available at https://www.ipcc.ch/sr15/).

35 Naomi Oreskes, Michael Oppenheimer, Dale Jamieson, 'Underestimating the Pace of Climate Change', *Scientific American*, 19 Aug 2019, a short article on their book *Discerning Experts*, referred to above.

36 Fiona Harvey, '"Tipping points" could exacerbate climate crisis, scientists fear', *Guardian*, 9 Oct 2018.

37 David Wallace-Wells, *The Uninhabitable Earth: Life After Warming* (New York: Tim Duggan Books, 2019), especially Part II, 'Elements of Chaos'.

38 Nick Watts et al., 'The 2019 report of the Lancet Countdown on health and climate change', *The Lancet* (2019), 394/10211:1836-78.

39 See Elizabeth Kolbert's excellent account in *The Sixth Extinction: An Unnatural History* (New York: Henry Holt & Co., 2014). George Monbiot,

'The big polluters' masterstroke was to blame the climate crisis on you and me', *Guardian*, 9 Oct 2019.

40 See Carrington, Grooten, Preface, note 1, above.

41 See IPBES, Watts, Preface, note 1, above.

42 Francisco Sanchez-Bayo and Chris A. G. Wyckhuys, 'Worldwide decline of the entomofauna: A review of its drivers', *Biological Conservation* (2019), vol. 232: 8–27. Damian Carrington, 'Plummeting insect numbers "threaten collapse of nature"', *Guardian*, 10 Feb 2019.

43 See Martin Schönfeld, 'The Fork in the Road', Editorial, *Journal of Global Ethics* (2018), 14/3: 305–13.

44 On 'dangerous anthropogenic interference', see UNFCCC (1992), Article 2. James Hansen, 'Is There Still Time to Avoid "Dangerous Anthropogenic Interference" with Global Climate?', available at http://www.columbia. edu/~jeh1/2005/Keeling_20051206.pdf (emphasis added).

45 Fred Pearce, *With Speed and Violence: Why Scientists Fear Tipping Points in Climate Change* (Boston: Beacon Press, 2008).

46 G. Myhre et al., 'Anthropogenic and natural radiative forcing', in T. F. Stocker et al., eds, *Climate change 2013: The physical science basis* (Cambridge: Cambridge University Press, 2013), 659–740. Available at http://www.climatechange2013.org/images/report/WG1AR5_Chapter08_ FINAL.pdf.

47 Simon L. Lewis, et al., 'The 2012 Amazon Drought', *Science* 331 (2011): 554; L. A. Parsons et al., 'The Threat of Multi-year Drought in Western Amazonia', *Water Resources Research* (2018) vol. 54/9: 5890–904; Carol Rasmussen, 'NASA finds Amazon drought leaves long legacy of damage', NASA: Global Climate Change, 9 Aug 2018, https://climate.nasa.gov/news/2780/nasa-finds-amazon-drought-leaves-long-legacy-of-damage/.

48 See the Editorial, 'Guardian view of Brazil's new president: a global danger', *Guardian*, 31 Oct 2018; Dom Phillips, 'Brazil records worst annual deforestation for a decade', *Guardian*, 24 Nov 2018; Jonathan Watts, 'Brazil's new foreign minister believes climate change is a Marxist plot', *Guardian*, 15 Nov 2018. Reuters, 'Brazil: Huge rise in Amazon destruction under Bolsonaro, figures show', *Guardian*, 3 Jul 2019.

49 James Hansen, *Storms of My Grandchildren: The Truth about the Coming Climate Catastrophe and Our Last Chance to Save Humanity* (New York: Bloomsbury, 2009), 99 (emphasis added).

50 Timothy M. Lenton et al., 'Climate tipping points – too risky to bet against', *Nature*, vol. 575 (2019): 592–5. Also Will Steffen et al., 'Trajectories of the Earth System in the Anthropocene', *Proceedings of the National Academy of Sciences*, 6 Aug 2018.

51 William J. Ripple et al., 'World Scientists' Warning of a Climate Emergency', *BioScience*, 5 Nov 2019.

52 Roy Scranton, *Learning to Die in the Anthropocene: Reflections on the End of a Civilization* (San Francisco: City Lights Books, 2015), 16.

53 Oliver Milman, 'James Hansen, father of climate change awareness, calls Paris talks "a fraud"', *Guardian*, 12 Dec 2015.

Chapter 2

1 *Zhuangzi*, ch. 3, in *Zhuangzi: The Essential Writings*, trans. Brook Ziporyn (Indianapolis: Hackett, 2009), 21. Subsequent references will be to the chapter of the original text followed by the page number of this translation.

2 For an excellent history (though not much on Prometheus, despite the title), see David H. Landes, *The Unbound Prometheus: Technological Change and Industrial Development in Western Europe from 1750 to the Present* (Cambridge: Cambridge University Press, 1969).

3 For many reasons why not, and an excellent overall assessment of geo-engineering, see Clive Hamilton, *Earthmasters: Playing God with the Climate* (New Haven: Yale University Press, 2013).

4 Kristin Shrader-Frechette, *What Will Work: Fighting Climate Change with Renewable Energy, Not Nuclear Power* (New York: Oxford University Press, 2011), 52 (emphasis added). Also J. M. Pearce, 'Thermodynamic limitations to nuclear energy deployment as a greenhouse gas mitigation technology', *International Journal of Nuclear Governance, Economy and Ecology* (2008), vol. 2, no. 1: 113–30.

5 Sallustius (fourth century CE), *De diis et mundo* (*Concerning the Gods and the Universe*) ed. and trans., A. D. Nock, (Cambridge: Cambridge University Press, 1926) sec. IV.

6 I discovered Bernard Stiegler's ingenious treatment of the Prometheus myth in relation to technology too late to discuss it here: the chapter 'Prometheus's Liver' in *Technics and Time 1: The Fault of Epimetheus* (Stanford: Stanford University Press, 1998).

7 Hesiod, *Theogony*, lines 517–616; *Works and Days*, lines 47–105.

8 See Stephen J. Pyne's excellent book, *Fire: A Brief History* (Seattle and London: University of Washington Press, 2001), 3. Pyne points out that volcanic discharges are 'faux fire', insofar as they consist in chemical processes that are quite different from those of fire, but that they can of course ignite real fires.

9 Pyne, *Fire*, xvi.

10 See *The Metamorphoses of Ovid*, trans. Allen Mandelbaum (New York: Houghton Mifflin, 1993), Book I, lines 5–150. For the original account of degeneration through four ages, see Hesiod, *Works and Days*, lines 109–201. Also Aeschylus,

Prometheus Bound, lines 450–505; 250–3. There's a mention of Prometheus's depriving men of knowledge of their death in Plato, *Gorgias*, 523d–e.

11 Pliny, *Natural History*, Book XXXIII, Ch. 1.

12 See, for example, Bill McGuire, *Waking the Giant: How a Changing Climate Triggers Earthquakes, Tsunamis, and Volcanoes* (Oxford and New York: Oxford University Press, 2012).

13 Lovelock, *The Revenge of Gaia*.

14 Plato, *Protagoras* 321c–d (emphasis added). I borrow Laurence Lampert's translation of these lines from his insightful discussion of *Protagoras* in *How Philosophy Became Socratic: A Study of Plato's* Protagoras, Charmides, *and* Republic (Chicago & London: University of Chicago Press, 2010), 52.

15 Hesiod, *Theogony*, lines 521–5. The image is most powerfully rendered by Rubens in his magnificent *Prometheus Bound* (1612).

16 Aeschylus, *Prometheus Bound*, lines 52–65.

17 William Nordhaus, responding to Andrew Revkin in 'Scientists Challenging Climate Science Appear to Flunk Climate Economics', Dot Earth, *New York Times*, 30 Jan 2012 (emphasis added).

18 See Steve Keen, 'Climate Change and the Nobel Prize in Economics: The Age of Rebellion', Brave New Europe, 4 May 2019, https://braveneweurope.com/steve-keen-climate-change-and-the-nobel-prize-in-economics-the-age-of-rebellion, and 'The Cost of Climate Change: A Nobel Economist's Model Dismantled', Evonomics, 14 Jul 2019, https://evonomics.com/steve-keen-nordhaus-climate-change-economics/.

19 Cited in Jamieson, *Reason in a Dark Time*, 106, 110 .

20 Nicholas Stern, *The Global Deal: Climate Change and the Creation of a New Era of Progress and Prosperity* (New York: PublicAffairs, 2009), whose subtitle reflects the author's optimism at the time that politicians would finally start to do something about global warming; and *Why Are We Waiting? The Logic, Urgency and Promise of Tackling Climate Change* (Cambridge, Mass.: MIT Press, 2015), whose title reflects his frustration that politicians still aren't doing anything to improve the situation. See also the illuminating discussion in Jamieson's *Reason in a Dark Time*, ch. 4, 'The Limits of Economics'.

21 Paul Krugman, 'Building a Green Economy', *New York Times Magazine*, 7 Apr 2010.

22 Ruth DeFries et al., 'The missing economic risks in assessments of climate change impacts', The Grantham Research Institute on Climate and the Environment, London School of Economics, Policy Publication (2019).

23 See Richard Heede and Naomi Oreskes, 'Potential emissions of CO_2 and methane from proved reserves of fossil fuels: An alternative analysis', *Global Environmental Change*, vol. 36 (2016): 12–20.

24 On carbon budgets and related issues, see the overview by the Carbon Tracker Initiative on their website at http://www.carbontracker.org/

resources/. Also James Leaton, 'Unburnable Carbon: Are the world's financial markets carrying a carbon bubble?' (Carbon Tracker Initiative, 2011).

25 M. Meinshausen et al., 'Greenhouse-gas emission targets for limiting global warming to 2°C', *Nature* (2009) 458:1158–62.

26 A list of sources criticizing the 2°C goal and advocating lower figures can be found on the homepage of the Climate Emergency Institute's website: http://www.climateemergencyinstitute.com/2c.html.

27 Bill McKibben, 'Global Warming's Terrifying New Math: Three simple numbers that add up to global catastrophe – and that make clear who the real enemy is', *Rolling Stone*, 19 July 2012.

28 Nicholas Stern, *The Economics of Climate Change: The Stern Review* (Cambridge: Cambridge University Press, 2007), 27. James Hansen et al., 'Assessing "Dangerous Climate Change"', PLoS ONE 8(12): e81648, https://pubs.giss.nasa.gov/abs/ha08510t.html.

29 Bill McKibben, *Eaarth: Making a Life on a Tough New Planet* (New York: Henry Holt, 2010), ch. 2; 'Global Warming's Terrifying New Math'.

30 Paul Roberts, *The End of Oil: On the Edge of a Perilous New World* (New York: Houghton Mifflin, 2005), 131–2.

31 Jason Channell et al., 'Energy Darwinism II: Why a Low Carbon Future Doesn't Have to Cost the Earth' (New York: Citigroup, 2015), 8, 21.

32 United Nations Environment Programme, *Emissions Gap Report 2019*, 'Executive Summary'.

33 Jonathan Watts et al., 'Oil firms to pour extra 7m barrels a day into markets, data shows', *Guardian*, 10 Oct 2019.

34 Stockholm Environment Institute et al., *The Production Gap Report 2019* , 'Executive Summary', http://productiongap.org.

Part Two

1 Josef Pieper, *Das Viergespann: Klugheit, Gerechtigkeit, Tapferkeit, Maß* (Munich: Kösel, 1964), 23; on 'Prudence' or 'Wisdom' as the first of the Four Cardinal Virtues.

Chapter 3

1 The Mont Pelerin Society, 'Statement of Aims' (Vaud, Switzerland: 1947), at https://www.montpelerin.org/statement-of-aims/.

2 George Monbiot in the 'Introduction' to the excellent collection of his articles for the *Guardian* (many on topics dealt with in this book of mine), *How Did We Get into This Mess? Politics, Equality, Nature* (London & New York: Verso, 2016).

3 Some fine accounts of neoliberalism are Noam Chomsky, *Profit over People: Neoliberalism and Global Order* (New York: Seven Stories Press, 1999), David Harvey, *A Brief History of Neoliberalism* (New York: Oxford University Press, 2005), Naomi Klein, *The Shock Doctrine: The Rise of Disaster Capitalism* (New York: Henry Holt & Co., 2007), and Jamie Peck, *Constructions of Neoliberal Reason* (New York: Oxford University Press, 2010).

4 See Howard Zinn, *A People's History of the United States, 1492-Present* (New York: Harper Collins, 2003), ch. 11, 'Robber Barons and Rebels'.

5 Thomas Piketty, *Capital in the Twenty-First Century*, trans. Arthur Goldhammer (Cambridge, Mass. and London: Harvard University Press, 2014), 173, 154.

6 Paul Krugman, 'Why We're in a New Gilded Age', *New York Review of Books*, 8 May 2014. See also Paul Krugman, *The Conscience of a Liberal* (New York: Norton, 2007); and an interview with Bill Moyers, 18 Apr 2014, http://billmoyers.com/episode/what-the-1-dont-want-you-to-know-2/.

7 Piketty, *Capital*, 514.

8 See Robert B. Reich, *Saving Capitalism: For the Many, not the Few* (New York: Knopf, 2015). Also the documentaries directed by Jacob Kornbluth and based on Reich's writings, *Inequality for All* (2013) and *Saving Capitalism* (2017).

9 Latour, *Down to Earth*, 1.

10 Latour, *Down to Earth*, 12-13.

11 L. Chancel and T. Piketty, 'Carbon and Inequality from Kyoto to Paris: Trends in the global inequality of carbon emissions (1998–2013) and prospects for an equitable adaptation fund' (Paris School of Economics, Nov 2015); Timothy Gore, 'Extreme Carbon Inequality: Why the Paris climate deal must put the poorest, lowest emitting and most vulnerable people first' (Oxfam International, Dec 2015).

12 Gore, 'Extreme Carbon Inequality', 1; Chancel & Piketty, 'Carbon and Inequality from Kyoto to Paris', 9. See also George Monbiot, 'For the sake of life on Earth, we must put a limit on wealth', *Guardian*, 19 Sep 2019.

13 Gore, 'Extreme Carbon Inequality', 2.

14 Deborah Hardoon, 'An economy for the 99%: It's time to build a human economy that benefits everyone, not just the privileged few', Summary (Oxfam International, Jan 2017), 2. 'Oxfam calculations using wealth of the richest individuals from Forbes Billionaires listing and wealth of the bottom 50% from Credit Suisse Global Wealth Databook 2016.'

15 Larry Elliott, 'World's eight richest people have same wealth as poorest 50%', *Guardian*, 16 Jan 2017.

16 Diego Pimental et al., 'Reward Work, Not Wealth: To end the inequality crisis, we must build an economy for ordinary working people, not the rich and powerful' (Oxfam International, Jan 2018). Larry Elliott, 'Inequality widens as 42 people hold the same wealth as 3.7bn poorest', *Guardian*, 22 Jan 2018. Max Lawson et al., 'Public Good or Private Wealth', Executive Summary (Oxfam International, Jan 2019), 9. For a critical analysis of the Oxfam reports, see Dylan Matthews, 'Are 26 billionaires worth more than half the planet? The debate, explained', *Vox*, 'Future Perfect', 22 Jan 2019, https://www.vox.com/future-perfect/2019/1/22/18192774/oxfam-inequality-report-2019-davos-wealth.

17 'The lives of the 0.0001%', *The Economist*, 7 Nov 2019. Gabriel Zucman, *The Hidden Wealth of Nations: The Scourge of Tax Havens* (Chicago and London: University of Chicago Press, 2015), 35.

18 Two excellent exposés are Jake Bernstein, *Secrecy World: Inside the Panama Papers Investigation of Secret Money Networks and the Global Elite* (New York: Henry Holt, 2017), and Oliver Bullough, *Moneyland: The Inside Story of the Crooks and Kleptocrats who Rule the World* (New York: St. Martin's Press, 2019).

19 Ann Pettifor, *The Case for the Green New Deal* (London & New York: Verso, 2019), xii-xiii.

20 Antony Fisher, cited by Richard Cockett in *Thinking the Unthinkable: Think-Tanks and the Economic Counter-Revolution, 1931–1983* (London: HarperCollins, 1994), 123–24 (emphasis added).

21 F. A. Hayek, 'Introduction', *The Constitution of Liberty* (Chicago: University of Chicago Press, 1960). On Hayek's extreme conservatism in this book, which was a favourite of Margaret Thatcher's, see Monbiot, *Out of the Wreckage*, ch. 2.

22 F. A. Harper, *The Writings of F. A. Harper, Volume 2: Shorter Essays* (Menlo Park: The Institute for Humane Studies, 1979), 236, 465, 388.

23 Oliver Smedley and Antony Fisher, cited in Cockett, *Thinking the Unthinkable*, 139, 131. See ch. 4, 'The Vision of a Chicken Farmer'.

24 On the transnational reach of the Atlas Network, see Marie Laure Djelic, 'Building an architecture for political influence: Atlas and the transnational institutionalization of the neoliberal think tank', in Christina Garsten, Adrienne Sörbom (eds.), *Power, Policy and Profit: Corporate Engagement in Politics and Governance* (Cheltenham: Edward Elgar Publishing, 2017). Milton Friedman, cited in Cockett, *Thinking the Unthinkable*, 122. Fraser in Wichita: 'An Interview with George Pearson', Atlas Highlights, Winter 2007/08, 16, https://www.atlasnetwork.org/assets/uploads/annual-reports/highlights/2008_winter_highlights.pdf

25 Peck, *Constructions of Neoliberal Reason*, 171; ch. 4 is good on Fisher's activities and influence.

26 James M. Buchanan, 'The Thomas Jefferson Center', *The University of Virginia Newsletter* (1958), vol. xxxv, no. 2. MacLean, *Democracy in Chains*, xix, 46. Academics associated with institutions criticized by MacLean have in turn criticised her book: see Mark Parry, 'Nancy MacLean responds to her critics', *The Chronicle of Higher Education*, 19 July 2017.

27 MacLean, *Democracy in Chains*, xiv, xxi–xxii, xxx.

28 See the thoughtful account by Gary Weiss in his *Ayn Rand Nation: The Hidden Struggle for America's Soul* (New York: St. Martin's Press, 2012). Also Jonathan Freedland, 'The new age of Ayn Rand: How she won over Trump and Silicon Valley', *Guardian*, 10 Apr 2017.

29 Ayn Rand, *Journals of Ayn Rand*, (New York: Plume, 1999), sec. 4, 4 Dec 1935.

30 See Weiss, *Ayn Rand Nation*.

31 United Nations, Rio Declaration on Environment and Development, June 1992, Principle 16, https://www.un.org/en/development/desa/population/migration/generalassembly/docs/globalcompact/A_CONF.151_26_Vol.I_Declaration.pdf.

32 Stern, *The Economics of Climate Change*, 27 (emphasis added).

33 Naomi Klein, *This Changes Everything: Capitalism vs. the Climate* (New York: Simon & Schuster, 2014), see especially chs 2, 'Hot Money: How Free Market Fundamentalism Helped Overheat the Planet', and 5, 'Beyond Extractivism: Confronting the Climate Denier Within'.

34 Klein, *This Changes Everything*, 40–1.

35 Mayer, *Dark Money*, 375, 119 (citing Michael Joyce, who was for many years the executive director of the John M. Olin Foundation).

36 The 'artillery' comes from James Piereson, a major figure in the conservative think tank world, cited by Mayer in *Dark Money*, 76. See Mayer, *Dark Money*, Part One, 'Weaponizing Philanthropy: The War of Ideas, 1970–2008', and MacLean, *Democracy in Chains*, chs 9 and 11.

37 Robert F. Kennedy, Jr., *Crimes against Nature: How George W. Bush and His Corporate Pals Are Plundering the Country and Hijacking Our Democracy* (New York: HarperCollins, 2004), 23–4.

38 See Robert J. Brulle, 'Institutionalizing Delay: foundation funding and the creation of U.S. climate change counter-movement organizations', *Climatic Change*, vol. 122/4: 681–94 (2013). Also the entries for the Heritage Foundation and the Mercer Family Foundation at DESMOG, https://www.desmogblog.com.

39 For information on Donors Trust, see DESMOG, https://www.desmogblog.com/who-donors-trust.

40 William Shawcross ('Rupert Murdoch', TIME, 18 Jun 2006) reports Murdoch as saying: 'What does libertarian mean? As much individual responsibility as possible, as little government as possible, as few rules as possible.'

41 Eric Boehlert, 'How Rupert Murdoch Pushed Australia into a Climate Change Retreat', MediaMatters for America, 24 Jul 2014; David Folkenflik,

'How Murdoch's Aussie Papers Cover Climate Change', NPR, 6 Apr 2012. Graham Readfern, 'What the World's Richest Woman, Gina Rinehart, Thinks about Climate Change', DESMOG, 27 Jun 2012.

42 See, in addition to chs 1 and 4 of Jane Mayer's *Dark Money* and ch. 9 of Nancy MacLean's *Democracy in Chains*, Daniel Schulman, *Sons of Wichita: How the Koch Brothers Became America's Most Powerful and Private Dynasty* (New York: Grand Central Publishing, 2015), and Christopher Leonard's *Kochland: The Secret History of Koch Industries and Corporate Power in America* (London & New York: Simon & Schuster, 2019).

43 See, for example, Jane Mayer, 'A Whistle-Blower Accuses the Kochs of "Poisoning" an Arkansas Town', *The New Yorker*, 9 Sep 2016.

44 Mayer, *Dark Money*, 140.

45 MacLean, *Democracy in Chains*, 195.

46 Barry G. Rabe and Philip L. Mundo, 'Business Influence in State-Level Environmental Policy', in Michael E. Kraft and Sheldon Kamieniecki, eds, *Business and Environmental Policy: Corporate Interests in the American Political System* (Cambridge, Mass.: MIT Press, 2007), 276.

47 See Alexander Hertel-Fernandez, *State Capture: How Conservative Activists, Big Businesses, and Wealthy Donors Reshaped the American States – and the Nation* (New York: Oxford University Press, 2019), ch. 4. The book's first four chapters give a comprehensive account of ALEC's activities.

48 Dave Levinthal, 'How the Koch Brothers Are Influencing U.S. Colleges', *TIME*, 15 Dec 2015, http://time.com/4148838/koch-brothers-colleges-universities/. Jim Tankersley, 'Inside Charles Koch's $200 million quest for "A Republic of Science"', *The Washington Post*, 3 Jun 2016.

49 Richard Fink, 'From Ideas to Action: The Role of Universities, Think Tanks, and Activist Groups', *Philanthropy Magazine*, Winter 1996.

50 See Leonard, *Kochland*, 400; and the conference flyer at KochDocs, an excellent source for all things Koched, https://kochdocs.org/2019/08/12/1991-cato-climate-denial-conference-flyer-and-schedule/. Videos of speakers at Heartland climate conferences are available at http://climateconferences.heartland.org.

51 See Greenpeace, *Koch Industries Secretly Funding the Climate Denial Machine* (Washington DC: Greenpeace USA, 2010). For more information on the activities of Koch Industries, see the Center for Media and Democracy's *Koch Exposed* website: http://www.kochexposed.org/.

52 Benjamin Franta and Geoffrey Supran, 'The fossil fuel industry's invisible colonization of academia', *Guardian*, 13 Mar 2017.

Chapter 4

1   Chris Mooney, *The Republican War on Science* (New York: Basic Books, 2005), on which I draw for the next few paragraphs.

2   See Mooney, *The Republican War*, ch. 6, 'Junking "Sound Science"'. On the obfuscatory tactics of Big Tobacco, see Robert N. Proctor, 'Agnotology: A Missing Term to Describe the Cultural Production of Ignorance (and Its Study)', and Jon Christensen, 'Smoking Out Objectivity: Journalistic Gears in the Agnotology Machine', in Proctor, *Agnotology*.

3   Rachel Carson, *Silent Spring* (New York: Houghton Mifflin Harcourt, 2002), 177, 259, 271.

4   See Linda Lear, *Rachel Carson: Witness for Nature* (New York: Henry Holt & Co., 1997), ch. 17.

5   Revelle, R., & H. E. Suess, 'Carbon dioxide exchange between atmosphere and ocean and the question of an increase of atmospheric CO2 during the past decades', *Tellus*, 9/1 (1957), 18–27.

6   Brannon, H. R., Jr. et al., 'Radiocarbon evidence on the dilution of atmospheric and oceanic carbon by carbon from fossil fuels', *Eos Transactions*, American Geophysical Union, 38/5 (1957), 643–50.

7   Jamieson, *Reason in a Dark Time*, 18. Jamieson's second chapter, 'The Nature of the Problem', provides a good overview of the development of climate science and of public awareness and discussion of the topic.

8   A good source on this topic is Neela Banerjee et al., 'CO2's Role in Global Warming Has Been on the Oil Industries' Radar since the 1960s', *Inside Climate News*, 13 Apr 2016. See also Bill McKibben, *Falter: Has the Human Game Begun to Play Itself Out?* (London: Wildfire, 2019), ch. 7.

9   Union of Concerned Scientists, *Smoke, Mirrors & Hot Air: How ExxonMobil Uses Big Tobacco's Tactics to Manufacture Uncertainty about Climate Change* (Cambridge, Mass.: 2007), and *The Climate Deception Dossiers* (Cambridge, Mass.: 2015).

10 Draft of 'Predicting Future Climate Change: A Primer', 1, 16 (emphasis added), attached to a memo from L. S. Bernstein, Environmental Health and Safety Department, Mobil Oil Corporation, 21 Dec 1995, in 'Deception Dossier 7', *The Climate Deception Dossiers*.

11 James E. Hansen, 'The Greenhouse Effect: Impacts on Current Global Temperature and Regional Heat Waves', 23 Jun 1988, https://climatechange. procon.org/sourcefiles/1988_Hansen_Senate_Testimony.pdf.

12 Sandra Laville, 'Top oil firms spending millions to block climate change policies, says report', *Guardian*, 22 Mar 2019; InfluenceMap, 'Big Oil's Real Agenda on Climate Change: How the oil majors have spent $1Bn since Paris on narrative capture and lobbying on climate', March 2019.

13 'What do we know about the top twenty polluters?' The Polluters, *Guardian*, 9 Oct 2019.

14 Naomi Oreskes and Erik M. Conway, *Merchants of Doubt: How a Handful of Scientists Obscured the Truth on Issues from Tobacco Smoke to Global Warming* (New York & London: Bloomsbury, 2010). See also James Hoggan with Richard Littlemore, *Climate CoverUp: The Crusade to Deny Global Warming* (Vancouver: Greystone Books, 2009), and Haydn Washington and John Cook, *Climate Change Denial: Heads in the Sand* (New York: Earthscan, 2011). And for a devastating snapshot from inside the Marshall Institute, see Matthew B. Crawford, *Shopcraft as Soulcraft: An Inquiry into the Value of Work* (New York: Penguin 2009), 82.

15 United Nations Framework Convention on Climate Change (New York: May 1992), Article 2, pdf available at http://unfccc.int/files/essential_background/background_publications_htmlpdf/application/pdf/conveng.pdf.

16 U. Mass. Amherst PERI, 'Greenhouse 100 Polluters Index' https://www.peri.umass.edu/greenhouse-100-polluters-index-2018-report-based-on-2015-data. For CSE and Rich Fink, see Mayer, *Dark Money*, 61.

17 See William Westermeyer, 'In 1993 my agency warned of climate change. In 1995 it was abolished', *New York Times*, 27 Dec 2018.

18 American Petroleum Institute, 'Global Climate Science Communications Action Plan', section 2, 'Victory Will be Achieved When . . .', at http://www.climatefiles.com/trade-group/american-petroleum-institute/1998-global-climate-science-communications-team-action-plan/.

19 Maxwell T. Boykoff and Jules M. Boykoff, 'Balance as Bias: Global warming and the US prestige press', *Global Environmental Change* 14 (2004): 125–36. Dana Nuccitelli, 'Rupert Murdoch doesn't understand climate change basics', *Guardian*, 14 Jul 2014.

20 Oliver Milman, '"Americans are waking up": two thirds say climate crisis must be addressed', *Guardian*, 15 Sep 2019.

21 Dana Nuccitelli, 'During the most important year for climate change, TV coverage fell', *Guardian*, 7 Mar 2016.

22 Alexander Michael Petersen et al., 'Discrepancy in scientific authority and media visibility of climate change scientists and contrarians', *Nature Communications* 10, no. 3502, (2019).

23 'The Top Talk Radio Audiences [2011]', *Talkers: The Bible of Talk Radio and New Talk Media*, https://web.archive.org/web/20110924132902/http://www.talkers.com/top-talk-radio-audiences/.

24 Rush Limbaugh, 'Friedman and Brooks', The Rush Limbaugh Show, 22 June 2011, https://www.rushlimbaugh.com/daily/2011/06/22/friedman_and_brooks_still_have_no_clue_who_barack_obama_really_is/; John K. Wilson, *The Most Dangerous Man in America:*

Rush Limbaugh's Assault on Reason (New York: St. Martin's Press, 2011), 166.

25 Wilson, *The Most Dangerous Man*, 174–5.

26 Sean Hannity, *The Sean Hannity* Show, 29 Jan 2014, reported in 'Hannity on New Climate Change Study: "I Don't Care" What Over 9100 Scientists Say', Media Matters for America, https://www.mediamatters.org/video/2014/01/30/hannity-on-new-climate-change-study-i-dont-care/197851.

27 Joe Bageant, *Deer Hunting with Jesus: Dispatches from America's Class War* (New York: Random House, 2007), 80–1.

28 James Delingpole, 'Global Temperatures Plunge. Icy Silence from Climate Alarmists', Breitbart, 30 Nov 2016; tweet from the House Committee on Science, 1 Dec 2016; Scott Johnson, ed., 'Analysis of "Stunning new data indicates El Nino drove record highs in global temperatures"', *Climate Feedback*, 2 Dec 2016.

29 Greenpeace, *Koch Industries: Secretly Funding the Climate Denial Machine* (Washington, DC: Greenpeace USA, 2010), 8, and *Koch Industries: Still Fueling Climate Denial 2011 Update*, Executive Summary, https://www.greenpeace.org/usa/global-warming/climate-deniers/koch-industries/.

30 Clive Hamilton, *Requiem for a Species* (New York: Earthscan, 2010), xiv.

31 Mayer, *Dark Money*, 1–18. The programme for the meeting in Aspen, Colorado in June 2010 can be found at https://images2.americanprogressaction.org/ThinkProgress/secretkochmeeting.pdf.

32 Mayer, *Dark Money*, ch. 9, 'Money is Speech: The Long Road to *Citizens United*'.

33 Global Commission on Elections, Democracy & Security (2012), 'Deepening Democracy: A Strategy for Improving the Integrity of Elections Worldwide'.

34 Oil Change International, 'Fossil Fuel Funding to Congress: Industry Influence in the U.S.', http://priceofoil.org/fossil-fuel-industry-influence-in-the-u-s/.

35 See the Center for Responsive Politics, at OpenSecrets.org, 'Outside Spending', https://www.opensecrets.org/outsidespending/; and 'Money-in-Politics Timeline', https://www.opensecrets.org/resources/learn/timeline.

36 Mayer, *Dark Money*, xx.

37 See Carole Cadwalladr, 'Our Cambridge Analytica scoop shocked the world', *Guardian*, 23 Dec 2018.

38 See Jane Mayer, 'The Reclusive Hedge-Fund Tycoon behind the Trump Presidency: How Robert Mercer exploited American's populist insurgency', *The New Yorker*, 27 Mar 2017.

39 Alan Zibel, 'The Koch Government: How the Koch Brothers' Agenda Has Infiltrated the Trump Administration' (Washington DC: Public Citizen, 2017). Also Mayer, *Dark Money*, 368, xx; and Alastair Gee, 'Democratic senators scrutinize Koch brothers' "infiltration" of Trump team', *Guardian*, 26 Apr 2018.

40 Freedom Partners, 'A Roadmap to Repeal: Removing Regulatory Barriers to Opportunity' (2017), available at https://freedompartners.org/wp-content/uploads/2017/01/Roadmap_To_Repeal_Removing_Regulatory_Barriers_to_Opportunity.pdf.

41 Koch Seminar Network, 'Efforts in Government: Advancing Principled Public Policy' (2017), https://www.documentcloud.org/documents/4364737-Koch-Seminar-Network.html. See also Lee Fang and Nick Surgey, 'Koch Document Reveals Laundry List of Policy Victories Extracted from the Trump Administration', *The Intercept*, 25 Feb 2018.

42 'Analysis: The Trump-GOP Tax Cuts One Year Later', Americans for Tax Fairness, 13 Dec 2018, https://americansfortaxfairness.org/analysis-trump-gop-tax-cuts-one-year-later/. See also Lawrence Summers, 'Trump's top economist's tax analysis isn't just wrong, it's dishonest', *Washington Post*, 17 Oct 2017, and Paul Krugman, 'The Trump Tax Cut: Even Worse than You've Heard', *New York Times*, 1 Jan 2019.

43 Koch Seminar Network, 'Efforts in Government'; see also Coral Davenport and Eric Lipton, 'How G.O.P. Leaders Came to View Climate Change as Fake Science', *New York Times*, 3 Jun 2017. Jane Mayer, 'In the Withdrawal from the Paris Climate Agreement, the Koch Brothers' Campaign Becomes Overt', *The New Yorker*, 5 June 2017.

44 Editorial, 'The Koch Attack on Solar Energy', *New York Times*, 26 Apr 2014; Tim Dickinson, 'The Koch Brothers' Dirty War on Solar Power', *Rolling Stone*, 11 Feb 2016. Hiroko Tabuchi, 'How the Koch Brothers Are Killing Public Transport Projects around the Country', *New York Times*, 19 Jun 2018.

45 Brad Plumer, 'How Big a Deal is Trump's Fuel Economy Rollback? For the Climate, Maybe the Biggest Yet', *New York Times*, 3 Aug 2018; Hiroko Tabuchi, 'The Oil Industry's Covert Campaign to Rewrite American Car Emissions Rules', *New York Times*, 13 Dec 2018.

46 David Cutler and Francesca Domenici, 'A Breath of Bad Air: Cost of the Trump Environmental Agenda May Lead to 80000 Extra Deaths per Decade', *Journal of American Medical Association*, The JAMA Forum, 12 Jun 2018.

47 Nadja Popovich et al., '95 Environmental Rules Being Rolled Back Under Trump', *New York Times*, 2 Jun 2019, which refers to studies by the Law Schools at Harvard, Columbia and New York University.

48 See Jeremy Berke, 'Trump's new pollution rules would cause hundreds more people to die prematurely each year, compared to the Obama plan it's designed to replace', *Business Insider*, 22 Aug 2018.

49 See Ariel Dorfman, 'Trump's War on Knowledge', NYR Daily, *New York Review of Books*, 12 Oct 2017. Also Brad Plumer and Coral Davenport, 'Science under Attack: How Trump is Sidelining Researchers and their Work', *New York Times*, 28 Dec 2019.

50 Michael Lewis, *The Fifth Risk* (New York & London: Norton, 2018), and the entertaining review by Fintan O'Toole, 'Saboteur in Chief', *New York Review of Books*, 6 Dec 2018.

51 Robert Booth, 'Rightwing UK think tank 'offered ministerial access' to potential US donors', *Guardian*, 30 Jul 2018. Concerning 'chickens coming home to roost', see (on video) Malcolm X, explaining his use of the phrase: https://www.youtube.com/watch?v=oD6aX3dHR2k.

52 *IEA Weekend Newsletter*, 28 Jul 2019, available at https://politicalemails.org/messages/8455.

53 See, for example, Timsbury Environment Group, 'Carbon Emissions and Climate Change' (2012), pdf at http://www.timsbury.org.uk/wp-content/uploads/2017/01/RM-summary-for-website-version2.pdf.

54 Felicity Lawrence et al., 'How the right's radical think tanks reshaped the Conservative Party', and Rob Evans et al., 'Wealthy US donors gave millions to right-wing UK groups', *Guardian*, 29 Nov 2019.

55 Rod Minchin, 'Brexit calamitous act of self-harm, warns Patten', Indepedent. ie, 9 Oct 2017.

56 See, for example, *The Republic of* Plato, trans. Allan Bloom (New York: Basic Books, 1968), 5a-376c, 410a-412a, 439b-441a..

Chapter 5

1 See Harold Bloom, *The American Religion: The Emergence of the Post-Christian Nation* (New York: Simon & Schuster, 1992). The focus is on Christian Science, The Church of Jesus Christ of Latter-Day Saints, Jehovah's Witnesses, the Seventh-Day Adventist Church, and the Southern Baptist Convention.

2 1 Thessalonians, 4:14–18.

3 Reverend S. J. Eaton, cited in Darren Dochuk, *Anointed with Oil: How Christianity and Crude Made Modern America* (New York: Basic Books, 2019), ch. 1.

4 See Philip J. Hilts, 'Creation vs. Evolution: Battle Resumes in Public Schools', *The Washington Post*, 13 Sep 1980.

5 See Russ Bellant, *The Coors Connection: How Coors Family Philanthropy Undermines Democratic Pluralism* (Boston: South End Press, 1988), especially 'The Coors Family and the Environment', 84–90.

6 See Daniel T. Rodgers, *Age of Fracture* (Cambridge, Mass. & London: Harvard University Press, 2011), 1. On the Heritage Foundation's history of climate denial and its libertarian funders, see the entry in DESMOG.

7 Mountain States Legal Foundation website, https://www.mountainstateslegal. org.

8 See Kennedy, *Crimes against Nature*, 28–9. Also David Helvarg, *The War Against the Greens: The 'Wise Use' Movement, the New Right, and the Browning of America* (San Francisco: Sierra Club Books, 1994).

9 Michael Weisskopf and David Maraniss, 'Forging an Alliance for Deregulation', *Washington Post*, 12 Mar 1995; Environmental Working Group, 'Project Relief: PAC contributions from Project Relief member companies and trade associations', Feb 1995, https://www.ewg.org/ research/project-relief.

10 '1991 Information Council on the Environment Climate Denial Ad Campaign', *Climate Files*, http://www.climatefiles.com/denial-groups/ ice-ad-campaign/; also Ross Gelbspan, *Boiling Point: How Politicians, Big Oil and Coal, Journalists and Activists Are Fueling the Climate Crisis – and What We Can Do to Avoid Disaster* (New York: Basic Books, 2004), 53.

11 See 'Greening Earth Society' at DESMOG.

12 Fred Palmer, cited by Naomi Oreskes, 'My Facts are Better than Your Facts', in Peter Howlett and Mary S. Morgan, eds, *How Well Do Facts Travel? The Dissemination of Reliable Knowledge* (New York: Cambridge University Press, 2011), 151–2; see also Jeff Goodell, *Big Coal*, 181-82, and Ross Gelbspan, *Boiling Point*, 51.

13 Fred Palmer, in an excerpt from *Staking the Globe: The Energy War is On* (1997), viewable at https://www.youtube.com/watch?v=Vr9kanvxa6A.

14 Suzanne Goldenberg, 'The truth behind Peabody's campaign to rebrand coal as a poverty cure', *Guardian*, 19 May 2015; 'Biggest US coal company founded dozens of groups questioning climate change', *Guardian*, 13 Jun 2016.

15 Fred Palmer, cited in Graham Readfearn, '"God Bless Trump"', DESMOG, 29 Jan 2017. See also the entry for Fred Palmer.

16 See Bernard Zaleha and Andrew Szasz, 'Why conservative Christians don't believe in climate change', *Bulletin of the Atomic Scientists* (2015), vol. 71(5): 19–30.

17 Evangelical Climate Initiative Statement, 'An Evangelical Call to Action' (2006), http://www.christiansandclimate.org/statement/.

18 Cornwall Alliance, 'Evangelical Declaration on Global Warming' (2009), 'What We Believe', article 1, 'What We Deny', article 1, 'A Call to Action', 3, available under 'Landmark Documents', https://cornwallalliance.org/ landmark-documents/.

19 Francis A. Schaeffer, *Pollution and the Death of Man*, second edition (Wheaton, Illinois: Crossway, 1992), 69, 71. E. Calvin Beisner, interview with Bill Moyers in *Moyers on America*, 'Is God Green?' (2006), https://www. youtube.com/watch?v=jwMsDVVahTA, at 43':05".

20 Sen. James Inhofe, television appearance when young, viewable at https:// www.youtube.com/watch?v=yHTSGDuO-j4.

21 See the Center for Responsive Politics entry, 'Sen. James M Inhofe', at opensecrets.org. Farron Cousins, 'Climate Denier Jim Inhofe Goes Full Conspiracy Theorist in Unhinged Rant about Global Warming', DESMOG, 2 Aug 2016.

22 My paraphrase of a passage in Sigmund Freud, *The Interpretation of Dreams*, ch. 2.

23 US Sen. James M. Inhofe, 'The Science of Climate Change: Senate Floor Statement', 28 Jul 2003, https://www.epw.senate.gov/public/index. cfm/2003/7/post-8070bc3a-6070-4bc1-8cc7-da6afe3e4740. Eleven key passages from Inhofe's text are refuted by John Cook in *Skeptical Science*, 'James Inhofe', https://skepticalscience.com/skepticquotes.php?s=30 (2 Apr 2013). Also Michael Mann, *The Hockey Stick and the Climate Wars: Dispatches from the Front Lines* (New York: Columbia University Press, 2012), ch. 8; Chris Mooney, *The Republican War*, ch. 7.

24 Inhofe, 'The Facts and Science of Climate Change', original version, seven paragraphs from the end; later version, 20 (emphasis added).

25 Ron Suskind, 'Faith, Certainty, and the Presidency of George W. Bush', *New York Times*, 17 Oct 2004.

26 Suskind, 'Faith, Certainty, and the Presidency of George W. Bush'.

27 Minority Staff, US Senate Environment and Public Works Committee, '"Consensus" Exposed: The CRU Controversy' (February 2010), 34, http:// www.inhofe.senate.gov/download/?id=ce35055e-8922-417f-b416-800183ab7272&download=1.

28 The findings and reports of the seven committees are well documented in the Wikipedia article, 'Climate Research Unit email controversy', https://en. wikipedia.org/wiki/Climatic_Research_Unit_email_controversy#Inquiries_ and_reports.

29 Mann, *The Hockey Stick*, 224-32; Rosslyn Beeby, 'Climate of Fear: Scientists Face Death Threats', *The Canberra Times*, 4 Jun 2011.

30 Minority Staff, '"Consensus" Exposed', 15.

31 See the characters described in Oreskes and Conway's *Merchants of Doubt*, and App. 5.1 for a discussion of Soon and Baliunas.

32 Senator James Inhofe, radio interview, 'Crosstalk', Voice of Christian Youth America, 7 Mar 2012; audible at https://www.youtube.com/ watch?v=EKd6UJPghUs.

33 James Inhofe, *The Greatest Hoax: How the Global Warming Conspiracy Threatens Your Future* (Washington, DC: WND Books, 2012), 68–71. The King James Version of Genesis 8:22 has 'seedtime' instead of 'springtime'.

34 Chris Castel, 'U.S. Senator Jim Inhofe's trips to Africa called a "Jesus Thing"', *The Oklahoman* NewsOK, 21 Dec 2008, https://newsok.com/article/3331838/us-senator-jim-inhofes-trips-to-africa-called-a-jesus-thing.

35 Robin McKie, 'Global heating to inflict more droughts on Africa as well as floods', *Guardian*, 16 Jun 2019.

36 Ralph Hall, in Jeffrey Mervis, 'Ralph Hall speaks out on climate change', *Science*Insider, 14 Dec 2011, http://www.sciencemag.org/news/2011/12/ralph-hall-speaks-out-climate-change.

37 United States Department of Defense, *Quadrennial Defense Review 2014* (Washington DC, 2014), 8 (emphasis added). See also Gwynne Dyer, *Climate Wars: The Fight for Survival as the World Overheats* (Oxford and New York: Oneworld Publications, 2010).

38 Kate Sheppard, 'House Directs Pentagon to Ignore Climate Change', *The Huffington Post*, 23 May 2014.

39 'Inhofe Announces Climate Hypocrite Awards', official Senate website, https://www.inhofe.senate.gov/climate-week.

40 Marc Morano, cited in Douglas Fischer, 'Cyber Bullying Intensifies as Climate Data Questioned', *Scientific American*, 1 Mar 2010.

41 See Michelle Goldberg, '"This Evil Is All Around Us"', *Slate*, 12 January 2017, and Edward Wong, 'The Rapture and the Real World: Mike Pompeo Blends Beliefs and Policy', *New York Times*, 30 Mar 2019 (emphasis added).

42 Dom Phillips, 'Bolsonaro declares "the Amazon is ours" and calls deforestation data "lies"', *Guardian*, 19 Jul 2019.

43 Jon Lee Anderson, 'Jair Bolsonaro's Southern Strategy: In Brazil, a budding authoritarian borrows from the Trump playbook', *The New Yorker*, 25 Mar 2019.

44 C. S. Lewis, *Mere Christianity,* revised edition (New York: HarperCollins, 2001), 59–60.

Transition

1 Nick Bilton, 'Silicon Valley's Most Disturbing Obsession', *Vanity Fair*, 5 Oct 2016.

2 Gary Cook et al., 'Clicking Clean: Who is winning the race to build a green Internet?' (Washington DC: Greenpeace Inc., 2017), 5, 15–16, http://www.clickclean.org/international/en/. Climate Home News, '"Tsunami of data" could consume one fifth of global electricity by 2025', *Guardian*, 11 Dec 2017.

3 Tom Bawden, 'Global warming: Data centres to consume three times as much energy in the next decade, experts warn', *Independent*, 23 Jan 2016.

Hugues Ferreboeuf et al., 'Lean ICT: Towards Digital Sobriety', The Shift Project (6 Mar 2019).

4 Naomi Xu Elegant, 'The Internet Cloud Has a Dirty Secret', *Fortune.com*, 18 Sep 2019.

5 Gregory Robinson, 'Most YouTube climate change videos "oppose the consensus view"', *Guardian*, 25 Jul 2019.

6 Stephanie Kirchgaessner, 'Revealed: Google made large contributions to climate deniers', *Guardian*, 11 Oct 2019.

7 Marshall McLuhan, *Understanding Media: The extensions of man* (New York: McGraw Hill, 1964).

8 Sherry Turkle, *Alone Together: Why We Expect More from Technology and Less from Each Other* (New York: Basic Books, 2011), 166–7, 293.

9 Guy Debord, *The Society of the Spectacle* (Detroit: Black & Red, 1983).

Part Three

1 Friedrich Nietzsche, *Unzeitgemäße Betrachtungen* (*Untimely Considerations*), 'Richard Wagner in Bayreuth', sec. 3; *Also sprach Zarathustra*, 'Von der Selbst-Überwindung' (On Self-Overcoming).

Chapter 6

1 Schumacher, *Small is Beautiful*, 31, 29 (emphasis added).

2 Thomas Hobbes, *Leviathan: Or, the Matter, Form and Power of a Commonwealth*; John Locke, *Two Treatises on Government*.

3 US Bill of Rights, https://www.archives.gov/founding-docs/bill-of-rights-transcript; United Nations General Assembly, Universal Declaration of Human Rights, http://www.un.org/en/universal-declaration-human-rights/index.html.

4 Henry Rosemont Jr., *Against Individualism: A Confucian Rethinking of the Foundations of Morality, Politics, Family, and Religion* (Lexington Books, 2015), 66. In the original the whole sentence is in italics.

5 See MacLean, *Democracy in Chains*, Introduction, Prologue, and ch. 1.

6 Rosemont, *Against Individualism*, 69 (again the whole quote is in italics).

7 Aristotle, *Politics*, trans. C. D. C. Reeve (Indianapolis: Hackett, 1998), 1253a. Secretary General of the United Nations General Assembly, 'Torture and

other cruel, inhuman or degrading treatment or punishment', sec. III, 'Solitary Confinement' (2011).

8 Rosemont, *Against Individualism*, 80.

9 See, for example, David L. Hall and Roger T. Ames, *The Democracy of the Dead: Dewey, Confucius, and the Hope for Democracy in China* (Chicago: Open Court, 1999), chs 6–8.

10 Charles Taylor, 'Atomism', in *Philosophy and the Human Sciences: Philosophical Papers 2* (Cambridge & New York: Cambridge University Press, 1985), 187–9.

11 Eno, 'Foreword', *Client Earth*, xiv.

12 See Piketty, *Capital in the Twenty-First Century*. Also Joseph E. Stieglitz, *The Price of Inequality: How Today's Divided Society Endangers Our Future* (New York: Norton, 2013), Walter Scheidel, *The Great Leveler: Violence and the History of Inequality from the Stone Age to the Twenty-First Century* (Princeton & Oxford: Princeton University Press, 2017), Branko Milanovic, *Global Inequality: A New Approach for the Age of Globalization* (Cambridge, Mass. & London: Harvard University Press, 2018).

13 The multiplicity of the self is the topic of my book *Composing the Soul: Reaches of Nietzsche's Psychology* (Chicago & London: University of Chicago Press, 1994).

14 See Nick Lane, *Power, Sex, Suicide: Mitochondria and the Meaning of Life* (Oxford and New York: Oxford University Press, 2005), 13.

15 Rob DeSalle and Susan L. Perkins, *Welcome to the Microbiome: Getting to Know the Trillions of Bacteria In, On, and Around You* (New Haven & London: Yale University Press, 2015), 118. National Institutes of Health, 'NIH Human Microbiome Project defines normal bacterial makeup of the body' (13 Jun 2012).

16 Scott F. Gilbert et al., 'A Symbiotic View of Life: We Have Never Been Individuals', *The Quarterly Review of Biology*, vol. 87/4 (2012): 325–41.

17 Schumacher, *Small is Beautiful*, 29.

18 John Tyndall, 'Address Delivered before the British Association Assembled at Belfast, with Additions' (1874), The Victorian Web, 60–1, http://www.victorianweb.org/science/science_texts/belfast.html.

19 Frank Newport, 'In U.S., 46% Hold Creationist View of Human Origins', GALLUP Politics, 1 Jun 2012; Megan Brenan, '49% of Americans Believe in Creationism', GALLUP Politics, 26 Jul 2019.

20 Nietzsche, *Beyond Good and Evil* 62.

21 Genesis 1:10–1. Also: 'All things were created by God, and for him: And he is before all things, and by him all things consist.' (Colossians 1:16–17)

22 Matthew 6:28–9.

23 Nietzsche, *Beyond Good and Evil* 188 (emphasis added).

24 See my essays, 'Staying Loyal to the Earth: Nietzsche as an Ecological Thinker', in John Lippitt ed., *Nietzche's Futures* (Basingstoke: Macmillan,

1999), 167–88, and 'Nature and the human "redivinised": Mahāyāna Buddhist themes in *Thus Spoke Zarathustra*', in John Lippitt and Jim Urpeth, eds, *Nietzsche and the Divine* (Manchester, UK: Clinamen Press, 2000), 181–99.

25 James W. Heisig, *Of Gods and Minds: In Search of a Theological Commons* (Nagoya: Chisokudō, 2019).

26 An excellent series 'Religions of the World and Ecology', edited by Mary Evelyn Tucker and John Grim, and published by Harvard University Press, includes multi-author volumes on Buddhism, Christianity, Confucianism, Daoism, Hinduism and Indigenous Traditions. See also the website of the Forum for Religion and Ecology at Yale: http://fore.yale.edu.

27 John Winthrop, 'A Model of Christian Charity' (1630).

28 Marilynne Robinson, 'Which Way to the City on the Hill?', *New York Review of Books*, 18 Jul 2019 (emphasis added).

29 On Pope Francis's background in Liberation Theology and its respect for the natural sciences, see Martin Schönfeld, 'Grounding Phenomenology in Laozi's *Daodejing*: The Anthropocene, the Fourfold, and the Sage', forthcoming in David Chai, ed., *Daoist Encounters with Phenomenology: Thinking Interculturally about Human Existence* (London: Bloomsbury, 2020).

30 Pope Francis, 'If we destroy Creation', catechesis in Rome, 21 May 2014, https://thewandererpress.com/pope-francis/if-we-destroy-creation-it-will-destroy-us/.

31 Pope Francis, 'Laudato Si'' (2015), 40, also 1, 4, 21; http://w2.vatican.va/content/francesco/en/encyclicals.index.html.

32 Zhang Zai, 'The Western Inscription', in Wing-Tsit Chan, ed., *A Source Book in Chinese Philosophy* (Princeton: Princeton University Press, 1963), 497.

33 Wang Yangming, 'Inquiry on the Great Learning', in Chan, *Source Book*, 659, 661.

34 Pope Francis, 'Laudato Si'', 1, 4, 21.

35 Pope Francis, 'Show Mercy to Our Common Home', Message for the celebration of the World Day of Prayer for the Care of Creation, 1 September 2016, http://w2.vatican.va/content/francesco/en/messages/pont-messages/2016/documents/papa-francesco_20160901_messaggio-giornata-cura-creato.html, accessed 1 September 2016.

36 Suzanne Goldenberg, 'Republicans' leading climate denier tells the pope to butt out of climate debate', *The Guardian*, 11 June 2015. James Inhofe, Plenary address, Heartland Institute, International Conference on Climate Change, June 2015, video available at http://climateconferences.heartland.org/james-inhofe-iccc10-keynote/ (7 Jul 2015).

37 Friedrich Engels, *Dialectics of Nature*, ch. 9. Xi Jinping brings a Neo-Confucian commentary by Cheng Yi on the *Yijing* together with a paraphrase of Engels: 'Everything has its counterpart' [Cheng Yi]. According to materialistic dialectics, things are universally related; they interact and constrain each other, and so do their composing elements; the world is an interrelated whole and also an interactive system.' Xi Jinping, *The Governance of China II* (Beijing: Foreign Languages Press, 2017), 225.

38 Engels, *Dialectics of Nature*, ch. 9.

39 The suggestion comes from David Satterthwaite of the International Institute for Environment and Development, cited by George Monbiot, *How Did We Get into This Mess?*, ch. 18.

40 E. Calvin Beisner, 'The Biblical Perspective of Environmental Stewardship: Subduing and Ruling the Earth to the Glory of God and the Benefit of Our Neighbors', sec. 20, under 'Landmark Documents' at cornwallalliance.org.

41 See William R. LaFleur's critique of 'fecundism' ('the attribution of religious value and significance to reproductivity') in his *Liquid Life: Abortion and Buddhism in Japan* (Princeton: Princeton University Press, 1992), and his open letter (1996) 'Dear Pope John Paul', *in Tricycle: The Buddhist Review*, Summer 2000, https://tricycle.org/magazine/dear-pope-john-paul/.

42 See Yana van der Meulen Rodgers, *The Global Gag Rule and Women's Reproductive Health* (New York: Oxford University Press, 2018).

43 Genesis 1:28, 9:1, 35:11.

44 Reverend Richard Cizik, cited in Alan Weisman, *Countdown: Our Last, Best Hope for a Future on Earth?* (New York: Little, Brown & Co., 2013), 427–9.

45 See Associated Press, 'Catholics don't have to breed "like rabbits", says Pope Francis', *Guardian*, 20 Jan 2015.

46 See, for example, the first chapter of Weisman's *Countdown*.

Chapter 7

1 Xi Jinping, *The Governance of China* (Beijing: Foreign Languages Press, 2014), and *Governance II* (note 36* above). The Publisher's Note to the first volume says that Xi's speeches 'embody the philosophy of the new central leadership', and that the aim of the book is 'to enhance the rest of the world's understanding of the Chinese government's philosophy'.

2 Mark Elvin, *The Retreat of the Elephants: An Environmental History of China* (New Haven & London; Yale University Press, 2004). Donald Hughes, *Pan's Travail: Environmental Problems of the Ancient Greeks and Romans* (Baltimore: Johns Hopkins University Press, 1994), chapter 3, and *An Environmental History of the World: Humankind's Changing Role in the Community of Life* (London & New York: Routledge, 2009), chapter 3.

3 Elvin, *Retreat of the Elephants*, 471 (emphasis added).

4 The traditional maxim is *Tian ren he yi* (Heaven and Humans are One), while Mao's slogans are *Ren ding sheng tian* (Man Must Conquer Nature) and *Zhansheng ziran* (Overcome the Natural). See Judith Shapiro, *Mao's War against Nature: Politics and the Environment in Revolutionary China* (Cambridge: Cambridge University Press, 2001), 10. Another excellent, and broader, study is Elizabeth C. Economy, *The River Runs Black: The Environmental Challenge to China's Future* (Ithaca & London: Cornell University Press, 2004). The pioneer in this field is Vaclav Smil: see his *China's Environmental Crisis: An Enquiry into the Limits of National Development* (London & New York: Routledge, 1993), and *China's Past, China's Future: Energy, Food, Environment* (London & New York: Routledge, 2004).

5 See Frank Dikötter, *Mao's Great Famine: The History of China's Most Devastating Catastrophe, 1958–62* (London: Bloomsbury, 2010).

6 In 1999, David Hall and Roger Ames wrote that we in the West 'need to enter a conversation with China in which the terms are set equally by both parties'. *Democracy of the Dead*, 10.

7 Scholars have shown that a conversation on this topic between our tradition and theirs is possible and could be fruitful, but we have to be flexible with the terms of the dialogue. See, for example, Daniel A. Bell, *East Meets West: Human Rights and Democracy in East Asia* (Princeton: Princeton University Press, 2000), William Theodore De Bary, *Asian Values and Human Rights: A Confucian Communitarian Perspective* (Harvard: Harvard University Press, 2000), and Stephen C. Angle, *Human Rights and Chinese Thought: A Cross-Cultural Inquiry* (Cambridge: Cambridge University Press, 2002).

8 Witness the popularity of sociopaths like Rodrigo Duterte, Viktor Orbán, Recep Tayyip Erdoğan and Jair Bolsonaro – and the tragic fiasco of Brexit.

9 See Stephen Platt, *Imperial Twilight: The Opium War and the End of China's Last Golden Age* (London: Atlantic Books, 2018).

10 On the ninety-fifth anniversary of the May Fourth Movement (1919), which was a response to the betrayal of China by the Triple Entente at the Versailles Peace Conference, Xi Jinping reminded students and faculty at Peking University of those sad chapters in Chinese history: 'The country was humiliated, its sovereignty was infringed upon, and its people were bullied by foreigners. . . . We must not let this tragic history repeat itself.' (Xi, *Governance*, 189).

11 For an excellent account of the Rebellion and its leader, see Jonathan Spence, *God's Chinese Son: The Taiping Heavenly Kingdom of Hong Xiuquan* (New York & London: Norton, 1996).

12 Orville Schell and Susan Shirk et al. , 'Course Correction: Toward an Effective and Sustainable China Policy' (New York: Asia Society, 2019), 9–10. The study is a collaboration between the Asia Society's Center on U.S.-China Relations and the 21st Century China Center at UC San Diego.

13 See Ben Parr and Don Henry, 'China Moves toward Ecological Civilisation', *Australian Outlook*, Australian Institute of International Affairs, 24 Aug 2016.

14 John Cook, 'Heat stress: setting an upper limit on what we can adapt to', *Skeptical Science*, 11 May 2010, https://skepticalscience.com/news. php?n=194.

15 S. F. Balica et al., 'A flood vulnerability index for coastal cities and its use in assessing climate change impacts', *Natural Hazards* (2012), vol. 64/1: 73-105.

16 See Gardner, *Environmental Pollution*, 167ff and 194ff.

17 See Barbara Finamore, *Will China Save the Planet?* (Cambridge: Polity Press, 2018).

18 Fan Gang, Nicholas Stern et al., *The Economics of Climate Change in China: Toward a Low-Carbon Economy* (London: Routledge, 2011), xvii-xviii.

19 Ren Peng et al., 'China's Involvement in Coal-Fired Power Projects along the Belt and Road', Global Environmental Institute (Beijing, 2017), at http:// www.geichina.org/_upload/file/report/China's_Involvement_in_Coal-fired_ Power_Projects_OBOR_EN.pdf.

20 I was intrigued by this consonance long before learning that Xi Jinping has actually read Plato's *Republic*: see Xi, *Governance II*, 371.

21 Confucius, *Analects* 12.22; compare Matthew 22:39. Zhang Fenzhi, *Xi Jinping: How to Read Confucius and Other Chinese Classical Thinkers* (New York: CN Times Books, 2015), VI.19, (source text, *Mencius* 1A.1), VIII.16 (*Mencius* 2A.6).

22 Robert B. Reich, *The Common Good* (New York: Knopf, 2018), ch. 3, 'The Origins of the Common Good'. See Lester J. Cappon, ed., *The Adams–Jefferson Letters* (Chapel Hill: University of North Carolina Press, 1988), 2:387–92 (emphasis added).

23 Edmund Burke, 'Letter to a Member of the National Assembly' (1791), in *The Works of the Right Honourable Edmund Burke*, vol. 4; also in *Reflections on the Revolution in France* (London: J. M. Dent & Sons, 1951), 281–2. Ophuls cites this passage frequently and to good effect.

24 Nietzsche, *Thus Spoke Zarathustra*, 2.12, 'On Self-Overcoming'. For the importance for Nietzsche of getting the optimal political regime established in oneself, see my *Composing the Soul*, Chapter IX.

25 *Mencius* 6A:14 and 15; see also 4B:19, 7B:35.

26 Plato, *Republic* 435b–442c; see also 588c–591d.

27 *Republic* 441e–442c, 589b, 590d.

28 *Republic* 341c, 342d.

29 See Atul Gawande, 'America's Epidemic of Unnecessary Care', *The New Yorker*, 11 May 2015.

30 As Socrates puts it: 'There isn't ever anyone who holds any position of ruler . . . who considers or commands his own advantage rather than that of what is ruled.' *Republic* 342e.

31 Plato, *Republic* 346e–347d. For a sobering account of a philosopher being drafted into politics and not fully prepared for the fray, see Michael Ignatieff's engaging memoir, *Fire and Ashes: Success and Failure in Politics* (Cambridge, Mass. & London: Harvard University Press, 2013).

32 See, for example, Tongdong Bai, *China: The Political Philosophy of the Middle Kingdom* (London & New York: Zed Books, 2012), 58-59. Also Daniel A. Bell, *The China Model: Political Meritocracy and the Limits of Democracy* (Princeton & Oxford: Princeton University Press, 2015), 97ff.

33 Plato, *Republic* 416d–417b, 420b.

34 Confucius, *Analects* 4:11, 4:12, 4:16, 14:12; *Mencius* 3A:3.

35 See, for example, Berggruen and Gardels, *Intelligent Governance*, and Bell, *The China Model*.

36 Confucius, *Analects* 4:18, 19:10.

37 For an excellent account of the role of ritual propriety in Confucian education see Geir Sigurdsson, *Confucian Propriety and Ritual Learning: A Philosophical Interpretation* (Albany: State University of New York Press, 2015).

38 The sixth art was mathematics, which was presumably involved physical training in the use of some kind of abacus. For a classic discussion of the Six Arts, see Xu Gan (171–281), *Balanced Discourses: A Bilingual Edition*, trans. John Makeham (New Haven & London: Yale University Press, 2002), ch. 7.

39 Confucius, *Analects* 12.1.

40 Plato, *Republic* 395d, also 377b. Confucius, *Analects* 19.9, 8.8.

41 *Li Chi: The Book of Rites*, trans. James Legge (Literary Licensing, 2014), Book XVII, 1.2–3; 1.23; 1.28.

42 Plato, *Republic* 432a; *Timaeus*, 36e, 47d, 90c–d.

43 *Xunzi* 10.4, in John Knoblock, *Xunzi: A Translation and Study of the Complete Works* (Stanford: Stanford University Press, 1988), 2:123. Xunzi also writes, 'The sage is the pitch pipe of the Way. The Way of the world has its pitch pipe in the sage', 8.7 (2:76).

44 See the discussions of the examination system, and of Singapore, in Bell, *The China Model*. Whatever your view of the current Chinese government, the top levels undeniably represent a robust political meritocracy and are far more competent than their American counterparts.

45 Sun Yat-sen, 'The Three People's Principles and the Future of the Chinese People', in Julie Lee Wei et al., eds, *Selected Writings of Sun Yat-sen, Prescriptions for Saving China* (Stanford: Hoover University Press, 1994), 49–50.

46 *The Most Venerable Book* (Shang Shu), trans. Martin Palmer (London: Penguin, 2014), 37.

47 Mencius ***; cited by Xi Jinping in *Governance*, 190.

48 Xi, *Governance*, 157, 162, 176, 433.

49 Zhang, *Xi Jinping*, II.14 (*Analects* 2.1). Also 'Govern the country with virtue', Xi, *Governance*, 190 (*Analects* 12.17), and *Analects* 12.19, 13.6, 13.13.

50 Max Weber, *The Theory of Social and Economic Organization*, trans. A. M. Henderson and Talcott Parsons (Free Press, 1924/1947), 328, 358ff.

51 On this idea, see Tingyang Zhao, *Redefining a Philosophy for World Governance* (Singapore: Palgrave Macmillan, 2019).

52 See Robert Eno, *The Great Learning and the Doctrine of the Mean: An online teaching translation*, I.B, indiana.edu/~ p374/Daxue-Zhongyong_(Eno-2016).pdf. See also Xi, *Governance*, 187.

53 Berggruen and Gardels, *Intelligent Governance*, 8–9, also ch. 6, 'Rebooting California's Dysfunctional Democracy'.

54 H. R. McMaster and Gary D. Cohn, 'America First Doesn't Mean America Alone', *Wall Street Journal*, 30 May 2017; Xi, *Governance*, 298.

Part Four

1 Nietzsche, *Die fröhliche Wissenschaft* (*The Joyful Science*), aphorism 339.

Chapter 8

1 See Alan Durning, *How Much Is Enough? The Consumer Society and the Future of the Earth* (New York & London: Norton, 1992).

2 Howard Frumkin, 'Beyond Toxicity: Human Health and the Natural Environment', *American Journal of Preventive Medicine* (2001): 20(3):234–40.

3 Ted Nordhaus and Michael Shellenberger, *Break Through: From the Death of Environmentalism to the Politics of Possibility* (Boston: Houghton Mifflin, 2007), 133.

4 See, for example, Philippe Descola's magisterial study *Beyond Nature and Culture* (Chicago & London: University of Chicago Press, 2013).

5 Bill McKibben, *The End of Nature* (New York: Random House, 1989), 104.

6 See William McDonough and Michael Braungart, *Cradle to Cradle: Remaking the Way We Make Things* (New York: North Point Press, 2002), ch. 4, 'Waste Equals Food'.

7 Nordhaus and Shellenberger, *Break Through*, 133.

8 In ancient Athens it was Epicurus (341–269 BCE), and Zeno of Citium (334–262 BCE, not to be confused with the earlier Zeno, of Elea and the famous paradoxes), who was the founder of the Stoic school of philosophy.

9 *Zhuangzi* 24, 103.

10 Cicero, *On the Nature of the Gods*, II.vii; III.xi (emphasis added).

11 Marcus Aurelius, *Meditations* 4.40–6, also 6.38, 7.9.

12 Zhu Xi, in Chan, *Source Book*, 643.

13 Nietzsche, *Beyond Good and Evil* 17.

14 Fritjof Capra drew attention to the analogies in his book *The Tao of Physics: An Exploration of the Parallels between Modern Physics and Eastern Mysticism* (1975), which remains a good introduction (though it would have worked better restricted to Chinese philosophy rather than the vast field of Eastern Mysticism).

15 Capra, *Tao of Physics*, 139–40, 209, 149–60.

16 William Ophuls has wise things to say about the new physics and its resonance with the principles of ecology, and even depth psychology. See William Ophuls with A. Stephen Boyan, Jr., *Ecology and the Politics of Scarcity Revisited* (New York: W. H. Freeman & Co., 1992) and William Ophuls, *Plato's Revenge: Politics in the Age of Ecology* (Cambridge, MA & London: MIT Press, 2011).

17 A. A. Long and D. N. Sedley, eds, *The Hellenistic Philosophers* (Cambridge: Cambridge University Press, 1987), 1:394–5; Marcus Aurelius, *Meditations* 12.26.

18 Marcus Aurelius, *Meditations* 1.9, 10.14.

19 Schumacher, *Small Is Beautiful*, 85.

20 Schumacher, *Small Is Beautiful*, 31.

21 *Zhuangzi* 6, 39; *Laozi* 51; *Zhuangzi* 19, 77; *Zhuangzi* 6.

22 *Handbook of Epictetus*, trans. Nicholas White (Indianapolis: Hackett, 1983), sec. 5.

23 Epictetus, *Handbook of Epictetus*, secs 5, 1.

24 Marcus Aurelius, *Meditations* 5.1.

25 Lucretius, *On the Nature of the Universe*, trans. Ronald Melville (Oxford: Oxford University Press, 1997), 1.76–7, 5.89–90; 1.584-86; 2.1116–17, 4.56–8.

26 Lucretius, *Nature of the Universe*, 5.1430–33.

27 *Laozi* 23, 9. On the relevance of the *Laozi* to the climate crisis, see Schönfeld, 'Grounding Phenomenology in Laozi's *Daodejing*'.

28 *Laozi* 40, 32, 44. The locus classicus for the operations of yin and yang is the *Book of Changes* (*Yijing*, or *Zhouyi*).

29 *Zhuangzi* 6, 43.

30 *Zhuangzi* 3, 21.

31 James Lovelock, *The Revenge of Gaia*, 34.

32 Ophuls, *Plato's Revenge*, 29; Kolbert, *The Sixth Extinction*.

33 Ophuls, *Plato's Revenge*, 63.

34 Will Steffen et al., 'Planetary Boundaries: Guiding human development on a changing planet', *Science*, 347 (6223), 2015; also Johan Rockström et al. 'Planetary Boundaries: Exploring the Safe Operating Space for Humanity', *Ecology and Society*, 14(2):32 (2009).

35 Ophuls, *Plato's Revenge*, 31.

36 Heraclitus, fragment LXVII, in Kahn, 59.

37 Plato, *Phaedo* 60b.

38 Epicurus, 'Letter to Menoeceus' 130b, in *Letters*, 56–7.

39 Epicurus, 'Vatican Sayings' XXI, 'Principal Doctrines' XXVI, XXIX, in *Letters*, 67, 63.

40 'Vatican Sayings' LXIII, in *Letters*, 71.

41 Confucius, *Analects* 9.3. On wealth and personal gain, see 4.5, 4.12, 4.16, 7.12, 7.16.

42 *Laozi* 46. Here's a translation that brings out different emphases:

There is no crime more onerous than greed,
No misfortune more devastating than avarice.
And no calamity that brings with it more grief than insatiability.
Thus, knowing when enough is enough is truly satisfying.

43 *Laozi* 78; 44, also 32; 3.

44 William Wordsworth, 'The World Is Too Much With Us'.

45 1 Timothy, 6:5–10.

46 Ian Ridpath, *Stars and Planets* (New York: DK Publishing, 1998), 64.

47 Blaise Pascal, *Pensées* 102.

48 For 'forest bathing' (Japanese, *shinrin-yoku*), see Yoshifumi Miyazaki, *Shinrin Yoku: The Japanese Art of Forest Bathing* (Portland, OR: Timber Press, 2018), and Qing Lee, *Into the Forest: How Trees Can Help You Find Health and Happiness* (New York: Penguin, 2019).

49 Wilson (1984) 85, 139.

50 See, for example, Shunryu Suzuki, *Zen Mind, Beginner's Mind* (New York & Tokyo: Weatherhill, 1970), and Charlotte Joko Beck, *Nothing Special: Living Zen* (New York: HarperCollins, 1993).

51 Emerson, 'Nature', in *Essays & Lectures*, 541.

52 Nietzsche, *The Joyful Science* 339.

Chapter 9

1 Henry David Thoreau, *Walden: or, Life in the Woods*, 'Spring', in *Thoreau: A Week etc.* (New York: Library of America, 1985), 568.

2 Aldo Leopold, 'The Land Ethic', in *A Sand County Almanac: And Sketches Here and There* (New York: Oxford University Press, 1968), 216 (emphasis added). See also J. Baird Callicott, ed., *Companion to* A Sand County Almanac: *Interpretive and Critical Essays* (Madison: University of Wisconsin Press, 1987), and *In Defense of the Land Ethic: Essays in Environmental Philosophy* (Albany: SUNY Press, 1989).

3 Leopold, *Sand County*, 203–07.

4 *Sand County*, 216–20. See also George Monbiot, 'We're treating soil like dirt. It's a fatal mistake, as our lives depend on it', *Guardian*, 25 Mar 2015.

5 Leopold, 'Thinking Like a Mountain', *Sand County*, 129-33.

6 James Lovelock, *Gaia: The Practical Science of Planetary Medicine* (New York: Oxford University Press, 2001), 153.

7 Jan Zalasiewicz et al., 'The geological cycle of plastics and their use as a stratigraphic indicator of the Anthropocene', *Anthropocene*, http://dx.doi.org/10.1016/j.ancene.2016.01.002. See also the numerous articles on plastics pollution in *The Guardian* from 2016 on.

8 Estimate by the Nature Conservancy; see Claire Le Guern, 'When the Mermaids Cry: The Great Plastic Tide', Coastal Care website (2018), http://plastic-pollution.org.

9 Plato, *Timaeus* 30b–c, 34b.

10 G. S. Kirk and J. E. Raven, *The Presocratic Philosophers: A Critical History with a Selection of Texts* (London: Cambridge University Press, 1957), 93–5.

11 E. R. Dodds, *The Greeks and the Irrational* (Berkeley & Los Angeles: University of California Press, 1962), ch. V.

12 Edward Burnett Tylor, *Primitive Culture: Researches into the Development of Mythology, Philosophy, Religion, Art, and Custom* (New York: Cambridge University Press, 2010), vol. 1, 260–1, 267, 431, 452.

13 Think of *prāṇa* in the Indian tradition, for instance, or *pneuma* in the Greek, the Hebrew *ruach*, Amerindian *orenda*, Polynesian *mana*, and *qi* energy for the Chinese. See Descola, *Beyond Nature and Culture*, Part III, 'The Dispositions of Being'.

14 Bruno Latour, *Politics of Nature: How to Bring the Sciences into Democracy*, trans. Catherine Porter (Cambridge, Mass. & London: Harvard University Press, 2004), 69, 75.

15 Lovelock, *The Revenge of Gaia*, 21.

16 See A. C. Graham, *Chuang-tzu: The Inner Chapters* (London: George Allen & Unwin, 1981), 18, 35, and chs 3, 63.

17 John Hay, *Kernels of Energy, Bones of Earth: The Rock in Chinese Art* (New York: China Institute in America, 1985), 173.

18 Jirō Takei and Marc P. Keane, *Sakuteiki: Visions of the Japanese Garden* (Boston: Tuttle Publishing, 2001), 3, 153. For the dry landscape garden, see François Berthier with Graham Parkes, *Reading Zen in the Rocks: The Japanese Dry Landscape Garden* (Chicago & London: University of Chicago Press, 2000). Takei and Keane, *Sakuteiki*, 183–4.

19 See my essay 'Kūkai and Dōgen as Exemplars of Ecological Engagement', in J. Baird Callicott and James McRae, eds, *Japanese Environmental Philosophy* (New York: Oxford University Press, 2017), 65–86.

20 Dōgen, 'Valley Sounds, Mountain Colors' and 'Mountains and Waters as a Sutra', in Kazuaki Tanahashi, ed., *Treasury of the True Dharma Eye* (Boston & London: Shambhala, 2010), 1:85, 1:156.

21 Dōgen, 'Instructions on Kitchen Work', in *Treasury of the True Dharma Eye*, 2:764.

22 'Instructions for the Tenzo', in Kazuaki Tanahashi, ed. and trans., *Moon in a Dewdrop: Writings of Zen Master Dōgen* (New York: Farrar, Straus & Giroux, 1985), 55. For the Japanese Buddhist notion of 'home ground', where things are there 'in themselves' rather than as represented by human beings, see Keiji Nishitani, *Religion and Nothingness*, trans. Jan Van Bragt (Berkeley & London: University of California Press, 1982).

23 Dōgen, 'Instructions for the Tenzo', 56.

24 Thoreau, *Walden*, 'Where I Lived, and What I Lived For', 394–5.

25 *Walden*, 'Economy', 332–3; 351.

26 Nietzsche, *The Wanderer and His Shadow*, aphorisms 5, 6, 11, 16.

27 Marie Kondo, *The Life-Changing Magic of Tidying Up: The Japanese Art of Decluttering and Organizing*, trans. Cathy Hirano (Berkeley: Ten-Speed Press, 2014). Her first name is Japanese, not French, and so is pronounced with three syllables, ma-ri-e, corresponding to three Japanese characters.

28 Kondo, *Life-Changing Magic*, ch. 4. For an excellent philosophical account of Shinto, see Thomas P. Kasulis, *Shinto: The Way Home* (Honolulu: University of Hawaii Press, 2004).

29 Kondo, *Life-Changing Magic*, ch. 3.

30 *Life-Changing Magic*, ch. 4.

31 *Life-Changing Magic*, ch. 5. Kondo doesn't say much about what happens to the vast amount of stuff that she helps her clients get rid of, although there are several mentions of recycling, most of them in the form of 'discard or recycle' along with a few 'donate or recycle'.

32 James Hillman and Michael Ventura, *We've Had a Hundred Years of Psychotherapy – and the World's Getting Worse* (New York: Harper Collins,

1991), 3. Since Hillman long ago encouraged me not to give up working on my PhD dissertation, I am pleased to return to his ideas in a much later work.

33 James Hillman, *Inter Views: Conversations with Laura Pozzo on Psychotherapy, Biography, Love, Soul, Dreams, Work, Imagination, and the State of the Culture* (New York: Harper & Row, 1983), 130–1.

34 James Hillman, 'Anima Mundi: The Return of Soul to the World', *SPRING: An Annual of Archetypal Psychology and Jungian Thought* (1982): 71–95, 77.

35 Cited in Dillard, *Pilgrim at Tinker Creek*, 198.

36 Hillman, *Inter Views*, 134.

37 James Hillman, *Kinds of Power: A Guide to its Intelligent Uses* (New York: Currency Doubleday, 1995), 73; first discussed in *A Hundred Years of Therapy*, 131.

38 Hillman, *A Hundred Years*, 52.

39 Hillman, *Kinds of Power*, 78, 81.

40 Hillman, *A Hundred Years*, 178. See also the video interview on loving the beauty of the world, https://www.youtube.com/watch?v=rFa0X06hLOU.

41 *A Hundred Years*, 182–4.

42 Michel Serres, *The Natural Contract*, trans. Elizabeth MacArthur and William Paulson (Ann Arbor: University of Michigan Press, 1995), 48.

43 Serres, *The Natural Contract*, 49–50.

44 *The Natural Contract*, 29.

45 Hillman, *A Hundred Years*, 124, 183.

46 *A Hundred Years*, 183, 154, 184, 156.

Inconclusions

1 Rage against the Machine, 'Take the Power Back', *Rage against the Machine*, track 3.

2 UN News, 'World faces "climate apartheid" risk, 120 million more in poverty: UN expert', 25 Jun 2019; https://news.un.org/en/story/2019/06/1041261.

3 UN News, 'World faces "climate apartheid" risk, 120 million more in poverty: UN expert', 25 Jun 2019; Philip Alston, 'Climate Change and Poverty', paragraphs 51, 87, available at https://undocs.org/A/HRC/41/39.

4 See, for example, the Seasteading Institute's website at seasteading.org; Peter Thiel, 'The Education of a Libertarian', *Cato Unbound: A Journal of Debate*, 13 April 2009.

5 Solomon Israel, 'Artificial intelligence, human brain to merge in 2030s, say futurist Kurzweil', CBC Technology & Science, 5 Jun 2015; Mick Brown,

'Peter Thiel: the billionaire tech entrepreneur on a mission to cheat death', *The Telegraph*, 19 Sep 2014.

6 Evan Osnos, 'Doomsday Prep for the Super-Rich', *New Yorker*, 30 Jan 2017.

7 Oliver Wainwright, '"The next era of human progress": what lies behind the global new cities epidemic?', *Guardian*, 8 Jul 2019.

8 See Osnos, 'Doomsday Prep for the Super-Rich'; Oliver Wainwright, '"The next era of human progress": what lies behind the global new cities epidemic?', *Guardian*, 8 Jul 2019; 'Vision' at https://www.neom.com. Also Martin Lukacs, 'New, privatized African city heralds climate apartheid', *Guardian*, 21 Jan 2014.

9 Mario Savio, 'Speech before the Free Speech Movement sit-in', Berkeley, 3 Dec 1964, Free Speech Movement Archives, http://www.fsm-a.org/stacks/mario/mario_speech.html.

10 Somini Sengupta and Lisa Friedman, 'At U.N. Climate Summit, Few Commitments and U.S. Silence', *New York Times*, 23 Sep 2019.

11 See Jonathan Watts, 'Concrete: the most destructive material on Earth', *Guardian*, 25 Feb 2019, and the other articles from 'Guardian Concrete Week'.

12 IPCC, *Climate Change and Land Use: An IPCC Special Report on Climate Change, Desertification, Land Degradation, Sustainable Land Management, Food Security, and Greenhouse gas fluxes in Terrestrial Ecosystems*' (2019), at https://www.ipcc.ch/report/srccl/.

13 For an excellent account of the disasters of palm oil production, see Abrahm Lustgarten, 'Palm Oil Was Supposed to Help Save the Planet. Instead It Unleashed a Catastrophe', *New York Times*, 20 Nov 2018.

14 George Monbiot, 'The natural world can help save us from climate catastrophe', *Guardian*, 8 May 2019. For Natural Climate Solutions, see https://www.naturalclimate.solutions.

15 See Damian Carrington, 'Tree planting "has mind-blowing potential" to tackle climate crisis', *Guardian*, 4 Jul 2019, commenting on J.-F. Bastin et al., 'The global tree restoration potential', *Science* (2019), vol. 365, issue 6448: 76–9. For Technical Comments and 'Response to Comments', see vol. 366, issue 6463.

16 See Christopher Flavelle, 'Climate Change Threatens the World's Food Supply, the United Nations Warns', *New York Times*, 8 Aug 2019, and Damian Carrington, 'How climate's impact on land threatens civilisation – and how to fix it', *Guardian*, 8 Aug 2019.

17 Hans-Peter Schmidt, 'Biochar and PyCCS included as negative emissions technology by the IPCC', *the Biochar Journal* (2018), https://www.biochar-journal.org/en/ct/94. Dominic Woolf at al., 'Sustainable biochar to mitigate global climate change'. *Nature Communications*, 10 Aug 2010

18 IPCC, *Climate Change and Land Use*, 'Summary for Policymakers', B 6.2.

19 Eric Gimon et al., 'The Coal Cost Crossover: Economic viability of existing coal compared to new local wind and solar resources', Energy Innovation and

Vibrant Clean Energy (2019), https://energyinnovation.org/wp-content/uploads/2019/03/Coal-Cost-Crossover_Energy-Innovation_VCE_FINAL.pdf.

20 Bill McKibben, 'A Future without Fossil Fuels?', *New York Review of Books*, 4 Apr 2019.

21 See Somini Sengupta et al., 'How One Billionaire Could Keep Three Countries Hooked on Coal for Decades', *New York Times*, 15 Aug 2019.

22 Global Commission on the Geopolitics of Energy Transformation, 'A New World: The Geopolitics of the Energy Transformation' (IRENA, 2019), available at: https://irena.org/publications/2019/Jan/A-New-World-The-Geopolitics-of-the-Energy-Transformation.

23 Adam Morton, 'Super funds and investors with $34tn urge leaders to speed up climate action', *Guardian*, 26 Jun 2019.

24 J. Poore and T. Nemecek, 'Reducing food's environmental impacts through producers and consumers', *Science*, 1 Jun 2018, vol. 360(6392): 987–92; Marco Springmann et al., 'Options for keeping the food system within environmental limits', *Nature*, 10 Oct 2018.

25 See Daniel Boffey, 'Plan to sell 50m meals made from electricity, water and air', *Guardian*, 29 Jun 2019.

26 See, for example, Roger Tyers, 'It's time to wake up to the devastating impact flying has on the environment', *The Conversation*, 11 Jan 2017.

27 Sonia Sodha, 'A radical way to cut emissions – ration everyone's flights', *Guardian*, 9 May 2018.

28 Matt McGrath, 'Tourism's carbon impact three times larger than estimated', BBC News, 7 May 2018.

29 Hiroko Tabuchi, '"Worse than Anyone Expected": Air Travel Emissions Vastly Outpace Predictions', *New York Times*, 19 Sep 2019.

30 Fridays for Future: https://fridaysforfuture.org; Extinction Rebellion: https://rebellion.earth, and thegiganticchange.com ('Your guide to taking action on climate change'); Power Shift Network: https://www.powershift.org, Zero Hour: http://thisiszerohour.org, YouthStrike4Climate: https://ukscn.org/ys4c.

31 See https://climateoutreach.org, and https://350.org.

32 For the Mobilisation Lab, see https://mobilisationlab.org; Sunrise Movement, https://www.sunrisemovement.org; Climate Advocacy Lab, https://climateadvocacylab.org; Climate Mobilization, https://www.theclimatemobilization.org; PowerLabs, https://powerlabs.io/turning-grassroots-activism-into-durable-political-power-social-movement-theory/.

33 End Citizens United, at https://endcitizensunited.org.

34 Arabella Advisors, 'The Global Fossil Fuel Divestment and Clean Energy Investment Movement, 2018 Report'.

35 Damian Carrington, 'Healthy diet means a healthy planet, study shows', *Guardian*, 28 Oct 2019, reporting on Michael A. Clark et al., 'Multiple health and environmental impacts of foods', *Proceedings of the National Academy of Sciences* (2019).

36 See Sebastian Gorka (on video), Reuters, 1 Mar 2019, https://www.reuters.com/video/2019/03/01/dems-want-to-take-away-your-hamburgers-g?videoId=520628816.

37 Keith Bradsher, *High and Mighty: The Dangerous Rise of the SUV* (New York: PublicAffairs, 2002).

38 Laura Cozzi and Apostolos Petropoulos, 'Growing preference for SUVs challenges emissions reductions in passenger car market', IEA Newsroom, 15 Oct 2019.

39 Eliza Mackintosh, 'Finland is winning the war on fake news', CNN, May 2019. DNC website: https://democrats.org/who-we-are/what-we-do/disinfo/.

40 Oliver Milman and Fiona Harvey, 'US is hotbed of climate change denial, major global survey finds', *Guardian*, 8 May 2019.

41 Ankita Rao and John Mulholland, 'If America wants to be the world's leading democracy, it should start acting like one', *Guardian*, 7 November 2019. For *The Guardian*'s series on Voter Suppression in the US, see https://www.theguardian.com/us-news/series/us-voter-supression.

42 For the No Fossil Fuel Money Pledge, see http://nofossilfuelmoney.org. As of March 2019, the pledge had 1386 signatures by incumbents or candidates for political office in the US. For Represent US, see www.represent.us, and the film at https://www.youtube.com/watch?time_continue=208&v=TfQij4aQq1k.

43 US crude oil: U.S. Energy Information Administration, 'The United States is now the largest global crude oil producer', Today in Energy, 12 September 2018. Lee Wasserman, 'Why Are We Still Looking for Oil and Gas?', *New York Times*, 25 Jul 2019.

44 George Monbiot, 'There is an antidote to demagoguery – it's called political rewilding', *Guardian*, 18 Dec 2019; *Out of the Wreckage*, especially chapters 8 and 9.

45 Kate Raworth, *Doughnut Economics: Seven Ways to Think Like a 21st-Century Economist* (White River Junction, Vt.: Chelsea Green Publishing, 2017), introduction and ch. 1. For some further reflections on needed innovations in economics along similar lines, see chapters 6 and 7 of George Monbiot's *Out of the Wreckage*.

46 See Schumacher, *Small Is Beautiful*, and Herman Daly, *Steady-State Economics* (San Francisco: W. H. Freeman, 1977).

47 See Catherine Kling, 'Polluting Farmers Should Pay', New York Times, 26 Aug 2019.

48 See Pettifor, *Green New Deal*, ch. 2.

49 Naomi Klein, *On Fire: The (Burning) Case for a Green Nezw Deal* (New York: Simon & Schuster, 2019), Introduction. Klein wrote a Foreword for Kate

Aronoff et al., *A Planet to Win: Why We Need a Green New Deal* (London & New York: Verso, 2019).

50 Available at https://www.congress.gov/bill/116th-congress/house-resolution/109.

51 Klein, *On Fire*, 264–71, and the Epilogue.

52 Pettifor, *Green New Deal*, xiii. The second chapter offers an informative history of the privatisation and globalisation of finance.

53 *Green New Deal*, chs 3 and 4.

54 *Green New Deal*, chs 5 and 6.

55 Brian Eno cited in Lorenzo Marsili, 'Europe now has a Green New Deal', DiEM25, 27 Jan 2019.

56 Yanis Varoufakis and David Adler, 'It's time for nations to unite around an International Green New Deal', *Guardian*, 23 Apr 2019. Karl Marx and Friedrich Engels, *The Communist Manifesto* (London: Vintage Classics, 2018), xxviii

57 AOSIS is an intergovernmental organisation whose aim is to cope with climate change.

58 See *United Nations Framework Convention on Climate Change* (New York, 1992), http://unfccc.int/files/essential_background/background_publications_htmlpdf/application/pdf/conveng.pdf.

59 Christian Holz et al., 'Fairly sharing 1.5: national fair shares of a 1.5°C-compliant global mitigation effort', *International Environmental Agreements* (2018) 18: 117–34.

60 See German Advisory Council on Global Change, 'Solving the Climate Dilemma: The budget approach', https://www.wbgu.de/en/publications/publication/special-report-2009.

61 See Iman Ghosh, 'All the World's Carbon Emissions in One Chart', Visual Capitalist, 31 May 2019, https://www.visualcapitalist.com/all-the-worlds-carbon-emissions-in-one-chart/.

62 See Robert Ireland (US International Trade Commission), 'Carbon Tariffs: A Climate Necessity', *Regulation for Globalization*, 13 Mar 2018.

63 See Erica Chenoweth & Maria J. Stephan, W*hy Civil Resistance Works: The Strategic Logic of Nonviolent Conflict* (New York: Columbia University Press, 2011).

64 Robert Reich, 'There is no "right" v "left": it is Trump and the oligarchs against the rest', *Guardian*, 7 Jul 2019. For more detail, see Reich's *Saving Capitalism*, the third part of which, 'Countervailing Power', contains many helpful suggestions for economic and political reform.

65 Socrates asks, 'And what about when a man believes he's being done injustice? Doesn't his spirit in this case boil and become harsh and form a battle alliance with what seems just?' (Plato, *Republic* 440c).

66 Serres, *The Natural Contract*, 121–2.

Select Bibliography

Bageant, Joe. *Deer Hunting with Jesus: Dispatches from America's Class War.* New York: Random House, 2007.

Bell, Daniel A. *The China Model: Political Meritocracy and the Limits of Democracy.* Princeton & Oxford: Princeton University Press, 2015.

Berggruen, Nicolas and Nathan Gardels. *Intelligent Governance for the 21st Century: A Middle Way between West and East.* Cambridge UK: Polity Press, 2013.

Bloom, Harold. *The American Religion: The Emergence of the Post-Christian Nation.* New York: Simon & Schuster, 1992.

Callicott, J. Baird. *In Defense of the Land Ethic: Essays in Environmental Philosophy.* Albany: SUNY Press, 1989.

Callicott, J. Baird and James McRae, eds. *Japanese Environmental Philosophy.* New York: Oxford University Press, 2017.

Carson, Rachel. *Silent Spring.* New York: Houghton Mifflin Harcourt, 2002.

Chomsky, Noam. *Profit over People: Neoliberalism and Global Order.* New York: Seven Stories Press, 1999.

Cockett, Richard. *Thinking the Unthinkable: Think-Tanks and the Economic Counter-Revolution, 1931–1983.* London: HarperCollins, 1994.

Coetzee, J. M. *Elizabeth Costello.* London: Secker & Warburg, 2003.

Coetzee, J. M. et al. *The Lives of Animals.* Princeton: Princeton University Press, 1999.

Confucius, *Confucius, The Analects (Lun yü).* Trans. D. C. Lau. Hong Kong: The Chinese University Press, 1979.

Debord, Guy. *The Society of the Spectacle.* Detroit: Black & Red, 1983.

Descola, Philippe. *Beyond Nature and Culture.* Trans. Janet Lloyd. Chicago & London: University of Chicago Press, 2013.

Dillard, Annie. *Pilgrim at Tinker Creek.* New York: Harper's Magazine Press, 1974.

Dochuk, Darren. *Anointed with Oil: How Christianity and Crude Made Modern America.* New York: Basic Books, 2019.

Dōgen. *Moon in a Dewdrop: Writings of Zen Master Dōgen.* Ed. and trans. Kazuaki Tanahashi. New York: Farrar, Straus & Giroux, 1985.

Dōgen. *Treasury of the True Dharma Eye.* Ed. Kazuaki Tanahashi. Boston & London: Shambhala, 2010.

Elvin, Mark. *The Retreat of the Elephants: An Environmental History of China.* New Haven & London; Yale University Press, 2004.

Emerson, Ralph Waldo. *Essays & Lectures.* New York: The Library of America, 1984.

Gang, Fan and Nicholas Stern et al., *The Economics of Climate Change in China: Toward a Low-Carbon Economy.* London: Routledge, 2011.

Gelbspan, Ross. *Boiling Point: How Politicians, Big Oil and Coal, Journalists and Activists Are Fueling the Climate Crisis – and What We Can Do to Avoid Disaster.* New York: Basic Books, 2004.

Goodell, Jeff. *Big Coal: the Dirty Secret behind America's Energy Future.* Boston: Houghton Mifflin Co., 2006.

Goodell, Jeff. *The Water Will Come: Rising Seas, Sinking Cities, and the Remaking of the Civilized World.* New York: Little, Brown & Co., 2018.

Goodman, Martin and James Thornton. *Client Earth: Building an Ecological Civilisation.* Melbourne & London: Scribe, 2017.

Graham, A. C. *Chuang-tzu: The Inner Chapters.* London: George Allen & Unwin, 1981.

Graham, A. C. *Disputers of the Tao: Philosophical Argument in Ancient China.* LaSalle, Ill.: Open Court, 1989.

Hall, David L. and Roger T. Ames. *The Democracy of the Dead: Dewey, Confucius, and the Hope for Democracy in China.* Chicago: Open Court, 1999.

Hamilton, Clive. *Requiem for a Species: Why We Resist the Truth about Climate Change.* New York: Earthscan, 2010.

Hamilton, Clive. *Earthmasters: Playing God with the Climate.* New Haven: Yale University Press, 2013.

Hamilton, Clive. *Defiant Earth: The Fate of Humans in the Anthropocene.* Cambridge UK & Medford Mass.: Polity Press, 2017.

Harvey, David. *A Brief History of Neoliberalism.* New York: Oxford University Press, 2005.

Hertel-Fernandez, Alexander. *State Capture: How Conservative Activists, Big Businesses, and Wealthy Donors Reshaped the American States – and the Nation.* New York: Oxford University Press, 2019.

Hillman, James. *Inter Views: Conversations with Laura Pozzo on Psychotherapy, Biography, Love, Soul, Dreams, Work, Imagination, and the State of the Culture.* New York: Harper & Row, 1983.

Hillman, James and Michael Ventura. *We've Had a Hundred Years of Psychotherapy – and the World's Getting Worse.* New York: Harper Collins, 1991.

Jamieson, Dale. *Reason in a Dark Time: Why the Struggle Against Climate Change Failed – And What It Means for Our Future.* New York: Oxford University Press, 2014.

Klein, Naomi. *The Shock Doctrine: The Rise of Disaster Capitalism.* New York: Henry Holt & Co., 2007.

Klein, Naomi. *This Changes Everything: Capitalism vs. the Climate.* New York: Simon & Schuster, 2014.

Klein, Naomi. *On Fire: The (Burning) Case for a Green New Deal.* New York: Simon & Schuster, 2019.

Kolbert, Elizabeth. *The Sixth Extinction: An Unnatural History.* New York: Henry Holt & Co., 2014.

Kondo, Marie. *The Life-Changing Magic of Tidying Up: The Japanese Art of Decluttering and Organizing.* Trans. Cathy Hirano. Berkeley: Ten-Speed Press, 2014.

Latour, Bruno. *Politics of Nature: How to Bring the Sciences into Democracy.* Trans. Catherine Porter. Cambridge, Mass. & London: Harvard University Press, 2004.

Latour, Bruno. *Facing Gaia: Eight Lectures on the New Climatic Regime.* Trans. Catherine Porter. Cambridge UK & Medford Mass.: Polity Press, 2017.

Latour, Bruno. *Down to Earth: Politics in the New Climatic Regime.* Cambridge: Polity Press, 2018.

Leopold, Aldo. *A Sand County Almanac: And Sketches Here and There.* New York: Oxford University Press, 1968.

Lovelock, James. *Gaia: A new look at life on Earth.* Oxford: Oxford University Press, 2000.

Lovelock, James. *Gaia: The Practical Science of Planetary Medicine.* New York: Oxford University Press, 2001.

Lovelock, James. *The Revenge of Gaia: Why the Earth is Fighting Back – and How We Can Still Save Humanity.* London & New York: Penguin Books, 2007.

MacLean, Nancy. *Democracy in Chains: The Deep History of the Radical Right's Stealth Plan for America.* Melbourne & London: Scribe Publications, 2017.

Mann, Michael. *The Hockey Stick and the Climate Wars: Dispatches from the Front Lines.* New York: Columbia University Press, 2012.

Marx, Karl and Friedrich Engels. *The Communist Manifesto.* London: Penguin, 2018.

Mayer, Jane. *Dark Money: The Hidden History of the Billionaires behind the Rise of the Radical Right.* New York: Doubleday, 2016.

McKibben, Bill. *The End of Nature.* New York: Random House, 1989.

McKibben, Bill. *Falter: Has the Human Game Begun to Play Itself Out?* London: Wildfire, 2019.

Mencius. *Mencius.* Trans. D. C. Lau. London: Penguin Classics, 2004.

Monbiot, George. *How Did We Get into This Mess? Politics, Equality, Nature.* London & New York: Verso, 2016.

Monbiot, George. *Out of the Wreckage: A New Politics for an Age of Crisis.* London & New York: Verso, 2017.

Mooney, Chris. *The Republican War on Science.* New York: Basic Books, 2005.

Nietzsche, Friedrich. *Thus Spoke Zarathustra.* Trans. Graham Parkes. Oxford: Oxford University Press, 2005.

Ophuls, William. *Plato's Revenge: Politics in the Age of Ecology.* Cambridge, MA & London: MIT Press, 2011.

Ophuls, William and A. Stephen Boyan, Jr. *Ecology and the Politics of Scarcity Revisited.* New York: W. H. Freeman & Co., 1992.

Pearce, Fred. *With Speed and Violence: Why Scientists Fear Tipping Points in Climate Change.* Boston: Beacon Press, 2008.

Pettifor, Ann. *The Case for the Green New Deal.* London & New York: Verso, 2019.

Piketty, Thomas. *Capital in the Twenty-First Century.* Trans. Arthur Goldhammer. Cambridge, Mass. & London: Harvard University Press, 2014.

Plato. *The Republic of Plato.* Trans. Allan Bloom. New York: Basic Books, 1968.

Parkes, Graham. *Composing the Soul: Reaches of Nietzsche's Psychology.* Chicago: University of Chicago Press, 1994.

Proctor, Robert N. and Londa Schiebinger, eds. *Agnotology: The Making and Unmaking of Ignorance.* Stanford: Stanford University Press, 2008.

Pyne, Stephen J. *Fire: A Brief History.* Seattle & London: University of Washington Press, 2001.

Raworth, Kate. *Doughnut Economics: Seven Ways to Think Like a 21st-Century Economist.* White River Junction, Vt.: Chelsea Green Publishing, 2017.

Rosemont, Henry, Jr. *Against Individualism: A Confucian Rethinking of the Foundations of Morality, Politics, Family, and Religion.* Lanham, Md.: Lexington Books, 2015.

Schumacher, E. F. *Small Is Beautiful Economics as if People Mattered.* London: Vintage Books, 1993.

Scranton, Roy. *Learning to Die in the Anthropocene: Reflections on the end of a civilization.* San Francisco: City Lights Books, 2015.

Serres, Michel. *The Natural Contract.* Trans. Elizabeth MacArthur and William Paulson. Ann Arbor: University of Michigan Press, 1995.

Shapiro, Judith. *Mao's War against Nature: Politics and the Environment in Revolutionary China.* Cambridge: Cambridge University Press, 2001.

Shapiro, Judith. *China's Environmental Challenges,* second edition. Cambridge: Polity Press, 2016.

Singer, Peter. *Animal Liberation.* New York: HarperCollins, 1975.

Stern, Nicholas. *The Economics of Climate Change: The Stern Review.* Cambridge: Cambridge University Press, 2007.

Stern, Nicholas. *The Global Deal: Climate Change and the Creation of a New Era of Progress and Prosperity.* New York: PublicAffairs, 2009.

Stern, Nicholas. *Why Are We Waiting? The Logic, Urgency and Promise of Tackling Climate Change.* Cambridge, Mass.: MIT Press, 2015.

Stieglitz, Joseph E. *The Price of Inequality: How Today's Divided Society Endangers Our Future.* New York: Norton, 2013.

Thoreau, Henry David. *Henry David Thoreau: A Week on the Concord and Merrimack Rivers, Walden, The Maine Woods, Cape Cod.* New York: The Library of America, 1985.

Turner, David P. *The Green Marble: Earth System Science and Global Sustainability.* New York: Columbia University Press, 2018.

Wallace-Wells, David. *The Uninhabitable Earth: Life After Warming.* New York: Tim Duggan Books, 2019.

Watts, Jonathan. *When a Billion Chinese Jump: Voices from the Frontline of Climate Change.* London: Faber & Faber, 2010.

Weisman, Alan. *Countdown: Our Last, Best Hope for a Future on Earth?* New York: Little, Brown & Co., 2013.

Xi Jinping. *The Governance of China.* Beijing: Foreign Languages Press, 2014.

Xi Jinping. *The Governance of China II.* Beijing: Foreign Languages Press, 2017.

Zhuangzi, *Zhuangzi: The Essential Writings*. Trans. Brook Ziporyn. Indianapolis: Hackett, 2009.

Zinn, Howard. *A People's History of the United States, 1492-Present*. New York: Harper Collins, 2003.

Suggestions for Further Reading

The suggestion for this section came in some time after completion of the manuscript, so I've included a few titles that I was unaware of while writing it. Given the size of the literature on the topics dealt with in the book, this is a small – but still, I hope, salubrious – slice of it.

Analytic philosophy

I haven't made much mention of analytic philosophy, which continues to dominate the profession worldwide, because treatments from that perspective have been overly theoretical, with relatively little traction on the ground of real-world events. But here are a few fine exceptions. Peter Singer's *One World: The Ethics of Globalization* (2002) has a good chapter on global warming, 'One Atmosphere'. The approach of Stephen Gardiner's *A Perfect Moral Storm: The Ethical Tragedy of Climate Change* (2011) is, as the subtitle suggests, ethical – with a special focus on global and intergenerational justice. John Broome's *Climate Matters: Ethics in a Warming World* (2012) takes a similar approach: it's especially strong on the economics, and at the same time confronts both individuals and governments with the practical implications of the author's sophisticated ethical arguments. By the time Dale Jamieson wrote *Reason in a Dark Time: Why the Struggle Against Climate Change Failed – and what it means for our future* (2014), the situation had become serious enough to merit the bold subtitle. This work combines a clear presentation of the relevant historical background in economics and politics with penetrating philosophical analysis.

Broader approaches

The first book on global warming for a general audience was written by Bill McKibben: *The End of Nature* (1989). The title announced the sad fact that, by intensifying the natural 'greenhouse effect' and spewing pollution into the atmosphere, human beings had left their dirty mark on every square foot of the Earth – leaving nothing in a natural state. Ten years later, sadly aware that human activity was bringing about changes that were making the planet increasingly difficult to live on for more and more people, McKibben published *Eaarth: Making a Life on a Tough New Planet* (2010). One of the keenest minds thinking about the climate crisis had concluded that it's going to get really bad – but that there are still things we can do to mitigate the worst consequences. His latest book, *Falter: Has the Human Game Begun to Play Itself Out?* (2019), inclines toward a positive answer to the question of the subtitle – unless we get our act together very soon. Grounds for hope are the solar panel, and its potential for replacing fossil fuels, and the nonviolent social movement, to which the author has been a major contributor 'on the ground' as they say.

Clive Hamilton's *Requiem for a Species: Why We Resist the Truth about Climate Change* (2010) was one of the first books by someone who understands the science as well as the geopolitics to say explicitly, 'It's too late: we've already blown it' (though not in those exact words). Hamilton shows that it's still worth shifting to clean and renewable energy sources, and argues cogently against carbon capture and storage and geoengineering as viable solutions. He expands the treatment of geoengineering in *Earthmasters: Playing God with the Climate* (2013), which draws on Earth System science to show how serious our situation is. Hamilton argues persuasively that geoengineering should be rejected as a dangerous (and Promethean) attempt to press on with business as usual – while conceding that judicious use of some of the technologies might help us adapt our behaviour to the new era of the Anthropocene. This last is the focus of *Defiant Earth: The Fate of Humans in the Anthropocene* (2017), where Hamilton again invokes the findings of Earth System science to show how radically we must rethink the human situation now that Earth is rising up against us.

Naomi Klein's *This Changes Everything: Capitalism vs. the Climate* (2014) may be the best single book on how to think about the climate crisis, and not simply because it's the biggest (at twice the length of mine). Klein gives a comprehensive account of the fundamental incompatibility between the neoliberal ideology that's driving us toward catastrophe and the economic and political steps we need to take to avoid it. She documents lamentable co-options of the environmental movement as well as admirable grassroots challenges to the powers that prevail, and concludes with sensible suggestions concerning how to avoid the worst. *On Fire: The Burning Case for a Green New Deal* (2019) contains a number of previously published essays (some of them gems) together with new material on the Green New Deal (all of it inspiring). The message is now more urgent: we have to change everything (almost) if we're to avoid the worst – and put special energy into launching powerful social movements for sane changes.

There's no mention in my text of an important precursor of Naomi Klein's work in the form of a first-rate book by John Bellamy Foster, *The Vulnerable Planet: A Short Economic History of the Environment* (1999), which many of my students have found eye-opening and is still very much worth reading. (There actually was a mention of it, in a discussion that I had to omit of Marxist perspectives on the environmental crisis.) Foster's follow-ups to *The Vulnerable Planet*, *Marx's Ecology: Materialism and Nature* (2000) and *Ecology against Capitalism* (2002) are also highly recommended.

Roy Scranton's *Learning to Die in the Anthropocene: Reflections on the End of a Civilization* (2015) is the best short book I've read on our topic, by a powerful writer who is well read in philosophy and literature. Drawing on his near-death experiences of fighting in Bush's disastrous war in Iraq, Scranton brings human mortality into the crux of the issue, where it rightly belongs. George Monbiot gathered many of his best pieces from *The Guardian* into a fine collection titled *How Did We Get into this Mess? Politics, Equality, Nature* (2016), and followed up the next year with a reply that offers intelligent suggestions concerning how to get out: *Out of the Wreckage: A New Politics for an Age of Crisis* (2017).

You can tell people how serious the climate crisis is getting and how much worse it's going to get, but there wasn't a single source you could point to until David Wallace-Wells came out with *The Uninhabitable Earth: Life after Warming* (2019). Highly recommended if you want a sober and comprehensive assessment of the consequences of our refusal to slow global heating. A precursor that had to rely on more extrapolation is Gwynne Dyer's *Climate Wars: The Fight for Survival as the World Overheats* (2010), which presents an array of frightening facts and convincing scenarios.

Returning to philosophy, this time in France: a foundational text is Michel Serres, *The Natural Contract* (1995), a short and profound book that considers what was lost when Western political philosophy made some kind of social contract central – and proceeded as if all politics didn't always take place in the context of the natural world. Serres's ideas were a major influence on the sociologist and philosopher Bruno Latour, who writes brilliantly about the politics of nature, incorporating the findings and insights of Earth System science and Gaia theory. *Facing Gaia: Eight Lectures on the New Climatic Regime* (2017) is a brilliant tour de force, though some readers may find the going rather heavy in places. Latour's *Down to Earth: Politics in the New Climatic Regime* (2018) is equally brilliant, but shorter and eminently accessible.

Climate science

James Lovelock first proposed his idea of the Earth 'as a kind of living organism' that is capable of regulating its climate in *Gaia: A New Look at Life on Earth* (1979), shortly before the emergence of Earth System science. Some two decades later, he warned that human activity was disrupting the Earth's climate regulation to the point of making it sick: *Gaia: The Practical Science of Planetary Medicine* (2001). The import of his next two books is clear from their titles: *The Revenge of Gaia: Why the Earth is Fighting Back – and How We Can Still Save Humanity* (2007), and *The Vanishing Face of Gaia: A Final Warning: Enjoy It While You Can* (2009).

The year 2009 also saw the publication of two good books for a general audience by distinguished climate scientists: David Archer, *The Long Thaw: How Humans Are Changing the Next 10,000 Years of Earth's Climate*, and James Hansen, *Storms of My Grandchildren: The Truth About the Coming Climate Catastrophe and Our Last Chance to Save Humanity*. A first-rate introduction is still Archer's book with Stefan Rahmstorf, *The Climate Crisis: An Introductory Guide to Climate Change* (2010). Another distinguished climate scientist, Michael Mann, wrote an eye-opening account of what bad things can befall you if you persist in telling the truth about global heating: *The Hockey Stick and the Climate Wars: Dispatches from the Front Lines* (2012). An accessible introduction to Earth System science is David P. Turner, *The Green Marble: Earth System Science and Global Sustainability* (2018).

If you're inclined to ignore the books mentioned in the previous paragraph, you might especially enjoy George Marshall's *Don't Even Think about It: Why Our Brains Are Wired to Ignore Climate Change* (2014) instead. 'Please read this book,' says Bill Nye (the Science Guy), 'and think about it.' Because Marshall's message turns upbeat toward the end: with a little tweaking, we can get wired into apt action. But some people, as we saw, have been weaponizing ignorance. For a more recent account than Chris Mooney's *The Republican War on Science*, there is Shawn Otto, *The War on Science: Who's Waging It, Why It Matters, What We Can Do About It* (2016). Naomi Oreskes weighs in at a high level of intellectual sophistication with *Why Trust Science?* (2019), to which six top scientists and scholars contribute reactions and reflections.

Ancient Greek philosophy

A first-rate study of the earliest philosophies of nature is *Greek Natural Philosophy: The Presocratics and their Importance for Environmental Philosophy* by J. Baird Callicott, John van Buren and Keith Wayne Brown (2018). The closest ancient Greek thinker to a Daoist sage may be Heraclitus, and for me the best edition is Charles Kahn's *The Art and Thought of Heraclitus: An Edition of the Fragments with Translation and Commentary* (1979). For Plato's *Republic* I prefer Allan Bloom's *The Republic of Plato, with Notes and an Interpretive Essay* (1960) because it's the translation that's closest to the original, and thus philosophically most helpful. (This means that Socrates and his colleagues don't sound like contemporary academics as they converse, which is perhaps just as well.) Two outstanding treatments of Plato in the spirit of ecology are Melissa Lane's *Eco-Republic: Ancient Thinking for a Green Age* (2011), and William Ophuls, *Plato's Revenge: Politics in the Age of Ecology* (2011).

The best introduction to Stoic and Epicurean philosophy in the context of resonances with ancient Chinese thought is Pierre Hadot's *Philosophy as a Way of Life: Spiritual Exercises from Socrates to Foucault* (1995). Another relevant masterpiece by Hadot is *The Veil of Isis: An Essay on the History of the Idea of Nature* (2006); and for an in-depth study of the stoicism of Marcus Aurelius, *The Inner Citadel: The Meditations of Marcus Aurelius* (1998) is highly recommended.

East Asian philosophy

There is now a substantial literature on Chinese philosophy, of which I can mention only a small portion. A reliable and highly accessible introduction to the field is *The Path: A New Way to Think about Everything* by Michael Puett and Christine Gross-Loh (2016).

On the Confucian (or, more accurately, Ruist) philosophical tradition, one of the earliest thoughtful contributions was Herbert Fingarette's slim volume, *Confucius: The Secular as Sacred* (1972). An eminent Chinese interpreter of the tradition who writes in English is Tu Weiming, whose *Confucian Thought: Selfhood as Creative Transformation* (1985) covers a range of relevant topics. The collaborations between David L. Hall and Roger T. Ames approach Confucian thought from the standpoint of process philosophy and American pragmatism: *Thinking through Confucius* (1987), *Anticipating China: Thinking through the Narratives of Chinese and Western Culture* (1995) and *The Democracy of the Dead: Dewey, Confucius, and the Hope for Democracy in China* (1999).

Robert Eno's *The Confucian Creation of Heaven: Philosophy and the Defense of Ritual Mastery* (1990) is an insightful treatment of the human relation to the natural world. Eno has also produced translations of all the major classics for the purposes of his teaching, which he has generously made available on Chinatxt, hosted by Indiana University (https:// chinatxt.sitehost.iu.edu/Resources.html). In the field of environmental philosophy, there's a valuable collection edited by Mary Evelyn Tucker and John Berthrong, *Confucianism and Ecology: The Interrelation of Heaven, Earth, and Humans* (1998).

Roger Ames has produced two 'philosophical translations' of Ruist classics with Henry Rosemont, Jr.: *The Analects of Confucius* (1998) and *The Chinese Classic of Family Reverence: A Philosophical Translation of the Xiaojing* (2009), and with David Hall a philosophical translation of the Laozi titled *Daodejing: 'Making This Life Significant'* (2003). Another fine version of the Laozi, from a different philosophical perspective, is Hans-Georg Moeller's *Daodejing: A Complete Translation and Commentary* (2007). Moeller's *The Philosophy of the Daodejing* (2006) provides more commentary and background, while his *The Moral Fool: A Case for Amorality (2009)*, which argues on Daoist grounds that moral judgments are usually superfluous and often dangerous, was one reason for my avoiding moral discourse – for which there are also Nietzschean grounds, as laid out in the two volumes of *Things Human, All-too-Human* (1878–80).

The versions of the Chinese classics by the great D. C. Lau are, well, classics by now, and highly reliable and readable: *Lao Tzu: Tao Te Ching* (1963), *Mencius* (1970), *Confucius: The Analects* (1979).

Another great pioneer in the field of Anglophone Chinese philosophy was Angus Graham, whose *Disputers of the Tao: Philosophical Argument in Ancient China* (1989) is an erudite account of the major figures and schools. His 1961 translation of the third Daoist classic (after *Laozi* and *Zhuangzi*), the *Liezi*, remains the philosophically most insightful version: *The Book of Lieh-Tzŭ: A Classic of Tao*. Graham's translation with commentary of the *Zhuangzi*, *Chuang Tzŭ: The Inner Chapters* (1981), is itself a classic, which contains quite a few of the 'outer' and miscellaneous chapters as well. A version that is in some respects even better is Brook Ziporyn's *Zhuangzi: The Essential Writings, with Selections from Traditional Commentaries* (2009), which has a most helpful introduction and notes.

A comprehensive multi-author volume is *Daoism and Ecology: Ways within a Cosmic Landscape*, edited by N. J. Girardot, James Miller and Liu Xiaogan (2001). Although his title uses 'religion' rather than 'philosophy', James Miller's *China's Green Religion: Daoism and the Quest for a Sustainable Future* (2017) contains much that is philosophically satisfying. *Yinyang: The Way of Heaven and Earth in Chinese Thought and Culture* (2012) by Robin Wang is a clear and detailed account of the development of the polarity that underlies so much of Chinese philosophy and culture.

Many books on Chinese philosophy by François Jullien, who often develops illuminating comparisons with ancient Greek thought, are available in English: perhaps the most relevant to the present topic is *The Propensity of Things: Toward a History of Efficacy in China* (1995). A good introduction to ancient Chinese political philosophy is Tongdong Bai, *China: The Political Philosophy of the Middle Kingdom* (2012).

Buddhism

A pathbreaking collection edited by Mary Evelyn Tucker and Duncan Ryūken Williams is *Buddhism and Ecology: The Interconnection of Dharma and Deeds* (1998). Peter Hershock's *Chan Buddhism* (2005) provides an enlightening introduction to the school of Chinese Buddhism that was the precursor of Zen in Japan.

My own interest in Zen philosophy was sparked by *The Way of Zen* (1957) by Alan Watts, which remains a reliable introduction, and for Zen practice the inspiration was Shunryū Suzuki's *Zen Mind, Beginner's Mind* (1970), now regarded as a classic of the genre. Also recommended:

Thomas P. Kasulis, *Zen Action/Zen Person* (1987), Charlotte J. Beck, *Everyday Zen: Life and Work* (1989), and Peter Hershock, *Public Zen, Personal Zen: A Buddhist Introduction* (2014). On more general issues of cross-cultural philosophy, see Tom Kasulis's excellent study, *Intimacy or Integrity: Philosophy and Cultural Difference* (2002).

Index

commons, 'Tragedy of the', 7–8
  atmospheric, 207
  extension of, 211
  theological, 111
communitarianism, 99, 105–6
community, 60, 86, 89, 102, 108, 113, 130,
    132, 187–8, 196, 199, 204
  biotic, 166–7
  global, 46, 106, 112, 138
  scientific, 30, 85
competence, 80
  in governing, 128, 131–2, 135, 138, 198
Competitive Enterprise Institute, 71, 97
complementarity, 147
concrete (and cement), 53, 189, 196, 245
Confucian (Ruist) philosophy, 104–5, 117,
    124, 126–33, 137, 172
Confucian (and Neo-Confucian) thinkers,
    115–16, 128, 136, 145
Confucianism, 124, 172, 234
  see also ritual propriety
Confucius, 128, 134–6, 158, 184
conspiracy theories, 2–3, 5, 74–5, 196–7
consumer goods, 140, 162
consumers, 77, 79, 102, 114, 118, 140, 162,
    202
consumerism, xi, 13, 98, 158–9, 164, 184
consumption, 13, 17, 96, 139, 142, 158,
    186, 193, 201
  high-level, 59, 98, 140
contrast effect (pleasure/pain), 156
control, 2, 37, 42, 59, 180, 202
  divine, of climate, 92
Coors, Joseph, 56, 64, 84–5, 88
corruption, 1, 28, 56, 123, 135, 159, 197–8
cost-benefit analysis, 38, 49
Creation (God's), 10, 83, 86–7, 99, 116–17
  beauty of, 111–12, 114
  (humans as) custodians/stewards of,
    86–7, 114
  science (creationism), 84, 110
  story of, 9, 74, 110
cryosphere, 30
cyborg, 151

Daly, Herman, 203
Dangers, see risks
dao (way), 145, 183
Daodejing, xv, 234, 240, 259
Daoism, 6, 99, 115, 144, 157, 260
  against anthropocentrism, 172–3, 178
  and fluidity of perspective, 147–9
  and the inorganic, 163
  and interactivity, 115, 117, 145
  and moderation, 157–8
  and physics, 147

as a religion, 111, 260
  and technology, 167–8
Darwin, Charles, 110
de (power, virtuosity), 30, 72, 136, 145, 170
de Gaulle, Charles, 136
death, x, 90, 144, 151, 166, 170
  blind hopes in the face of, 44, 188, 218
  as fated, 153
  by heat, 23, 34
Debord, Guy, 98
deception, 70–1
deforestation, xi, 1, 7, 37–8, 44, 95, 118,
    190, 210, 216, 231
democracy, in chains, 60
  and China, 121, 123
  as communicative community, 105
  inadequacy of American, 123, 135, 197
  making it work, 100, 121, 207
  social, 199
  under threat, 76, 85, 196
Democracy in Europe Movement 2025,
    203
Department of Defense (United States),
    94, 214, 231
deregulation, 37, 57
Descartes, René, 184
  see also Cartesian, post-Cartesian
desires, 150–1, 158, 184
  domination by, 128–30
  fulfillment of , 98
  necessary, 157
Dewey, John, 105
differentiated responsibilities (for global
    heating), 30, 205–6
divestment (from fossil fuels), 195, 246
Dōgen (Zen Master), 10, 174–5, 178–9,
    183
Donors Trust, 64, 222
dynamic equilibrium, 29, 153

Earth, central life of, 164–5, 167–8, 183
Earth Summit, see United Nations Earth
    Summit
Earth System, 28–32, 35, 37, 42, 164–5,
    168, 189, 201
  boundaries within, 38, 154–5
Earth System science (ESS), ix, 28, 30–2,
    49, 87, 155, 200
ecological ceiling, 201
ecological civilization, 125, 198
ecological conversion, 117
ecological impact (of synthetic products),
    12, 143, 169
ecological response, 183
ecology, deep, 171
  and interconnection, 2

soul, 141, 222–33, 237, 244, 250–1
  care for, 182
  Christian/Cartesian understanding
    of, 170–1
  as exclusively human, 165
  immortal, 83, 99, 112
  Orphic/Pythagorean notion of, 170
  sparks of, 182, 185
  'spirited' soul (Plato), 130, 133
  tripartite (Plato), 130, 133–4
  see also world soul
Southern Baptists, 86–7
Spectacle, the, 98, 162
species extinction, ix, 7, 33, 35, 143, 153–4,
    191
spirit(s), 32, 116, 172, 174, 185
  of the dead, 45
  in nature, 9, 111, 146, 171, 179
  see also Promethean spirit
sport utility vehicle, see SUV
steady state economy, 203
Steffen, Will, 155
Stern, Nicholas, 47–8, 50, 62
Stoic philosophy, 117, 144–7, 150–1, 154,
    157
stone(s), 170, 173, 177, 182
  as substitute for concrete, 190
  see also rocks
stranded assets, 50
sufficiency, 156–8, 164, 184
Sun Yat-sen, 135
sunk costs, 50
Supreme Court (US), 76–7
sutra, 174, 243
SUV, 195–6
symbiosis, 32, 108
sympathetic resonance, 136–7, 145, 150,
    164, 167, 172
synthetic(s), 12, 68, 143, 169

taiji quan (t'ai chi ch'uan), 6
Taiping Rebellion, 124
talent, 23, 128
Tax Cuts and Jobs Act (2017), 78–9
tax havens, 58–9
taxes, 60–1, 78, 198
  on carbon emissions, 2, 47–8, 65, 70,
    72, 201
  libertarians and, 55–6, 63–4, 72, 76, 96,
    104, 106, 188
Tech Titans, 96, 98, 102, 198
technological 'fixes', 34, 40–1, 97, 155
technologies, Promethean, 44, 46–7, 155, 167
technology, guidelines for sensible use of,
    167–9
  in China, 122, 144

Thales, 170
Thatcher, Margaret, 55, 61, 81
Thiel, Peter, 61, 96, 188
things
  beauty of, 183–4
  befriending, 115–16, 165, 171, 174–5,
    177–8
  boundaries/limits of, 151
  careful attention to, 172, 177, 180–3
  closest (Nietzsche), 178
  dysfunctional human relationship
    with, 165, 169
  freeing, from human purposes, 178
  as manifesting the world soul, 182–5
  mind of all, 146
  motivation issuing from, 133
  as naturally expressive, 174–5,
    184
  as putatively 'inanimate', 165, 170–3
  sympathetic resonance with, 164
  as teachers, 182
  unity/interconnectedness of all, 10, 99,
    116, 144–5, 147, 149, 173, 178, 235
think tanks, 25, 28, 60, 63–4, 66, 69, 71, 81,
    97
Thomas Jefferson Center for Political
    Economy and Social Philosophy,
    60–1, 69
Thoreau, Henry David, 165–6, 177, 179
Thornton, James, 198
threat multiplier, 32, 94
Three Obstructions, 67, 82, 98, 100, 121,
    140, 198
Thunberg, Greta, x
Timaeus (Plato), 134, 145
tipping points (climate, Earth System), ix,
    xv, 18, 34, 36–8, 49, 52, 155, 205
tools, 166, 170, 172, 181–2
tourism, xiii, 194
tree planting, 190, 292, 245
Trump, Donald, 23, 33, 37, 47, 74–5, 77, 81,
    123
  denial of global heating, 3
  digs coal, 191
  rescinding of environmental
    regulations, 80, 85
  under the influence of libertarian
    billionaires, 55–6, 61, 78–80, 207
  withdrawal from Paris climate
    agreement, 99
  and post-truth politics, 90
  and the war against science, 80
Tucker, Mary Evelyn 234, 259-60
Turkle, Sherry, 98
Tylor, E. B., 171
Tyndall, John, 26, 109–10